MW00480017

The Horseshoe Virus

The Horseshoe Virus: How the Anti-Immigration Movement Spread from Left-Wing to Right-Wing America

©2020 Bob Worsley. All Rights Reserved. No part of this publication may be reproduced, stored in a retrieval system or transmitted in any form by any means electronic, mechanical, or photocopying, recording or otherwise without the permission of the author.

The views and opinions expressed in this book are solely those of the author. These views and opinions do not necessarily represent those of the publisher or staff.

For more information, please contact:
Amplify Publishing
620 Herndon Parkway #320
Herndon, VA 20170
info@amplifypublishing.com

Library of Congress Control Number: 2020910488

CPSIA Code: PRF0820A
ISBN-13: 978-1-64543-650-8

Printed in Canada

To my wife, Christi. A woman with an open heart without a trace of guile. Without her steadfast support and love, I wouldn't have followed my dreams. I owe her my happiness each new day.

The

HORSESHOE VIRUS

How the Anti-Immigration Movement
Spread from
Left-Wing to Right-Wing America

BOB WORSLEY

Former Arizona State Senator

CONTENTS

PREFACE

"WHAT WAS THAT BREAKFAST MEETING about this morning?" my wife Christi asked.

We had been in the car about ninety minutes, driving up to Camp Lo Mia, a beautiful recreation center about ninety miles from our home in Mesa, Arizona. Christi and I run a biomass energy business and we'd been talking nonstop about work. Even our visit to the camp was work-related. The camp was located in a heavily forested box canyon with one way in and one way out. Five hundred girls attended a church camp there every week of the summer and so the members of our Church who run the camp wanted to reduce any fire hazards. We had offered to donate machinery and labor to clean it up, and to take the biomass slash to our electrical power generation plant that runs on forest waste material. It was the middle of March 2012, and the sooner we started on the project, the better.

I had brushed aside the meeting that began my day. "Oh," I said, "they asked me to run against Russell Pearce in the Senate primary."

I laughed. The idea of me running for office struck me as humorous on several levels. I had never been heavily involved or focused on politics. I didn't know the first thing about running a campaign. It just didn't seem like something anyone would ever ask me to do. It seemed absurd.

In addition, Russell Pearce, as former state Senate president, was widely considered the most powerful and well-recognized politician in Arizona. Talk about uphill battles.

I parked our Ford Raptor and Christi turned to me. "You should consider doing it," she said. "We've seen the damage Pearce has done. His laws. His rhetoric. We've witnessed it first-hand, lived with it, and we're the lucky ones."

I knew exactly what she was talking about. Over the last six years, I had helped start two Latino Mormon congregations in Mesa. I loved working with a thriving community of about 150 families. But these congregations had been devastated since Russell Pearce had forced through an innocuous-sounding Arizona state law—SB 1070—that targeted the state's immigrant community. In the previous eighteen months, Christi and I had repeatedly driven three hours south to take mothers with babies and young children to the border so they could reconnect with a deported father. We had bought church members—wonderful, loving, hard-working people—tickets to go back to their homes in southern Mexico, all because a new law written by Pearce essentially forced them to flee Arizona— just as he intended.

"I just never really thought about being a politician," I said. "But maybe I should."

"Let's talk about it when we're done here," she said.

A few hours later, we were back in the truck. I told Christi about the meeting in more detail. It was set up by politically-active associates of our friend, Jerry Lewis, the Mesa state senator who had unseated Pearce four months earlier, in the first recall of a sitting state Senate president in American history. We both knew and admired Jerry, a leader in our Mormon community in Mesa. We considered him a hero for unseating Pearce.

I get calls from plenty of political groups. That's what happens when the fund-raising world identifies you as someone with money and even a smidgeon of generosity. So, I showed up expecting to hear a pitch and make a donation. But after a nice breakfast, Jerry stood up. He said, "I'm really sorry. I've got to be on the Senate floor at nine o'clock. You can visit with these other guys. But, Bob, the reason we called you here is we want you to run against Russell Pearce." Jerry had defeated Pearce in the 2011 recall election for the 18th District, but rumor had it that Pearce was planning a primary comeback in an adjacent district—the one I lived in.

"That's a really nice way to exit and leave me the check," I laughed, shaking my head at the bomb that had just been dropped. But the guys at the table—Tyler Montague, Chad Haywood, Brent Ellsworth, and Ken Smith—weren't laughing with me.

"Guys," I said, "I brought my checkbook, but I never anticipated this kind of request."

Tyler spoke for the group. "Bob, we can't find anyone that is in your financial position, that has no political baggage, that we could put up against Russell Pearce in the primary. We really want you to seriously think about this."

"You *should* take it seriously," Christi said, when I finished my tale. And we started weighing the idea of Bob Worsley, candidate for the Arizona State Senate.

I was a little hesitant. For most of my life, I had focused on my family, my church, and my work. Publicity and personal fame were never my goals. If people knew my name at all, it was likely because I had started a successful catalog company, SkyMall, in 1989. To be honest, as that business took off, I was never completely comfortable with the public side of being a CEO. I loved the company, but I didn't necessarily love being *the face* of the company—schmoozing, cheerleading for investors, and talking to the press. When I was awarded the 1999 Entrepreneur of the Year honors by Ernst & Young, I found the recognition gratifying, but it left me feeling a bit awkward and slightly embarrassed. I wasn't used to the attention and I didn't like it.

During the drive home, I got a call from Tyler Montague inviting

Christi and me to Brent Ellsworth's home. Brent and his wife, Linda, hosted about thirty people with a nice dinner. Soon, the conversation turned to combatting Russell Pearce.

Or rather, me combatting Russell Pearce.

Tyler and others restated their case: I was the perfect candidate: I had enough money to challenge Pearce and zero baggage. I didn't have to be at work every day. I cared about the issues. I had seen the damage done to families, to the community, to the church.

You can probably imagine me wincing reluctantly—wanting to say "no," but also not wanting to say it. "Guys, I'm not a political person. I've never done this before. I have no idea what I'm doing. I'm very competent in certain areas, but this is not one of them."

They pushed back. I was an innovator. I ran major businesses. If I could negotiate with Rupert Murdoch, then I could handle anyone in the state legislature. This was just the right thing to do.

We had started the evening early, at about six o'clock. Now it was nearing eleven. I said, "Before we go, I just need to hear why each one of you is here. Why are you so interested in this election? What's your story?"

We were utterly blown away by what we heard. One person after another shared stories about people they knew who had been uprooted by Pearce's cruel law. The stories were about kids at school who suddenly vanished, their families fleeing in the middle of the night; beloved nannies getting deported; a neighborhood family who decided to flee after years of building a successful landscaping and cabinetry business. As people told their stories, some were moved to tears. Even now, when I think back on this evening, the emotions come flooding back. There was a great deal of pain and empathy in that room, and we, as my wife had said, were the lucky ones. No law was going to uproot our lives.

The next morning, still moved by what we heard and what we knew in our hearts was the right thing to do, we made the decision. Although I had spent my entire life never exhibiting an iota of political ambition and only a casual interest in politics, I was going to run for Arizona State Senate against Russell Pearce. In three days, we moved from a cold call to answering the call. When I started my political journey that spring, I knew almost nothing, other than SB 1070, about the anti-immigration movement in the United States and its long, complicated history.

At the time, Pearce's statute was the most restrictive anti-immigration law ever passed at a state level. It essentially green-lighted racial profiling by giving local police the right to arrest any alien, legal or not, who failed to produce residency documents. It also made it a crime for anyone to shelter, employ, or just drive an illegal alien to the store or even to church. I had witnessed the law's impact. But the complex, insidious movement that spawned this destructive legislation was unknown territory to me.

With my decision to run for office, I realized I would have to actively seek the spotlight and be comfortable in it. No other event has overtaken my life with such speed and importance. I began a crash course in campaigning and Arizona politics and, unfortunately, the politics of division. I learned that the same SB 1070 law that spurred me to action had also made Arizona ground-zero for a growing, national anti-immigrant movement that was spreading throughout our country—a movement that by 2016 had entrenched itself in some segments of mainstream national politics.

My unexpected entry into politics in 2012 began a new phase in my career—working to stop further anti-immigrant legislation in my state. Now, more than eight years later, that movement is rarely far from my mind.

The vilification of immigrants in America and the rise of white nationalism has forced my hand when it comes to my own privacy. I am no longer a politician; I am a retired one in spite of never losing any of my six elections. But I must share my experience—not only what I've learned about the history of this movement, but how it can be combated.

The United States of America is under assault by the Horseshoe Virus, my term for this toxic, anti-immigration legislative and ideological strategy. It is a strategy borne by the collision and strange attraction of far right and far left motivations.

The shape of a horseshoe has been used in political science discussions as a metaphor conveying the idea that the radical ends of the political spectrum often have more in common with each other than they do with the moderate political center. Put another way, if two ideas line up side-by-side, and one idea keeps turning to the right while the other keeps turning to the left at the same trajectories, they will inevitably run smack into each other, or at least face each other. The shape of a horseshoe implies that, barring any change in direction, the two ends will approach each other like opposite poles of a magnet. Ideologues on both sides of the spectrum may refuse to admit they have come to the same radical position because they have very different motivations. The history and development of the anti-immigration movement—the spread of the Horseshoe Virus, if you will—reveals that this is precisely what has happened over the last 150 years in America.

To be clear: when I am discussing the left-wing of the virus, I am talking about a group of people who have diverged from the standard liberal platform. They kept turning left, desperate to push specific segments of their agenda—radical environmentalism, abortion rights, and population control agendas—and hit on targeting immigrants. I realize that many on the left are pro-immigrant; indeed, Senator Bernie Sanders has advocated halting deportations and decriminalizing border crossings. In other words, I am talking about a specific segment of liberals, not all liberals. And the same goes for conservatives. Many on the right are also pro-immigration, including me. The subgroups at both extremes who oppose all immigration were or are racists or zero population growth environmentalists, or, in many cases, both. Their collaboration—initially a union of right-wing brawn and left-wing brains—has forged the Horseshoe Virus.

The horseshoe shape also provides an apt metaphor for the ultimate result of this particular anti-immigrant right-wing and left-wing collision. The two ends of a horseshoe always approach each other, but what lies between those ends?

Emptiness.

How fitting for an ideology built on nativism, which historian John Higham defined as the intense opposition to an internal minority based on its foreign—in our nation's case, "un-American"—connections.[1]

The Horseshoe Virus infecting America has been building up steam for decades. This book will reveal that the roots of the current U.S. anti-immigration movement go back hundreds of years. The strands that make up the virus started with misguided social theorists in Europe in the 1700s. They grew with the eugenics movement that started in England in the 1800s. In the U.S., eugenics took root and gave rise to a slew of official organizations in the first quarter of the 1900s. They got a boost from a wealthy, politically-connected racial theorist named Madison Grant. As author of *The Passing of the Great Race*, a touchstone text for white supremacists, Grant influenced both Congress' early twentieth century immigration laws *and* Hitler's social theories. These coalesced in Nazi Germany, resulting in the most horrific ethnic cleansing in history. Eventually, immigrant-hating fans of eugenics and Nazism found a home in a bucolic town on Long Island, New York, and a sponsor in millionaire and staunch racist Wickliffe Draper, who launched a "charity," the Pioneer Fund, to pay for dubious scientific studies, pro-Nazi films, and countless racist publications.

Draper's fund made payouts of over one million dollars to organizations run by a northern Michigan ophthalmologist named John Tanton, a rabid environmentalist who also supported abortion as a means of population control.

Tanton was a fan of radical, earth-first, far-left ideas. Eventually, he shifted his focus from attacking the unborn to attacking immigrants. His dangerous, cynical, and—I say this with utmost reluctance—brilliant mind conceived of a manufactured movement to seed hatred and fear of foreigners.

From the 1970s until his death in July 2019, Tanton honed the Horseshoe Virus—although he never called it that. He married his radical left population control ideas, dedicated to shrinking the immigrant population of America, to the nativist, white supremacy, and xenophobic agendas of far-right nationalists that also targeted immigrants. He wrangled funds, literally hundreds of millions of dollars, from some of the wealthiest people in America and used the money to propel the virus forward via his network of organizations devoted to espousing anti-immigrant propaganda and misinformation.

Over the years, Tanton created many think tanks, political action groups, strategy groups, and pseudo-scientific associations to give gravitas and fake depth and breadth to his movement. These bodies have been used as political tools to launder and legitimize false, widely discredited economic, scientific, and sociological claims about immigrants, effectively sanitizing prejudice by fabricating facts to paint immigrants as an economic and social plague on America. To get an idea of Tanton's modus operandi, imagine a network of organizations that are similar to the NRA (in terms of relentless, single-minded lobbying) but one that actively promotes hatred and fear of all non-northern European-Americans.

The donors and ideologues behind this movement now aim to strip our nation of the protections and aspirations codified in the Declaration of Independence and in our Constitution. Their agenda seeks to turn the United States of America—a nation of immigrants founded on the self-evident idea that all men are created equal—into a racist, Protestant white-majority. Their end goal is a nationalist country, undoing our shared history and a political identity that has been a beacon of justice and liberty for much of the world.

As I was finishing this book, another virus—an infectious agent called COVID-19—was crippling our country. This disease moved silently, secretly. It started in China. According to one theory, it may have jumped from, coincidentally enough, horseshoe bats, and replicated and immigrated quickly, infecting millions and killing hundreds of thousands.

In this light, COVID-19 is relevant. Tracking the movement of people over international borders during epidemics is a must. That is a responsible thing to do. But I mention the pandemic to make a larger point about the nature of deadly viruses. They hurt everyone. Even individuals who don't catch the disease have been hurt. They've lost jobs. They've seen their businesses collapse. Short- and long-term plans have been shattered and destroyed. The Horseshoe Virus is a political and social virus, not a biological one. But the damage threatens to hurt us all. Its presence and the actions taken by those infected with it will damage our nation, our security, our unity, and economy, as reducing the flow of people to America has vast fiscal implications.

I started my working life as an accountant. I am used to dealing with facts. For years, I spent my days looking at numbers. I analyzed the history of transactions. I pored over deliverables and receivables. I examined inventory. I went line-by-line over expenses. I studied organization charts. And I even dragged myself through mind-numbingly boring tax laws to make sure everything was on the up-and-up. My goal in checking and double-checking all those financial records was to arrive at an accurate picture of a company's fiscal health. I was assigned several forensic audits during my career at Price Waterhouse, based on my skills at finding fraud, malfeasance, and the hidden truth.

This book is a forensic audit, an account of the discoveries I've made about how and why this toxic, anti-immigrant, ideological virus has spread. It is a frightening tale, one that at its core is simultaneously an un-American and yet very American story. Our immigration history is uglier than the myths and aspirations that often feed our handsome, righteous, national self-image. But I believe we come by that image honestly; it has been shaped by our foundational documents, the Declaration of Independence and the Constitution, which have served to point us toward a better version of our country—a theoretical democratic republic utopia. So, the story of the Horseshoe Virus needs to be shared across our nation, along with the vaccine we developed in Arizona—our SANE immigration policy coupled with using the ballot box to replace anti-immigrant policies—to counteract the virus and ensure the future health of our union.

Uncovering the Horseshoe Virus and decoding its vast implications for our nation is an exponentially larger audit than any I have previously undertaken. It is also vastly more important than anything I've ever done. I believe the anti-immigration movement is one of the most poisonous, inflammatory issues facing our nation. Our fiscal, moral, and constitutional health depend on exposing this campaign for what it is. The virus is a political and economic weapon used to divide and conquer by promoting tribalism over national unity and by fueling hate. It is the opposite of a government by, and for, all. I hope readers will absorb this story and recognize the manipulative, divisive forces that threaten to tear our great nation apart. Sharing this history and combating the destructive forces of the anti-immigrant movement is vital to safeguarding the American dream our founders set in motion so many years ago. It is vital to safeguarding the national motto that must remain our American identity:

E pluribus unum. Out of many, one.

PART ONE

Chapter One

MY IMMIGRANT STORY

Despite laws guaranteeing the freedom of worship, religion has been weaponized in the war against immigrants throughout much of American history. In my case, it provided a wake-up call. You might even say it weaponized me, or, to use a more peaceful term, focused me.

Let me explain.

I am a Mormon. Sometime between 1850 and 1900, my forefathers joined The Church of Jesus Christ of Latter-day Saints (LDS) and migrated from Manchester and Liverpool in northern England and Scotland via New Zealand. At that time, becoming an American citizen meant meeting two requirements, which were set down in the Naturalization Act of 1790. The law stated that any free white person of "good character," who had lived in the United States for two years or longer could apply for citizenship.[1] So, when the first generation of Worsleys stepped on U.S. soil, like millions before them, they were what today we might term undocumented immigrants.

My ancestors arrived in Salt Lake as part of a massive Mormon migration movement begun by Brigham Young, after church founder Joseph Smith was murdered by a mob while awaiting trial in Carthage, Illinois in 1844. Over the next few decades, tens of thousands of immigrants arrived in the Salt Lake Valley, building a city that quickly rivaled the population of San Francisco. Over 65,000 Mormons traveled via horse and wagon trains to Salt Lake before rail service was established in 1869. Even more astounding, as documented in the book, *Handcarts to Zion*, from 1856 to 1860, three thousand church members arrived on foot pulling handcarts—human-powered wagon trains with not a single horse or mule—along the 1,300-mile Mormon trail from St. Louis to Salt Lake.[2] Way-stations were established to aid the teams of LDS travelers as they crossed the plains. When they arrived in Salt Lake, these exhausted pioneers were greeted with open arms and an elaborate welcome dinner—likely the first good meal they'd had since leaving St. Louis. The newcomers were also directed to paying work and places to live. Brigham Young would arrange for land to be provided where they could hew timber and build log houses.

I'm a fourth- and fifth-generation Utahan and LDS member on both sides of my family. Although I was born in Salt Lake, I grew up in a nurturing, supportive Mormon community in Boise, Idaho. As a kid, I was a typical math nerd. I enjoyed excelling in school and was proud that I could handle an accelerated math program from seventh grade through high school without breaking a sweat. Out of school, I was an Eagle Scout. I loved fishing, hunting, hiking and camping. I was also a budding entrepreneur. When I was ten, I sold *Grit* newspapers door-to-door for a dime a copy and saved my money. When I was thirteen, my dad suggested I diversify into real estate. Actually, he didn't say that. He said, "Son, you've saved up a couple thousand dollars. We can buy this lot close to our home. How would you like to buy it with me?" So, I did.

I neither ran nor wanted to run for any student body office in junior high or high school. I got good grades and minded my own business. I had one unspoken interest that I kept to myself. A pretty, charming, blonde-haired girl named Christi Armstrong had caught my eye in the hallways of Capital High School. She was a sophomore and I was a senior. That difference in age and the fact I was raised to be respectful meant I kept my distance. But I felt a definite connection.

My interest in public service or civics really didn't extend beyond my Eagle Scout achievement and volunteering for the church. As I aged out of my troop, I became an Explorer—a senior division of the Boy Scouts—and was selected to represent the organization at a meeting in Washington, D.C. I made the trek with several other Explorers from Idaho to Washington, D.C. to meet our senator, Frank Church. During the visit, we were invited to meet President Nixon at the White House. It was a powerful experience at the time. Not long after, however, that thrill became a bit of an embarrassment when Nixon resigned from the presidency for misconduct. None of this exposure to politics and the Capitol managed to light any fire in my soul to ever run for any office or even to play a meaningful role in our political process.

When I graduated from high school, I signed up for a two-year stint as a Latter-day Saint missionary in Uruguay and Paraguay where I served most of my time near the border these two countries share with Brazil. The church does not offer financial backing for these missions. Most are individually or family-funded. I was able to support my time abroad by renting out a trailer home I had purchased.

PERFECT POLITICAL TRAINING

Going on a mission in 1975 at the age of nineteen was a tremendously empowering and eye-opening event in my life, particularly my time in Paraguay. I had taken our American standard of living for granted. I had never given a second thought to the clean water that sustains us every day nor the electricity that powers our modern conveniences—kitchen and home appliances, lights, and entertainment systems. In Paraguay, a land-locked country between Argentina, Brazil, and Bolivia, most people I encountered lived in shacks with dirt floors. Access to running water and electricity was the exception, not the rule. In Boise, every family—every eighteen year old, come to think of it—seemed to have a car. In Paraguay, none of the people we met or worked with had such a luxury. Ox-drawn carts with two large wooden wheels were the predominant vehicles.

By comparison, Uruguay was a more developed nation, but I often felt I was in a time warp there, too. The cars on the road seemed to have been driven straight out of the 1950s and the neo-colonial architecture in the capital of Montevideo seemed like a holdover from a previous century.

Ultimately, living in both countries was an enriching cultural experience. I arrived in Montevideo, Uruguay, in May 1975 during political unrest. In fact, my first night, while getting photographed with other new missionaries in the capital, I was caught in a face off between military troops on horseback with weapons and sign-waving protestors in the main plaza of the city. Fortunately, we ducked into a store and avoided the clash. I had never seen such things in Boise, Idaho. I came to love and admire the different cultures I encountered. My Spanish language skills soared, and I became fluent. I didn't realize it at the time, but the rigorous schedule of missionary work—studying scripture for several hours a day and then going door-to-door deep into the evening to share our faith with others—was great training for a future politician knocking on thousands of doors in my district in Mesa, Arizona. We were taught to make sure we were presentable in our dark pants, crisp white shirts, ties and name tags over our breast pockets. To help us connect with complete strangers, we were taught to find common ground, empathize, and to exude the warmth and confidence that so often comes with embracing faith. We were even instructed on how to deal with hecklers who sometimes regarded us with distrust and hostility.

There is one last thing about my time abroad that is important to mention. Given the strong Catholic roots of the two countries I worked in, my dozen or so volunteer mission companions and I expected to be greeted with some derision and antagonism. But these instances were few and far between. I attribute part of that to the fact we were taught to never demean another religion. The articles of faith that are at the core of Mormonism make this clear. Here's what #11 says:

> We claim the privilege of worshiping Almighty God according to the dictates of our own conscience, and allow all men the same privilege, let them worship how, where, or what they may.[3]

MAKING MY WAY

I returned to the U.S. and enrolled at Brigham Young University where I decided that my interest in math might best be monetized by studying accounting like my dad. That pretty much sums up my conservative state of mind. In the late 1970s, accounting was a "sure thing" path to moderately paid employment and I definitely needed a career.

Remember Christi—the girl back in Boise before my mission? We got married in 1977, during my sophomore year at BYU.

My decision to become a CPA served me well. In 1980, I landed a job with Price Waterhouse, one of the premier accounting firms in the world. Christi and I had a choice of moving to Denver, San Francisco, or Phoenix. We chose Phoenix and settled in the suburb of Mesa, located about twenty miles from the capital. Mesa got its start when Mormon leaders asked Daniel Webster Jones to establish a town in Arizona in the 1870s. The area went through a succession of names from Fort Utah to Jonesville to Lehi, which was Brigham Young's suggestion.[4] Eventually, the settlement became Mesa, the Spanish word for table or plateau, and morphed into a sprawling city encompassing 140 square miles and a population of over 510,000. Mesa has more people and takes up more square mileage than Pittsburgh, Atlanta, or Miami.[5] But in 1980, Christi and I settled in Mesa, lured in part by its family-friendly, active Mormon community.

We raised six children in that community. And after five years at Price Waterhouse, I had enough confidence to strike out on my own. Later, when I was just thirty-five, I started SkyMall, a catalog company that distributed our merchandise-filled magazines on 95 percent of all commercial airplanes crisscrossing America. After a few iterations, we got our business model right, and the company went public in 1996. The stock eventually hit a valuation high of half a billion dollars before falling victim to the 2000 stock crash. After thirteen years of running SkyMall, we sold the company to Rupert Murdoch's Gemstar/TV Guide group in 2001 for a substantial profit.

I now had enough money to pursue my interests without financial pressure. But that entrepreneurial spirit that first surfaced when I was just a kid never vanished. I own two established privately held companies. One, Novo Power, is a renewable energy company that uses wood waste—the tons of slash, dead and pre-commercial small timber—as our primary fuel source. The other, NZ Legacy, is a land, mineral, and energy development company that controls the surface land rights to over 100,000 acres and the mineral rights to another one million acres in the four corners area of Utah, Colorado, New Mexico, and Arizona. I am proud of both these ventures, which actively engage in biomass, solar and wind renewable energy, and forest conservation.

MY AWAKENING

Owning these successful ventures meant I could use my time as I saw fit. And that is what led, indirectly, to my awakening regarding the anti-immigration movement. Volunteering is a central part of the Latter-day Saints infrastructure. Mormon churches operate as "lay churches." Every congregation is run by unpaid volunteers, from a church's clergyman—we call them bishops—to our stake presidents who oversee five or more wards. (To be clear, an LDS bishop, while especially important at the grassroots level, does not have the same scope of authority or prestige bestowed on a Catholic or Anglican bishop.)

In early 2004, I was called on by my stake president to dedicate twenty hours a week to found, build, and strengthen two Hispanic congregations in our area. Mesa has many legal immigrants, thanks in part to legislation championed by President Ronald Reagan as part of the 1986 Immigration Reform and Control Act, which made undocumented aliens who entered the U.S. before 1982 eligible to obtain legal status.[6] But we also had a lot of undocumented immigrants who had arrived after 1986. The housing market was red-hot in Arizona from 2002 to 2008. Add that to Arizona's proximity to and border with Mexico, and the large Hispanic presence already in the state, and you have a magnet for people desperate for good jobs that pay significantly higher wages than those available south of the border.

Initially, my primary job as branch president was to create an outreach program and Spanish-speaking congregation for the Hispanic community in my area of Mesa. In no time at all, I found myself working with Peruvians, Argentinians, Central Americans, and Mexicans. Eight years into the project, we had grown from zero congregations to two thriving wards with several hundred families. It was an incredibly gratifying experience. I was involved in these families' lives. It comes with the territory when you work closely with a population that's underserved and poor. This community needed support and guidance forging a life in America. We helped our members with housing, jobs, and school advice for their children. We started youth groups, which are so elemental to instilling kids with a sense of community and fellowship. I estimate that half of our members were either first or second-generation Americans or legal residents. The other half were undocumented immigrants. Some of these families had mixed status; one parent might be legal, but their partner wasn't.

Just because some of our church members didn't have papers, visas or green cards doesn't mean they were drains on our society. In fact, it was quite the opposite. For example, we counseled undocumented immigrants who were working locally to file their taxes every year. Immigration experts told us it was better to file than be in denial, and we passed that advice along.

Millions of undocumented immigrants obtain Individual Taxpayer Identification Numbers; others buy fake IDs and Social Security Numbers. In 2015, 4.35 million people with ITINs paid $13.7 billion, according to an American Immigration Council report based on IRS data.[7] Unfortunately, without legal status, these taxpayers aren't eligible for many benefits.

Ironically, making contributions for Social Security, unemployment insurance, and taxes bolstered society in two ways. First, every contribution boosted coffers, and second, because many of those people filing were undocumented, the taxes and other funds they paid went straight to the government's bottom line. This happened because there's no way to tie the contributions back to the people—the immigrants—who made them. These people had no "legitimate" ID, so they couldn't claim unemployment benefits or recoup the Social Security benefits later in life despite making contributions. Nevertheless, they were trying to adhere to rules required of all legal employees in the U.S.

The anti-immigration movement often claims that illegal aliens drain local resources. But in my experience, this was not the case. Many of our parishioners would avoid going to doctors, dentists and hospitals because they lacked the documentation and insurance needed to get procedures done.

I also learned that many undocumented immigrants refused to call the police when they were victims of violence, abuse, or fraud—fearful that any interaction with law enforcement or government bureaucracy might result in being turned over to federal immigration authorities. Unscrupulous employers would defraud them of overtime or even real hours worked or paid them below the legal minimum wage. Protesting this abuse would frequently be met with threats to alert immigration officials.

Many people ask why undocumented immigrants overstay visitor's visas or cross illegally into America. The short answer is that time is of the essence. Going through established legal channels at U.S. embassies and consulates in Mexico and other Central and South American nations to obtain work visas can take years because of our broken, antiquated immigration laws. Many migrants had leads for jobs that could be filled *immediately*. Waiting two or five or ten years was not a viable option. So, they came. About 50 percent flew or drove to America with visitor's visas and, at the end of six months, simply overstayed. The other fifty percent found ways to cross the border illegally in order to stay.

This was my world in 2012. It had been so gratifying that I had begun talking about applying for a foreign church mission assignment with Christi, who had not gone on a mission as a young woman. Given that we were running three businesses and had more than twenty grandchildren (with more on the way), it would have been difficult to pull off, but we were very engaged with the idea.

Then my world began to change. Russell Pearce, the president of the Arizona Senate, pushed the passage of SB 1070, a bill with a law-and-order alias: the Support Our Law Enforcement and Safe Neighborhoods Act. In that moment, without realizing it, my "mission" to help my Hispanic friends began to take a non-traditional and totally unexpected turn.

The new law had an immediate and destructive impact on Arizona as a whole. And I got an up-close look because of my work with two burgeoning Mesa congregations.

Our membership dwindled immediately. The idea that every police officer was now able to stop, question, and arrest our members was terrifying. Even those who were here legally could conceivably be picked up if they didn't have their paperwork with them. Families that had lived in Mesa for years without papers fled to Denver, Salt Lake City, California, and New Mexico, while a few went back to Central America. At least a third of our congregation was deported or effectively chased out of state.

I am a firm believer in law and order. But what about laws that are poorly written, sporadically enforced, widely panned, and not adhered to? What about laws that many employers ignored in order to fill openings that citizens would not apply for? When you witnessed the devastation of SB 1070 first-hand, you had to ask, why was this law passed? What good was it doing? What was the point of targeting these hard-working families, who were anxious to contribute to society, to pay taxes, to love and serve others, and, frankly, do work others didn't want to do?

One man in our church—I'll call him Carlos—just disappeared. For five days, his wife and three young children had no idea what had happened to him. The police had picked him up on his way home from work and deported him without allowing him a phone call. He was sent to a detention center in Eloy, Arizona, and then deported to Nogales, Mexico. He was broke. He had no means of support. What did he do? What would you do if your wife and kids were 181 miles away? He crossed the border into the U.S. and began to walk across the desert. A day or two later, a Border Patrol officer found him passed out and barely alive, just 150 yards from Rio Rico, Arizona, in the paltry shade of a mesquite bush. Rio Rico is only a nine-mile drive from Nogales. But there's no telling how many miles Carlos had walked to avoid detection.

Untold thousands of migrants have likely perished in the desert trying to walk to a new, better life in America. One fascinating and frightening book, *The Land of Open Graves: Living and Dying on the Migrant Trail* by anthropologist Jason De León, reveals that the Sonoran Desert—the area straddling Mexico and Arizona and the hottest stretch of land in North America—is filled with evidence of humans: backpacks, phones, letters, photos, clothes, and other things migrants would be unlikely to leave behind on their journey. De León wondered if the owners of these items had perished in the lethal, blistering climate and, if they had, why human skeletons were such a rarity on the empty terrain. It seemed as if the owners of the abandoned items had suddenly vanished into thin air.

De León had a hunch about what might have happened to the missing migrants. He conducted a series of experiments, killing five pigs at separate intervals, dressing the carcasses in human clothes, training motion-activated cameras around the dead animals, and leaving their bodies to decompose in the desert. After two-week intervals, he returned to inspect the carcasses and the camera footage. What he found was brutal and shocking and yet completely natural. Turkey vultures feasted on the pigs for days, shredding the clothes from the bodies, picking apart bones. In one instance, coyotes and domestic dogs from a nearby residence feasted on an animal.[8]

The scavengers had obliterated each pig carcass, first skeletonizing the bodies in a matter of days, and then dismantling the bones. The clothes that each pig wore were shredded, often found many yards from the initial spot of the carcasses. In one instance, a note that had been placed inside a pocket was found twenty yards from the carcass, with no clothes nearby. De León's experiments humanized death in the desert. This is what happens to the men, women, and children who succumb to the dry, blistering temperatures while trying to cross the border and come to America.[9]

This is what would likely have happened to Carlos, had he not been rescued. He was air evacuated to a Tucson hospital, where a Border Patrol agent stayed in the room with him for three days while his condition stabilized. This was a salt-of-the earth carpenter, not a drug trafficker or gang member. He was a father determined to reunite with his wife and children. But border agents needed to watch him to make sure he didn't flee.

As soon as he was back on his feet, he was deported to Nogales once again. This time he stayed put while Christi and I drove his wife and kids to reunite with him. It was a heart-breaking reunion. They hugged and kissed and cried. It was a joyful moment, and it was impossible not to celebrate and give thanks after enduring so much uncertainty and anxiety. It seemed miraculous that Carlos, who had been arrested and banished with barely any money in his pocket, who wandered in the desert without a canteen, a compass or a map, was alive and able to embrace his children.

But undercutting the triumph of survival was a crushing reality: this family had been ripped apart and further destruction seemed inevitable. A foreigner who has been deported from the United States needs to apply for a waiver to be considered for reentry called "consent to reapply." The normal waiting period for previously deported applicants to apply is five to ten years. Even though Carlos and his wife were married, reuniting north of the border would take time, money for lawyers, and luck. If his wife and kids stayed in Mesa, it would be years before Carlos could legally return and they could all live under one roof. I was devastated thinking about this. Ultimately, Carlos and his wife decided to go back to Mexico City.

Carlos' family was one of many I knew that was sent into a downward spiral by SB 1070. By 2011, we had lost two-thirds of our congregations. Distressingly, that was the law's intent. Summarizing the strategy of SB 1070's author, the *New York Times* reported, "For years, Russell Pearce, Arizona's most powerful legislator and the architect of its tough immigration law, has sought to make life so uncomfortable for illegal immigrants in the state that they pack up and go."[10]

Or as Pearce himself said about his legislative philosophy, "Disneyland learned a long time ago that if you want the crowd to go home, you shut down the rides and turn off the lights. That's what we're doing."[11] Pearce's goals were extremely frustrating to me. Good, hardworking families were being treated like criminals. They were being split up and placed in artificial hardship in order to scare the rest of the Latino community. This was not my America. Pearce's policies sowed the seeds of destruction for the community I was helping. And they reflected directly—and problematically—on our congregation. Russell Pearce was a member of the LDS Church and represented my district in Mesa. His statements created a stupefying case of cognitive dissonance. Here was a politician who supposedly shared my faith and was supposed to represent our interests in community building, and yet he had declared war on the very people in his district of Mesa he should have been treating as kin or constituents.

After being criticized about the damaging effects of SB 1070, Pearce made the outrageous claim that he had the support of his church. A video surfaced on the Internet of Pearce telling a group of Republicans that the LDS Church had approved SB 1070. "I got hold of the church headquarters in Salt Lake," Pearce stated. "And they said they absolutely do not oppose what Arizona is doing."[12]

When a TV reporter contacted LDS spokesman Michael Purdy to

confirm Pearce's claim, Purdy stated that the church had not taken a stand "on any specific immigration legislation in Arizona."[13]

The church's attitude toward immigration grew even clearer on November 11, 2010, when business leaders, politicians, and community advocates in Salt Lake issued the Utah Compact, a five-point statement on immigration that said it regarded policing immigration as a federal matter and that local law enforcement resources should not focus on civil violations of federal code. It also opposed "policies that unnecessarily separate families" and recognized the "economic role immigrants play as workers and taxpayers." Later that day, the LDS press office announced that it regarded the "the declaration of the Utah Compact as a responsible approach to the urgent challenge of immigration reform. It is consistent with important principles for which we stand."[14] Those principles included "loving our neighbors... all of God's children, in all places at all times." It also indirectly attacked the divide-and-conquer, immigrant harassment strategy behind Arizona's draconian law:

> We recognize an ever-present need to strengthen families. Families are meant to be together. Forced separation of working parents from their children weakens families and damages society.
>
> We acknowledge that every nation has the right to enforce its laws and secure its borders. All persons subject to a nation's laws are accountable for their acts in relation to them.[15]

So why would Russell Pearce claim he had the approval of the church? The polite, short answer is that Pearce has had a unique perspective on reality. He justified everything with a "Rule of Law!" mantra—applying this cliché to broken, antiquated federal laws that were not being enforced consistently and the new laws he drafted with the assistance of paid, anti-immigrant consultants. After being aligned with radical white supremacists and anti-immigrant groups for years, he appeared to be obsessed with political power. Now it seemed he believed that he had license to vilify immigrants, to promote false narratives designed to appeal to, manipulate, and inflame voters. Somehow it became okay to deceive outright, accept dark money donations, enact an inhumane agenda, and provide a template to extend the anti-immigrant movement beyond Arizona. The wild, crazy, and craven story of Russell Pearce's rise and fall could fill a book. For our purposes, a chapter or two will have to suffice.

Chapter Two
RAZING ARIZONA

To FULLY UNDERSTAND THE RISE and fall of SB 1070 and how it fits into the larger, national, anti-immigration movement requires a deep dive into several complex factors. These include Arizona's economy and housing market, the shifting demographics of Mesa and the rest of the Grand Canyon State, and religious guidance from LDS Church leaders regarding immigrants. Other forces shape immigrant issues, too: Homeland Security Border Patrol policy, the history of anti-immigration legislation in Arizona, campaign finance realities, and the rise of social media. There are other factors at play, as well, including the role of Russell Pearce himself, the unapologetic architect of the incendiary bill. His influence is hard to overestimate.

But before we get to him, some history is in order.

CRUNCHING NUMBERS AND SHAPING IMMIGRATION POLICY

For most of its existence, Arizona has been a big state with a small population. On Valentine's Day in 1912, it became the last of the lower forty-eight states in the continental U.S. to be admitted to the union. At that time, its landmass made it the sixth-largest state in the union and the fourth most sparsely populated. The dry and scorching environment of the Sonoran Desert had a lot to do with Arizona's low population density. Before the advent of electricity and air conditioning, and the creation of a water system that relies on a multibillion-dollar network of dams, pumping stations, and canals, the state was not exactly a magnet for newcomers. But with modernization came people. By 1980, it was the twenty-ninth most populous state with 2.7 million residents. Over the next few decades, Arizona's population exploded. There are many reasons for this. Inexpensive real estate led to low cost housing, which translated into a booming market for bedroom communities outside urban centers like Phoenix and Tucson. It also fed a growing retiree market as older Americans were lured by the winter's perfect weather, affordable housing, luxury communities and one of the lowest state income taxes in the U.S.[1] But the biggest demographic surge wasn't gray-haired transplants; it was Latinos.

Arizona's population more than doubled between 1980 and 2010, totaling 6,392,017 people, according to the 2010 Census. From 2000 to 2010, the Latino population nearly doubled to account for nearly 30 percent of the total population.[2] And twenty-eight percent of the 1,950,000 Latinos in Arizona's Latinos were born outside the U.S.[3]

The remarkable influx of Latinos in Arizona did not happen in a vacuum. The housing boom that started in the 1980s meant there were plenty of construction jobs and a robust market for both skilled and unskilled laborers. So, a humming economy was one factor as (news flash!) a strong job market obviously attracts people. That attraction multiplies for people who are earning far lower wages in developing economies. Put another way, if you discovered you could make ten times the wages for the same work by traveling a few hundred—or even a thousand—miles, what would you do?

When folks ask me, "Why are immigrants coming here?" I ask if they understand the law of hydraulics. That law dictates that water always finds its way to lower elevations. No wall or other barrier can withstand the wage differential between Mexico and the USA. Meanwhile, because wages are similar on both sides of the U.S. border with Canada, no one is calling for the federal government to build a wall on our northern perimeter. It is, however, also worth mentioning the U.S. and Canada's founders and traditional ruling class share common Anglo-Saxon ancestry, language, race, religion and other similarities with the American groups that have consistently attacked immigrants. Just as important—or arguably *more* important—when it comes to Arizona's growing Latino population was the launch of a program in El Paso, Texas, in 1993. This initiative installed fences and hundreds of Border Patrol agents along a twenty-mile stretch of the Rio Grande that separates El Paso from Ciudad Juarez. "This mass posting of agents created an imposing line, if not a virtual wall, of agents along the river, which was supplemented by low-flying and frequently-deployed surveillance helicopters," reported Timothy J. Dunn in *The Militarization of the U.S.-Mexican Border*.[4]

The strategy, dubbed "Operation Blockade," greatly reduced illegal border-jumping within El Paso proper, which had hit an estimated 8,000 undocumented crossings a day.[5] The number of chaotic, frightening chase scenes involving border jumpers and lawmen in El Paso, and embarrassing wrongful arrests—the result of Border Patrol officers mistakenly apprehending legal residents—plummeted. Illegal immigration within city limits was no longer a major issue. I want to clarify something about "border jumping" in El Paso or any other municipality. The vast majority of these people were coming here to work. Many were likely motivated to cross to join family members who were already here. I think it is easy to fall into a false assumption that immigrants might be "jumping" or running from Border Patrol because they are "bad" or engaged in criminal behavior. Or, are they trying to circumvent immigration law and policy? Yes.

Does that mean they are all smugglers, drug mules, crooks, and killers? No. Again, they are coming here with a vision of better life, not a life of crime. And many from destabilized countries like Honduras and El Salvador are actually fleeing the effects of crime in their communities.

Ultimately, Operation Blockade was a cosmetic, localized solution for illegal immigration. Once again, the law of hydraulics came into effect; like a small dam placed in the middle of a huge river, the blocked water simply flowed downstream elsewhere. Its mastermind, an agent named Silvestre Reyes, devised it as a solution for driving unsanctioned and unwanted migrant traffic away from the city, which is exactly what happened. The increased security measures forced the flow of illegal crossings outside city limits. It didn't solve any long-term immigration problems beyond improving the quality of life in El Paso—admittedly an achievement—but it was a "not in my backyard" crackdown that exported the problem to someone else's yard.[6]

In a world where perception is too frequently confused with reality, it's easy to see how Operation Blockade was viewed as a terrific success. Within a matter of months, the Immigration and Naturalization Service (INS), which is a division of Homeland Security, adopted Operation Blockade's tactics, deploying similar programs along the borders of California, Texas and, yes, Arizona.

Less than a year later, the INS codified its strategy in a document called "Border Patrol Strategic Plan 1994 and Beyond," which included an attempt at a mission statement:

> The mission of the United States Border Patrol is to secure and protect the external boundaries of the United States, preventing illegal entry and detecting, interdicting and apprehending undocumented entrants, smugglers, contraband, and violators of other laws.[7]

The document also unveiled a new name for the strategy used in El Paso: "The Border Patrol will improve control of the border by implementing a strategy of 'prevention through deterrence.'"

It goes on:

> The Border Patrol will achieve the goals of its strategy by bring-
> ing a decisive number of enforcement resources to bear in each
> major entry corridor. The Border Patrol will increase the number
> of agents on the line and make effective use of technology,
> raising the risk of apprehension high enough to be an effective
> deterrent. Because the deterrent effect of apprehensions does
> not become effective in stopping the flow until apprehensions
> approach 100 percent of those attempting entry, the strategic
> objective is to maximize apprehension rate. Although a 100
> percent apprehension rate is an unrealistic goal, we believe we
> can achieve a rate of apprehensions sufficiently high to raise the
> risk of apprehension to the point that many will consider it futile
> to continue to attempt illegal entry.

Because "prevention through deterrence" focused on "major entry" corridors, it has had a huge impact on Arizona, which has the United States' second-longest border with Mexico. The 370-odd mile stretch crosses often mountainous desert terrain with an extremely low population density and extremely high desert temperatures. As I've already noted, the risks of crossing—and not surviving—such scorching, inhospitable and unforgiving terrain are offset by the sparse population, wide open spaces, and a dearth of visible Border Patrol agents.

By not massing agents along the no man's land of the Sonoran Desert, the Border Patrol seemed to be consciously using Arizona's deadly environment to deter migrant traffic, in a sense outsourcing border patrol to the treacherous, shadeless, waterless—murderous, if you will—terrain. It almost feels like a green light to enter here. During my visits to the border with sheriff's agents, I was shocked how small the law enforcement presence was in this vast area. It felt like I was surveying an informally approved path for the illegal entrance to America. Technology would provide an easy, inexpensive way to monitor the area.

But the effect of this policy has been to allow the desert to become the go-to porous entry corridor for migrants and drug runners. There is no getting around the fact that drug cartels and criminals do mix in with the hard-working job seekers engaged in border crossings. This makes the strategy of Operation Blockade more problematic. By pushing the flow of migrants—both good guys and bad—to the Arizona desert, there is evidence that we may be inadvertently strengthening the cartels. During my tenure in the Senate, I visited with Sheriff Joe Arpaio and accompanied his deputies on patrol of the Vekol Valley. According to law enforcement officials, cartels had taken control over the Arizona desert gauntlet into the USA. By controlling the territory on the south side of the border, they were able to bolster their primary business, human smuggling and drug running. They would "eliminate" independent coyotes (human traffickers) for leading "unauthorized" crossings as a way of sending a message to rivals that this was cartel territory. They would often require immigrants passing through their "turf" to become one way temporary "mules," essentially drafting them to bring Mexican weed, meth, cocaine, and black tar (heroin) on their desert journey. Once they dropped the goods at an appointed place, they were free to move safely on to their destination. I also heard that women and girls had to provide "other benefits" to the male cartel workers and coyotes to get passage—something that has been well documented.[8] Add all this up, and it becomes clear the decision to push immigrant traffic to the desert has allowed a brutal criminal element to police U.S. entry lands instead of policing it ourselves.

This channeling of immigrants toward death's door is by design, charges *The Land of Open Graves* author Jason De León: "If they can't stop the huddled masses, at least they can funnel them into remote areas where the punishment handed out by difficult terrain will save money... and get this unsightly mess out of public view."[9]

Add these circumstances up, and Arizona became the center of a perfect immigration storm: For millions of immigrants, it was the entry point, the first stop on the way to other destinations throughout the U.S. But it was also the home to a booming economy in need of low-skilled hard workers—located beside Mexico that struggles with high unemployment and low wages. Meanwhile, we hosted a massive, porous border—sandwiched between more tightly-policed territories in California and Texas. This made it the chosen path for predatory, profiteering coyotes who lead migrants northward, and for the drug smugglers who traffic crystal meth, cocaine, and other drugs into the U.S.

This goes a long way to explaining why, between 2000 and 2010, nearly five million people were arrested in the Tucson and Yuma sectors of the border trying to illegally cross into the United States—about half of all those apprehended crossing the entire U.S.-Mexico border.[10] "It's no wonder Arizona hates immigrants," De León writes. In his view, the federal government has been using Arizona's desert as something of a killing field, "a gauntlet to test the endurance of millions of border crossers."[11]

Seen in this ugly light, there is a tendency to recoil. It is hard to argue with De León's analysis and yet I find it equally difficult to fully accept his interpretation that our national immigration policy is specifically designed to push unwanted people toward death in a desert moat around our nation. Have our policy makers become that desensitized to the human cost of this policy? I often wondered why there weren't news stories about the human deaths. Media outlets and activists should turn the murders, rapes and accidents that occur under cartel control into headlines to pressure policy makers to drive down this human tragedy. Instead, like the silence that persisted for so long regarding slavery and segregation in the South, the abuse and deaths of brown people at our borders is something too many pretend doesn't exist.

INS policies are designed to stop unauthorized crossing of our borders using a number of deterrence methods. If we flooded Arizona's Sonoran corridor with thousands of troops, would that be more humane? In this era of post-9/11 national security concerns, tightening economies, and rampant drug smuggling, that might seem to be a prudent strategy to monitor our borders. Interestingly, monitoring of the desert border is technologically quite easy to do. After 9/11, every major utility facility in the country rapidly executed surveillance strategies, including perimeter electronic fences, around substations, power plants and dams. The U.S. government has wasted decades and billions of dollars failing to devise effective perimeter protection. It almost seems like the desire to know or see what's crossing the Arizona border was a low priority for Washington, D.C.

There are many other geopolitical, economic, security, and humanitarian concerns that must be factored into constructing a wise immigration policy. Once we have examined the long history of the anti-immigration movement and the motivations that have driven this ominous moment in America, we'll get to those issues.

ARIZONA ANTECEDENTS

As the Grand Canyon State's population expanded, so did local politicians' ability to snag headlines with controversial legislation rooted in racial and anti-immigrant issues. On March 18, 1986, Governor Bruce Babbitt declared Martin Luther King Jr. Day an Arizona state holiday. Babbitt's move came three years after Ronald Reagan signed a 1983 bill creating a federal holiday honoring the slain civil rights leader. Babbitt's action meant both state and federal workers in Arizona would have a paid holiday, but that didn't happen. Just weeks before the first holiday for Dr. King, newly-elected governor Evan Mecham overturned the bill, claiming Babbitt's executive order had been illegal.

When civic leaders protested, Mecham insisted the move had nothing to do with race and everything to do with finances. But it's hard not to wonder if the decision was influenced by voter demographics and racial politics. Of Arizona's 3,665,000 population in 1990, 2,626,185 were white, 688,388 were Hispanic, and 104,809 were black, according to the U.S. Census.[12] In other words, less than 3 percent of Arizona's population was African-American, barely a blip of a voter bloc. You can see that Mecham might have made a calculated decision to ignore that particular constituency and appeal to white voter prejudices.

Warren H. Stewart Sr., pastor of the First Institutional Baptist Church in Phoenix and a leader of Arizonans for a Martin Luther King Jr. State Holiday, met with Mecham to protest the decision. "He told us, black people need jobs, not a holiday," Stewart told the *Tucson Sentinel*. "From then it was on."[13]

That wasn't the only battle that was "on" with regard to racially inflammatory measures coming from the state capitol. In 1988, the Arizona ballot contained Proposition 106, a referendum on making English the official state language. This measure was conceived and promoted by an out-of-state figure, Michigan resident John Tanton, who would later prove to be a kind of ideological guru and enabler for Russell Pearce and much of the modern American anti-immigration movement. Tanton's first attempt to insert divisive legislation into Arizona worked—at least temporarily. The vote to make English the official language of the state passed but was later struck down as unconstitutional.[14]

Mecham's MLK Day decision turned into a PR nightmare. A national boycott of the state began. Pop stars like Stevie Wonder refused to perform in Arizona. In the biggest blow of all, the NFL announced it was considering pulling the 1993 Super Bowl, scheduled to be played in Tempe's Sun Devil Stadium. State politicians and business leaders went into damage-control mode but that effort was undercut when the legislature passed a measure to install the King holiday in place of Columbus Day, which caused an outcry from Italian-Americans. Eventually, a new bill was put on the statewide ballot to keep both holidays, but a stunning 76 percent of voters rejected the King holiday.

The vote reverberated across America, and not in a good way. The NFL threat morphed into a reality, as the Super Bowl was relocated to Pasadena, California. That decision—along with the vanished multi-million-dollar cash infusion that usually floods Super Bowl host cities—seemed to affect voter thinking. Another referendum was rushed onto the ballot in 1992. This time, voters okayed the holiday. When Arizona finally celebrated its first Martin Luther King Jr. Day on January 18, 1993, it was hard not to think about the damage that had been done to the state. Thirteen days after the holiday, the Dallas Cowboys, the closest thing to a home team for many Arizonans at the time, lost to the Buffalo Bills in the Super Bowl game that had been relocated to Pasadena.

I mention this detail because the MLK Day legislation story has, in a sense, repeated itself in Arizona many times over the years whenever legislation and referendums with prejudiced and anti-immigrant overtones have surfaced. There is a constant push-and-pull—with good reason. Laws that target or impact minorities are often designed to appeal to white voters. Our state was a popular destination for white, midwestern retirees, including many farmers. We also have a large, white, blue-collar population that own and operate many of the trades in the booming construction industry. Even if they hire immigrants, these folks often agree on one thing: brown people are not like them. Immigrants speak a different language, listen to strange music, and play sports with their feet. The perception of this white voter segment is that "they" do not seem to be integrating into the fabric of American life with any real urgency. It's ironic that, 170 years ago, members of the Know-Nothing Party had similar complaints about the Irish, German, and Italian immigrants working in our cities, who have by now become part of that fabric. Acculturation takes time.

These controversial, racially-loaded bills get introduced to activate Arizona's white voter bloc and, once passed, result in a national outcry and, often, economic boycotts. This backlash frequently resulted in the offensive law being legally challenged, overturned, or de-fanged.

Sometimes it takes longer than expected to undo the damage. In 2000, a new ballot initiative, Proposition 203, which was dubbed English for the Children, was put before the Arizona electorate. It followed in the footsteps of California's Proposition 227, a 1998 measure that banned bilingual education programs and prohibited public schools from even minimal communication in Spanish and other languages with non-English-speaking students. The campaign was led by immigrant Silicon Valley millionaire Ron Unz who believed English-only schooling would help immigrants assimilate and improve their lot in American society.

Unz denied having anti-immigrant motivations.[15] His co-chair, Gloria Tuchman, however, had been a board member of John Tanton's U.S. English organization, as was another Unz associate, Linda Chavez.[16]

The language of the Arizona measure made the case for the primacy of English in its opening paragraph:

> 1. The English language is the national public language of the United States of America and of the state of Arizona. It is spoken by the vast majority of Arizona residents, and is also the leading world language for science, technology, and international business, thereby being the language of economic opportunity;[17]

The measure was passed with a 63 percent majority. The results have been underwhelming, to say the least. Making English the only legal language for schools not only demeaned the legitimacy and validity of the first language of many Arizona residents, it also introduced a steep learning curve for schoolchildren who weren't fluent in English. English Language Learning (ELL) has been an unmitigated disaster for first generation children in Arizona since it removes targeted kids from normal math, science, and literature classes to go to ELL classes. It's not surprising then that these kids fall further and further behind and too often land in the bottom percentile of classes. Mesa public schools were 94 percent white when we moved there in 1980, but now are 50 percent Hispanic. The testing scores and graduation rates have been awful since then. I attribute most of that decline to ELL, and I'm not alone.

Since Prop 203 was enacted, studies have challenged the educational effectiveness of zero-tolerance for non-English languages. Kathy Hoffman, the state's superintendent of public instruction, issued a blistering critique of the law in the *Arizona Republic*, noting, "In 2018, only 47 percent of our state's 83,000 EL (English Learner) students graduated high school in four years. That's nearly 20 percent below the national average for EL students, and more than 30 percent below Arizona's general student population." Hoffman also shared that Arizona EL students had considerably lower standardized test scores, "with just 5 percent passing the English reading portion and 9 percent passing the math portion in 2018-19," and the language restriction has left English Learners to struggle with other subjects like math and science.[18] What good could possibly come from nearly 50 percent failure rates for EL Hispanic students?

California's Proposition 227 measure was overturned in 2016 and a similar Massachusetts law got the boot in 2017. A movement to repeal the Arizona law made it through the state House but was stymied in the state Senate in 2019. Hoffman is pushing for the repeal in 2020. One linguistic law Hoffman isn't challenging, however, is an act that was passed in 2006. It was called Proposition 103, which once again made English the official language of Arizona. That measure, which carved out other language exceptions to meet federal requirements and avoid being overturned by the courts, was drafted and promoted by a then-member of the State House of Representatives named Russell Pearce.

THE PEARCE FACTOR

With a thick neck, thinning grey hair, and the bulging biceps that suggest a man with a fixation with pumping iron, Russell Pearce physically embodies the role he has come to play. If Hollywood were looking for someone to portray an archetypal tough ex-cop who morphs into a demagogue politician, Central Casting could do a lot worse than send over Pearce. But Pearce is no actor, despite a continually demonstrated flair for the dramatic, as his record of patriotic pronouncements, sky-is-falling warnings, Tea Party zealotry, and fact-challenged speeches attests. He got his start in public service after working for two decades as a sheriff's deputy in Maricopa County, eventually becoming the now-famous Sheriff Joe Arpaio's chief deputy. In his years as a beat cop, he established a reputation as an officer with an overly zealous, take-no-prisoners, authoritative style. That background in police work shaped his image, and his views on immigrants and public policy, which can be distilled into three words: Rule of Law.

Unfortunately, from the moment he took office, Pearce has used his "Rule of Law" mantra to cloak a racist, politically divisive agenda that appeals to white nationalists by vilifying and persecuting Arizona's Latino population. But I'm getting ahead of the story.

Russell Pearce is not without impressive accomplishments, having overcome a good deal of hardship in life. Born in 1947, he grew up in the north Mesa town of Lehi, in a blended Mormon family of thirteen with roots going back five generations. His father was an alcoholic and the family endured extreme poverty. Stories about Pearce's hardscrabble early years are the stuff of legend to those who track the controversial figure, including a tale that he used to bathe in the irrigation ditch in front of the family home. Pearce himself has spoken about finding bags of groceries left outside his home by neighbors, which he says his mother refused to accept.[19]

When it comes to a work ethic, Russell Pearce has been relentless. He started working in junior high school and has never stopped. He was a member of the Arizona National Guard from 1965 to 1972. He worked in construction as a framing contractor until 1970, when he joined the sheriff's office where he spent the next twenty-one years. The resume on his website lists several highlights from his career as a sheriff's deputy, including five nominations for Deputy of the Year honors. (It does not say if he ever actually won this award.) In 1984, he drafted legislation to require city and state governments to pay prisoner costs for all misdemeanor arrests made by the county, a law that he claims resulted in saving "hundreds of millions for counties."[20]

Long before Pearce became a state politician, he was an activist. While he was a sheriff's deputy in 1985, he pushed for legislation to create a state-wide fingerprinting system to aid in "identifying thousands of bad guys through automated fingerprinting identification." Later, according to his resume, he was responsible for banning cigarettes from those same jails, and coming up with the plan for the county's infamous Tent City plan—a decision to cope with over-burdened jails by putting prisoners in army surplus tents to bake in the desert, surrounded by barbed wire and armed guards.[21]

Pearce was finally able to fully flex his might in the Maricopa County jail system because of a new alliance.

In 1992, Joe Arpaio, a former special agent in charge at the Phoenix office of the Drug Enforcement Agency ran for the office of Maricopa County Sheriff. He had perfect timing. Since retiring from the DEA in 1982, Arpaio had run a travel agency with his wife. But in late 1991, Maricopa County Sheriff Tom Agnos was reeling from a series of arrests involving one of the most brutal crimes in Phoenix history, the cold-blooded executions of six monks, two young initiates and an elderly nun at a Buddhist temple west of the city. Agnos' investigators had wrangled signed confessions out of four men who denied the charges as soon as they were appointed lawyers. Two months later, evidence surfaced that would lead to the conviction of two teenagers for the murders, and Agnos found himself in the hot seat, his reputation in tatters over accusations of forced confessions.

Contrasted with Agnos' troubles, Arpaio's resume—four years in the Army, three years as a Washington, D.C. police officer, and twenty-five years with the DEA—and his promise to be a one-term sheriff helped him connect with voters. When he took office in 1993, Arpaio appointed Pearce as his second in command. It was a fractious match, but it was also a meeting of minds.

The two men have had their differences—usually about taking credit for things like Tent City. Pearce has claimed the brutal incarceration camp was his idea—an inexpensive way to cope with an overflowing jail system. Arpaio, who has proudly referred to the makeshift jail as a "concentration camp" and bragged to the *New Yorker* that "I put them up next to the dump, the dog pound, the waste-disposal plant," insisted that as the boss of county penal enforcement, he was the man who made things happen. "Sure, I don't come up with all the ideas;" he admitted. "I do delegate responsibility. But I'm the sheriff, and nothing gets done without my approval."

However, the issue that reportedly drove Pearce to quit the force involved a campaign promise. Initially, Arpaio had vowed to be a one-term sheriff and stated that he thought the position should be filled by appointment, echoing the widespread political wisdom that arcane elections of county sheriffs, clerks, assessors, and judges should be eliminated so that cities and states can ensure appointees have proper qualification and oversight. But his hardline position on that issue quickly evaporated once he ascended to the spotlight, and his one-term promise was broken. Pearce, who understandably might have thought he would be a logical successor to a one-term boss, resigned in 1995. At age eighty-seven, Joe remains a vocal supporter of sheriff elections and is trying to get this job back after losing his first election in twenty-four years to Paul Penzone. No one should be surprised. He loves the limelight like only one other person I have ever watched in politics, and I'll bet you can guess who that is.

Whatever their differences, Pearce and Arpaio have also been in ideological lock-step when it comes to what they view as the most serious issue in Arizona and America in general: undocumented aliens. In the short time they worked together, their entire penal focus was on making inmates—many of whom were illegal aliens or Hispanic—as uncomfortable as possible.

But Pearce's and Arpaio's methods diverged over time. Arpaio, to borrow a biting description from criminal justice expert Judy Greene, "became a media whore,"[22] a man who reveled in outrageous stunts—like forcing inmates to wear pink undergarments, ordering "chain gangs" that recall cruel slave labor practices, or calling his prisons concentration camps on national TV. The list of his dubious tactics, asinine antics, and over-the-top statements is endless and embarrassing. He recruited actor and martial artist Steven Seagal to train a volunteer posse; he led the absurd, disproven, and racist birther campaign accusing President Obama of having a forged birth certificate; and he posed for photo ops with neo-Nazis.

His intent with these stunts was, he insisted, a form of deterrence to let lawbreakers—crooks, drug runners and, yes, illegal immigrants, whose status made them de facto criminals in his mind—know his jails were brutal, cruel places. (Ironically, Russell Pearce's legislation to push the costs of county sheriff incarceration back to Arizona cities was so expensive under Arpaio that the City of Mesa outsourced its arrests to private prisons to avoid the gouging taking place by Maricopa County Sheriff's jail. Apparently, Arpaio's tents were very expensive.)

Pearce took a different tack, exiting law enforcement to quietly focus on policy, law, and accruing political power. Arpaio, not surprisingly given his credit-grabbing ways, says he called then-Arizona Governor John Fife Symington and wrangled an appointment for Pearce to become director of the Governor's Office of Highway Safety.[23] A year later, Pearce became the director of the Arizona Motor Vehicles Office. He was, even by the accounts of some of his sharpest critics, good at his job, at least initially. An aggressive administrator, he focused on making the DMV a more efficient operation, changing its reputation as a black hole where time and productivity disappeared. He largely succeeded, implementing cost-saving innovations including a program to renew vehicle registrations digitally. Administrative costs dropped and so did the DMV's notorious wait-times.

Four years later, Pearce was forced out of office when an investigation found driving records relating to a drunk driving charge had been tinkered with, apparently as a political favor. Although Pearce's supporters have claimed he was exonerated, the boss who axed him, Arizona Department of Transportation Director Mary Peters, has disputed that claim, and confirmed to *Phoenix New Times* that she fired Pearce because of the scandal, which involved a Tucson woman's DUI conviction and alleged license-record change. "There's a big difference between being cleared and choosing not to file criminal charges," she said.[24]

One other scandal surfaced tainting Pearce's DMV tenure: In 2000, his son Justin evidently made two fake state IDs for underage pals so they could furnish "proof" they were over the legal age to buy alcohol.[25]

These examples would not be the last scandals to blemish the law-and-order man's reputation.

MAN OF THE HOUSE

The embarrassing DMV disclosures didn't have much negative effect on Pearce's next big job: running for the Mesa seat in the Arizona House of Representatives in 2000. He won the race and spent a quiet first two years in office, biding his time. Although voters had pushed through the English-only bill the same year he took office, Pearce's only significant legislation was to co-sponsor a request for additional border patrol funds. There can be little doubt he had been keeping his eye on Sheriff Joe's antics and noting his former boss' growing popularity. As far back as 1996, Arizona poll results proclaimed Arpaio the most popular politician in Arizona. In 2002, pollsters determined Arpaio would be the man to beat if he entered the governor's race. While that will-he-or-won't-he drama was playing out, the novice legislator was busy readying his first explosive bills.[26]

Perhaps explosive is the wrong word. Pearce prepared two bills, both of which targeted the same segment of the population that Sheriff Joe loved to aim at: migrants. One bill, HB 2243, was far-reaching and broad. Among the proposals: all local police authorities would be required to enforce federal immigration laws; schools for kindergarten through twelfth grades would have to check the legal status of all students and report those without documentation to immigration authorities; and Arizona universities would be prohibited from admitting illegal immigrants—and check citizenship status of all students at the start of semesters. That bill was never pushed forward. Instead, it was filed away.

But Pearce evidently felt better about the chances for his second, narrower bill, HB 2246, which called for proof of citizenship for anyone registering to vote or to actually cast a ballot. He submitted it to the House Judiciary Committee.

The bill never made it past the committee stage and was rejected in a roll call vote. But for Russell Pearce, this was a dry run. A stake in the ground. A rough draft. He knew he needed a position of more power to push his agenda. He was laying the groundwork for his signature issue: anti-immigration. It was the first foray into a vicious sustained legal assault on the Hispanic communities of Arizona. And it opened a door for him to generate outside cash and support, attracting the attention of the Federation for American Immigration Reform, an organization with a misleading acronym—FAIR—and an agenda that advocates extreme immigration restrictions.

We will return to FAIR repeatedly in this book. It was masterminded by John Tanton, who married radical environmental and Planned Parenthood movements with the money and support of wealthy benefactors with ties to population control and white supremacy groups. This organization, borne of a very tight partnership of those two opposing extremes, made Arizona its temporary playground, where far-right types like Russell Pearce provided the *brawn* while Tanton's radical FAIR provided the *brains* for anti-immigrant policy and legislation in Arizona.

In 2003, FAIR ponied up $450,000 to support a new Pearce initiative which recycled his first failed bill: Proposition 200, the Arizona Taxpayer Citizen and Protection Act, also known as Protect Arizona Now (PAN). [27]It called for voters to furnish proof of citizenship and identification to cast a ballot, and proof of citizenship to receive public benefits. The referendum passed, but high courts struck down parts of the bill.

The involvement of FAIR wasn't the only divisive outside influence tied to Proposition 200. When PAN's financial backers tried to develop the initiative into a national movement, it chose Virginia Abernethy, a professor emeritus at Vanderbilt University School of Medicine in Nashville and self-proclaimed racial separatist, as the chairwoman of its advisory board. "I'm in favor of separatism—and that's different than supremacy," said Abernethy, who worked with avowed racist organizations like *Occidental Quarterly* and exchanged numerous letters with FAIR-founder Tanton. "Groups tend to self-segregate. I know that I'm not a supremacist. I know that ethnic groups are more comfortable with their own kind."[28]

WHAT MAKES RUSSELL RUN?

Russell Pearce has repeatedly denied that his work in law enforcement has shaped his racial views. He also denies any of his legislation was motivated by racism or prejudice. But his record, quotes, and life story suggest otherwise.

In 1977, when he was a young officer, Pearce was shot in the line of duty. Details of the shooting have frequently been reported in somewhat sketchy terms. The resume on his website says Pearce was shot by a .357 Magnum in the chest and hand and had "continued in pursuit of bad buys (sic)." This sentence omits an embarrassing detail—the Magnum was, in fact, Pearce's own weapon.

An *L.A. Times* article reported Pearce "wrestled with one of the youths who attacked him and chased two more before seeking medical help."[29] In a 2008 interview, Pearce said he stopped a teenager for suspected underage drinking and noted that the suspect might have been Mexican.[30] He lost the third finger on his right hand as a result of the gunshot and received a Medal of Valor for the incident. Reading these accounts, it seems we really know nothing about the shooter beyond the fact that Pearce thought he witnessed someone drinking who he suspected might be under-age and might be an illegal alien. He might have been eighteen, the drinking age at the time. He might have been a U.S. citizen. An *Arizona Republic* account furnishes more specifics. Peace stopped three kids in Guadalupe, a town south of Tempe in Maricopa County, for drinking. According to the account, "One sicced his Doberman on Pearce. Pearce clubbed the animal with his flashlight. As he struggled with the dog's owner, another kid grabbed Pearce's .357 Magnum and aimed." Pearce's ring finger was blown off, and the bullet entered his chest. "Still, he wrestled one kid into his squad car. The kid was covered with blood, and Pearce thought the kid was shot, too—until he saw the gushing stub on his own hand. That kid stayed put in the car as Pearce called for help... Deputies eventually tracked the kids down. The seventeen-year-old shooter got five years in prison. His sixteen-year-old brother went to jail for six months. The third youngster was not charged."[31]

While Pearce worked in law enforcement, the county he grew up in and worked for changed a great deal. When we moved to Mesa in 1980, it was a predominantly white, squeaky-clean, bedroom community. Family-minded Mormons made up a significant percentage of the city population, drawn to a town with a great public education system, affordable, modestly priced single-family tract housing, and the Church's historic ties to the area. Add all that up, throw in the great weather and the growing economy, and young Mormon couples flocked to this stable, burgeoning community. Mothers often stayed home, and the families relied on single-earners. That was the way it was in our house and the houses of most of our neighbors. In a sense, the community of Mesa echoed the *Father Knows Best,* 1950s vision of suburban America, complete with potluck dinners on the cul-de-sacs, Scout meetings, Little League baseball, and church activities.

By the 1990s, Mesa's population began to shift. The children of those large families that populated Mesa and thrived from its excellent education system, grew up, went off to college and got married. Many of them, if they stayed local, chose to move into more modern new homes in Gilbert's subdivisions, south of Mesa. Long-time residents, their houses now paid off and families dispersed, chose to downsize. Others moved to retirement communities or relocated to be near their far-flung children.

The housing market changed along with the population. The modest, small block single family houses erected in endless subdivisions in the 1960s–1980s began to age and decline in value. Areas that had been predominantly white began to morph into Latino neighborhoods. A derisive buzzword made it into the local lexicon: Mesa was often referred to as "Mesi-co." The same hallmarks that accompanied white-flight in cities like New York and Chicago in the 1950s and 1960s repeated themselves to some degree in Mesa and many areas of Arizona. Property values declined in older, rundown subdivisions. Investment slowed. The tax base shrank. The much-vaunted Mesa public schools began to decline in enrollment and ranking in the state.

In 1994, another shooting took place that rocked Pearce's world. His son Sean, then an eleven-year sheriff's deputy in Maricopa County, was shot in a December 16th SWAT team raid gone wrong. Sean Pearce was part of a team executing a search warrant tied to a murder investigation. The team, which reportedly encountered trouble opening the deadbolt lock before entering the mobile home, was greeted with gunfire. Pearce's body armor absorbed the first shot, but the second hit his abdomen and he went down. His fellow officers returned fire, wounding and arresting twenty-one-year-old Jorge Luis Guerra Vargas.

The younger Pearce survived, and later criticized Joe Arpaio for mismanaging Maricopa's SWAT team deployments and cutting down on training hours—another instance of bad blood between the two families. But I mention this shooting because it provides further evidence of an incident—like the shooting he experienced in 1977 by a suspected Latino—that may have shaped Russell Pearce's negative worldview of Hispanics.

CONFIRMATION BIASES

I've talked to police officers about how the daily grind of their job can take its toll on the psyche. They talked candidly about the life lessons that come with being in law enforcement. Nobody calls 911 to report happy, positive events. They aren't summoned to emergency graduations or charity events that honor kids getting scholarships or house parties for someone paying off their mortgage. The daily beat involves problems: domestic violence, drug sales, drug overdoses, drug turf wars, and drug-related murders, burglaries, robberies, noise complaints, and on and on, every day. Serve twenty years on the job and it's hard not to become jaded. Former officers told me they would start to think that everyone has a secret life, that everyone—in both high and low crime areas—is doing something illegal. One veteran told me he'd go to church and look around at the congregation members and wonder who was secretly selling drugs, who was in an abusive relationship or engaging in prostitution. "I really had a hard time trusting people," he told me. "I realized I was getting paranoid."

When I shared these police officers' stories with my wife, I realized that Pearce and I were on opposite ends of the spectrum. At our church, I was working with people who represented 95 percent of an immigrant population I viewed as inspiring—people who up and left their homelands and families, were trying to build a community, trying to find spiritual guidance, trying to study, finding a better life for their children, trying to grow. Pearce's time was spent among the 5 percent of that population who inhabit a dangerous, desperate underworld where violence and money rule, where the drug and human smuggling trade may seem like the only way out for people with limited resources and whom public schools have failed. Seen in this light, it almost made sense that a sheriff's deputy working in heavily Latino districts would view Latinos as criminals. And given my vastly different exposure to Mesa's Hispanic community, it made sense that my view of Latinos was exactly the opposite: most I encountered were hard working, law-abiding social and loving people. They were family people who would work in unbelievably brutal conditions to earn a paycheck and who would still give you the shirt off their back if you needed it.

Pearce would not be the first person to suffer from what researchers call confirmation bias—the very human habit of drawing conclusions based on interpreting information in a way that is consistent with one's existing beliefs and experience in life. I'm sure his defenders would say my perspective is tainted by the same trait. But there is at least one great difference between us and our perspectives. If asked, I would say that I do have prejudices. I think we all do. But nothing in those inherent prejudices nor anything I've experienced in my entire life would lead me to make a career out of targeting an ethnic group, breaking up families, bullying, and stirring racial animosity, all under the guise of maintaining "Rule of Law." I have the highest respect for the Rule of Law. But that doesn't mean locking people up at every turn; it means treating people fairly, with laws that are widely known, equally enforced, independently judged, and in compliance with internationally recognized human rights, while also offering due process. When laws extol hate over love and compassion and break up families, I am going to look for better laws and, if they don't exist, find ways to pass better ones.

PEARCE'S POLICY

There are plenty of other reasons to doubt Pearce's disavowals of racism. His mantra was "Illegal is a crime, not a race."[32] The constant focus of his legislation serves as my most compelling evidence. Here are highlights from his assault on Arizona's Latino population while he was in the Arizona House of Representatives.

- In addition to his infamous Proposition 200 legislation, Pearce introduced HB 2448, which called for the suspension of business licenses for any company that violated federal laws regarding the hiring of illegal immigrants. The bill didn't make it out of the House committee, but Pearce clung to its ideas.

- The following year, Pearce went into anti-immigration over-drive. His bill, known as Prop 100, which amended the state constitution to deny bail to anyone suspected of a felony who entered the country unlawfully, was approved to go on the ballot in 2006. (A young Hispanic woman in my church was raped by an illegal stepfather. He was denied bail under Pearce's bill and served his entire sentence in Arizona prisons without eligibility for early release—another Pearce bill. Seen in this light, the outrageous incarceration costs Pearce would rail about were a self-fulfilling cycle of his own legislation.) He also introduced two bills that tied eligibility to Medicaid and welfare programs to citizenship status and revisited the quest to make English Arizona's official state language after the 1998 referendum was ruled unconstitutional. These measures began their journeys through the legislature.

- In 2006, Prop 100 passed and so did Prop 103, Pearce's proposal to make English the official state language. His omnibus bill HB 2577 seeking major policy changes to the state's treatment of immigrants, however, made through both chambers but was vetoed by then-Governor Janet Napolitano. This law, a dry run for SB 1070, would have required local lawmen to enforce federal immigration laws, made trespassing on state property a state crime, denied the ability of an undocumented person to file a civil suit, receive financial assistance for childcare, or to attend university.

- In 2007, the Pearce-initiated Fair and Legal Employment Act was enacted, making it a violation to knowingly hire an undocumented person.[33]

This list, taken from a comprehensive article by future Arizona Congresswoman and Senator Kyrsten Sinema, who wrote it while finishing her Ph.D. and working as a state senator, is far from exhaustive—Pearce served four terms in the House, before running for the state Senate in 2010—but it is exhausting. And would be more tiring if it included measures of other House members who were inspired by Pearce's brazen tactics to introduce their own divisive, immigrant-targeting bills, like a measure Napolitano vetoed that would have made it a crime for day laborers to stand on a street corner looking for work—a common sight during Arizona's housing boom.

His legislation sought to strip undocumented immigrants of any protections or rights in Arizona. And these policies worked hand-in-glove with Sheriff Joe's strategy of making jail as unpleasant as possible for anyone accused of a crime. By making trespassing, hiring, receiving benefits, or just waiting on corners illegal, Pearce and his like-minded lawmakers were going to drive the people they deemed "undesirable" out of the state. These were the very same people who powered so much of Arizona's economic boom with their own blood, sweat, and dreams of a better life. Pearce was criminalizing the very existence of a major segment of the population and planned to drive that group into Sheriff Joe's jails to teach them a lesson. By 2011, Arpaio and Pearce's Arizona incarcerated more than twice the number of people than Washington State had in lockup—40,000 in Arizona and 17,000 in Washington, despite the fact that there are 500,000 more people in the Evergreen state than in Arizona.[34]

The marriage of a law enforcement "Rule of Law"-obsessed Senate president and an aggressive, for-profit prison industry was a disturbing union. Some of Pearce's political allies while he was in the legislature included Department of Corrections Executive Director Charles Ryan and the heads of for-profit prisons. Legislative cronyism abounded: pass laws that round up more immigrants and you will need more prison cells, which private prisons will be happy to provide to the state for a nice profit. Over time, they created overpopulated prisons and with that, enormous budget demands for the Department of Corrections. And who bears the brunt of all this? The taxpayers. Of course, what would you expect from an ex-cop who was shot by Latino—as was his son—and hung around with private prison owners?

Pearce was also very chummy with the towing industry, the slimiest folks that came to lobby me during my tenure. As chairman of Transportation in the state Senate, I saw them each session, sometimes with Russell Pearce at their side, pushing self-serving legislation. Towing and impounding the cars or work trucks of arrested undocumented workers was part of Pearce's hostile vision. When an undocumented worker was stopped and taken to a detention center, their vehicle would be carted off by a preapproved tow truck operator and then held for a hefty daily impound fee. This would climb while the apprehended worker was being held. Many of my friends went through this ordeal and ended up abandoning their vehicles in the tow yards since the towing and impounding fees were greater than the value of the vehicle. And so, the state would legally steal cars and trucks from undocumented aliens.

Interestingly, many of the measures described above were launched in the middle and end of Arizona's massive economic boom. In 2008, however, when the U.S. banking crisis hit, the local economy crashed, fracturing and upending the lives of millions of Arizonans. And now, with money tight, jobs scarce, and no recovery in sight, you had the perfect storm for racial politics to raise its ugly head and go into full attack mode.

PEARCE'S PALS

Russell Pearce has developed a number of alarming relationships with questionable figures over the years. Among the most disturbing was his association with a man named J.T. Ready.

With U.S. Border Patrol's policy unofficially channeling the flood of illegal aliens into Arizona, so came a flood of militarized, political extremists determined to stop them. Jason Todd Ready, born in 1973 and raised in Florida, was a former Marine who, in 1996, disappeared for eight days and was court-martialed for being absent without leave. After serving a three-month sentence, he was convicted again, this time of conspiracy, assault, and wrongful solicitation and advice. After a six-month sentence, he was discharged.[35]

His problematic Marine stint did not deter his obsession with military uniforms, weaponry, and war games. In the early 2000s, Ready had relocated to Arizona and crossed paths with Pearce, a man he would eventually call his "substitute father."[36] In 2004, as the Protect Arizona Now (PAN) movement gathered steam, Ready became a vocal and visible proponent of the plan to make proof of citizenship a requirement to vote and to receive public benefits. Soon, he was a fixture in local, right-wing Mesa politics. He was hard to miss. A large man with the gift of gab, Ready loved cameras and microphones and playing dress-up. He also loved extremist ideology.

By 2005, Ready became a spokesman for the Minuteman Project, a vigilante group that donned camouflage and semi-automatic weapons and patrolled the Arizona-Mexico border. The group's mission was to report—and stop—undocumented immigrants from Mexico entering the United States. At one point, Ready made a video calling for landmines to be planted at the border to blow people up. In April 2006, Ready staged a protest at the Mexican Consulate's office in Phoenix with United for a Sovereign America, an extreme anti-immigrant organization with reported ties to white supremacists. Ready's activity was flagged by the Anti-Defamation League, which tracks anti-Semitism and bigotry.[37]

The ADL was clearly on to something. The *Phoenix New Times* revealed that Ready had proclaimed *The Turner Diaries*, a novel beloved by white supremacists for its depiction of an American race war, as one of his favorite books.

Arizona political reporters understandably took notice when Ready appeared side-by-side with Russell Pearce at a June 16, 2007 anti-immigrant protest at the state capitol. There, Ready delivered a not-so-nuanced proposal to solve Arizona's border issues. His solution? Call in the very organization that kicked him out:

"All the politicians wanna say [immigration] is a complex problem," he proclaimed. "Well, I got it for you, one, two, three, four. Ya ready?

Number one: Put the 1st Marine Division on the southern border. Number two: Put the 2nd Marine Division on the northern border. Number three: Put the 3rd Marine Division at our ports and shores. Number four: Our 4th Marine division needs to be within the interior moppin' up these gangbangers and takin' 'em out of here."[38]

When photos emerged of Ready at neo-Nazi and white supremacist events that same year,[39] Pearce downplayed his relationship to the machine-gun-toting firebrand.

But another picture surfaced that indicated Pearce's relationship with Ready was indeed much closer than he was letting on. The photo, taken at Ready's LDS baptism and conversion ceremony sometime in 2003 or 2004, shows Pearce standing behind Ready and former state Senator Karen Johnson. Beaming beside Pearce were former state Representative Dean Cooley, local John Birch Society leader Jim Pinkerman, and late state House Speaker Jeff Groscost.[40]

"Johnson, Pinkerman, and Cooley all freely admitted they were at the baptism," wrote *Phoenix New Times* reporter Stephen Lemons, who further underscored the connection between the neo-Nazi and the state representative. Lemons established that Ready also asked Pearce, a church elder, to participate in the ceremony. In our Latter-day Saints ritual, the about-to-be ordained person has an option to choose the elder who he most admires and respects—very often his father—to conduct the ordination. That Ready chose Pearce again suggests close ties between the two men.

It is not clear if Ready had adopted his extremist views at the time of the ceremony, which predated the ADL report. And even if Ready had become a card-carrying neo-Nazi,[41] that doesn't mean Pearce would know about it. Still, the connection between the two men who clearly bonded over anti-immigrant passions was indisputable. Ready's extremist views cast a shadow over Pearce's reputation. Pearce was forced to disavow the man he had once brought into the LDS Church.

Unfortunately, it was not the last time Ready's actions would generate disturbing headlines.

Pearce also began working with another future headline maker. This associate, however, was from out of state. His name is Kris Kobach. He is a true believer nativist who has spent a good portion of his professional life beating the drums of anti-immigration.

Kobach grew up in Topeka, Kansas, and went to college at Harvard, where his faculty advisor was Professor Samuel P. Huntington, an international affairs expert. In another odd left and right collaboration, Huntington was a former Jimmy Carter advisor who courted controversy with his book, *Who Are We? The Challenges to America's National Identity*, which advocated that immigrants be forced to "adopt English" and warned that Latino and Islamic immigrants posed threats to "American" culture. Huntington's ideas evidently resonated with his student.

After obtaining his law degree at Yale, Kobach worked for George W. Bush's Attorney General John Ashcroft as an advisor on immigration issues. In 2004, while Russell Pearce was working with FAIR on Proposition 200, Kobach collaborated with the same organization, suing his home state of Kansas for granting in-state tuition to undocumented immigrants. From then on, Kobach was omnipresent at a national level and in Arizona, working with FAIR and Immigration Reform Law Institute, the legal assault entity created by John Tanton, to pressure state colleges in California to stop accepting undocumented immigrants and on a variety of other suits targeting undocumented immigrants.

It was only a matter of time before Pearce would cross paths with the bulldog legal strategist of John Tanton's burgeoning nativist movement. It's not clear when they first began collaborating. But according to Kyrsten Sinema's research, Kobach wrote earlier legislation for Pearce in 2007, 2008, and 2009. What's more, in 2009, Kobach signed an agreement with Pearce's old pal Sheriff Joe Arpaio on the Maricopa taxpayers' dime. "Dr. Kobach's services will be utilized primarily in analyzing the immigration enforcement activities of the Sheriff's Office of Maricopa County, Ariz. as well as the other law enforcement activities of other jurisdictions," said the contract, which was signed by Kobach and an employee of the Ogletree Deakins law firm, and paid Kobach a $1,500 monthly retainer.[42]

Talk about covering your bases. In 2009, Kobach's hands were everywhere, devising Pearce's divisive legislative masterwork and teeing up Sheriff Joe to unleash the hounds.

SB 1070 was ready to launch.

Chapter Three
ARIZONA RISING

IN 2009, ARIZONA GOVERNOR JANET Napolitano resigned to become secretary of Homeland Security. Secretary of State Jan Brewer assumed the governor's office to serve out the rest of the term. According to early polls, however, her chances of winning the upcoming election were not particularly strong. Her political consultants advised her to stick to the Arizona playbook of backing racially divisive legislation to galvanize the state GOP behind her. With that advice ringing in her ears, Governor Brewer signed Senate Bill 1070 into law on April 23, 2010. The crowning achievement of Russell Pearce's legal assault on immigrants was finally on the books.

I say "finally" because members of the Senate and House later told me it was an ordeal to endure Pearce's relentless bullying tactics. He would call members "pussies" and taunt them for not having the courage to vote for his bill. He tried to intimidate colleagues. Efforts to fix his bill in committee were met with badgering and more insults. In the end, it was bound for the governor's desk, and she signed it for political salvation, which is exactly what happened. She won the Republican nomination and then nabbed 55 percent of the vote in the 2010 gubernatorial election.

By vilifying the state's growing Latino community, the alleged "law-and-order" bill played on nativist fears to appeal to Arizona's white voters. All law enforcement officers in the state from any legal jurisdiction (city, county, or state) now had the legal right to stop anyone for any reason at all, and arrest them if they could not provide documents establishing their legal right to be on U.S. soil. In interview after interview and speech after speech, however, Pearce denied any implication that the measures targeted a specific population, insisting the goal of SB 1070 was solely to achieve his favorite refrain: Rule of Law.

"*I* will not quit until the laws are enforced. We are a generous nation. We have more people living in this country *legally* than every other developed country, combined," Pearce told an interviewer, evidently referring to green card and visa recipients. "But you must have a permission slip. And I want the laws enforced. And if you won't go home, I'll help you."[1]

But SB 1070 didn't just enforce existing laws, it made new ones. It created statutes on trespassing, on looking for work, on driving someone down the block, essentially providing excuses for lawmen to have "reasonable suspicion" to stop anyone and ask for their immigration papers.

The Senate-issued fact sheet framed SB 1070's purpose this way:

> [It] Requires officials and agencies of the state and political subdivisions to fully comply with and assist in the enforcement of federal immigration laws and gives county attorneys subpoena power in certain investigations of employers. Establishes crimes involving trespassing by illegal aliens, stopping to hire or soliciting work under specified circumstances, and transporting, harboring or concealing unlawful aliens, and their respective penalties.

The law called for police and anyone with ties to local government to determine the immigration status of an individual "if reasonable suspicion exists that the person is an alien who is unlawfully present in the U.S."

Reasonable suspicion is an amorphous term. It amounted to an official stop-and-frisk policy that provided cover for authorities to target anyone who looked Latino. Given that low bar, the law required that anyone stopped *had to have their immigration status verified.* And if that person had no documentation, then they had violated federal law. And SB 1070 then allowed "a law enforcement officer, without a warrant, to arrest a person if the officer has probable cause to believe that the person has committed any public offense that makes the person removable from the U.S."

There were other specific infractions specified by Pearce and Kobach's handiwork:

> A person is guilty of trespassing if the person is:
>
> a) present on any public or private land in the state and
>
> b) is not carrying his or her alien registration card or has willfully failed to register.

The statute also said there could be no reduction of sentence for those found guilty. Time had to be served and jail costs had to be paid along with a fine of "at least $500 for the first violation or at least $1,000 for subsequent offenses." Sounds pretty good for jails and prisons—especially for-profit prisons who were now the sole providers of all new prison beds in Arizona.[2]

Creating a policy that helped or challenged immigration enforcement was also now a crime, with penalties of up to $5,000 a day for any policy found to be obstructive. On the opposite end of the spectrum, law enforcement officers were "indemnified by their agencies against reasonable costs and expenses, including attorney fees, incurred by the officer in connection with any action, suit or proceeding" relating to the law, except if an officer is found "to have acted in bad faith."

How do you prove bad faith when you've just given lawmen *carte blanche* to stop anyone? The ambiguous nature of the law meant that just speaking Spanish or just "looking" Latino—i.e., having brown skin—could be termed probable cause for stopping someone.

IMMEDIATE IMPACT

As noted in the preface, SB 1070 had an immediate impact on the two Latino LDS congregations I worked with. Within three months, we lost about half our families. Some families told us where they were going—often to other states where they would not have to live in fear. Some just disappeared into thin air. Others, like Carlos and his family, whom I wrote about in chapter one, decided to move back home, south of the border. Experiences like this were replicated throughout the state.

SB 1070 also had an immediate impact on the Arizona economy, which in 2010 was still grappling with the 2008 financial meltdown and a stalled housing market. In a replay of the Martin Luther King Jr. holiday fiasco, the state's lucrative conference and convention business took a major hit, with tourist organizations reporting an immediate wave of cancellations that were a direct result of SB 1070. Kristin Jarnigan, a spokeswoman for the Arizona Hotel and Lodging Association, said the market was still struggling one year after the passage: "A lot of the meetings are bypassing Arizona because they just don't want to be associated with the controversy."[3]

Pearce, however, insisted his law had done nothing but good. He would crow about how his measure had caused illegal aliens to flee, boasting that caravans of immigrants were renting U-Haul trucks for one-way trips out of the state.[4]

Getting SB 1070 passed came with rewards attached—lobbyists representing prison interests, which figured the new law would boost incarceration numbers, donated generously to reelection campaigns for legislators who were supportive. Russell Pearce was a very popular man in state government. He was voted the president of the Senate in 2011 after serving just two years in the body. Giddy with power, he began to discuss a new measure to penalize undocumented immigrants, attacking a law that has been on the books since 1868 when the Fourteenth Amendment was ratified: that those born within our borders are American citizens. Pearce wanted to deny birthright citizenship to the American-born children of undocumented immigrants.

Russell Pearce's ascendance proved to be his undoing. One Sunday in 2011, the newly-minted Arizona Senate president appeared on *Sunday Square Off*, the state's long-running version of *Meet the Press*. As he blathered on, oozing confidence in his vision and agenda, Pearce had no way of knowing he was inadvertently sowing the seeds of his own destruction.

Watching Pearce's appearance was a long-time political activist and organizer named Randy Parraz. In 2010, Parraz launched an unsuccessful campaign to become the Democratic nominee in the race for Senate that would have pitted him against John McCain. He was looking around for a new cause and as he listened to Pearce talk, an idea began to crystallize.

"Something triggered me," Parraz recalls. "After a whole year of SB 1070 protests, calls for boycotts, marches in the streets, this guy was rewarded for bad behavior, and elected the president of the Senate. And I just knew then, as someone who was in politics, that this is one guy you couldn't just wait out because he was going to be worse. And he was—he was pushing some of the most anti-immigrant legislation there was, and I just said, 'No way.'

"It wasn't like I did a strategic analysis at first. I was just more like, 'Hell, no. This guy needs to go.' So, I quickly did some research and found out what we needed to do."[5]

Under Arizona law, any elected official can be subject to recall. A recall is triggered when organizers gather signatures of 25 percent of the total votes cast in the previous election for the position under recall. A total of 31,023 votes were cast in the Mesa District State Senate race. Pearce trounced Democratic candidate Andrew Sherwood 17,532 to 10,663, with Liberal party's Andrea Garcia getting the remaining 2,808 votes.

What Parraz needed to do was collect 7,756 qualified signatures to recall Pearce and force a special election.

Early on, Parraz never expected to remove Pearce from office. "From an organizer's point of view, I didn't get caught up in, 'Can we win the recall election?' I just wanted to put a stain on his record, that everyone would know he was recalled," he says.

Parraz launched a grassroots movement group called Citizens for a Better Arizona and set about gathering signatures in Pearce's district. They had 180 days to canvas against Pearce and get registered voters in the district to sign their recall petition. Initially, Parraz focused on registered Democrats and independent voters, going door-to-door. But a desk at the library provided a strong hint that the recall effort might be more than a gesture. "We got over 1,000 Republican signatures, people we didn't target, just from the library."

By the time Citizens for a Better Arizona were done, they had amassed 18,000 signatures from petitioners. Maricopa County's Board of Elections verified over 10,000 signatures, and the Secretary of State's office then approved the recall.[6] Parraz and his team had made history: It was the first time a president of any state Senate had been successfully recalled in the United States.

Governor Jan Brewer ordered a special election for November 2011. Anyone could run for the open Senate seat, according to recall law. The question for Parraz was who. Pearce's district was solidly Republican. "We needed a moderate Republican," says Parraz, a life-long Democrat. He began making inquiries. "As I got further involved in the process, I began to learn that there was a whole minority, at least 35 percent solid minority of Republicans that did not support Russell Pearce and his extreme views, but they could never get to the 50 percent they needed to get him out of office in a Republican primary."

Tyler Montague was one of those conservative Mesa residents who had had enough of Pearce. While he agreed that illegal immigrants who are convicted of a crime should be deported, Montague, who works for a national bank and is active in the Mormon community, was alarmed by the racist and extremist overtones of Pearce's legislation. "After SB 1070 passed, Pearce came out with five bills that would make hospitals and schools have to turn in people they suspected of being illegal immigrants," Montague said. "It felt like Nazi Germany—a kind of 'turning in your neighbors' thing—all these nonpartisan government entities were being turned enforcement mechanisms of Russell Pearce's anti-immigrant mission."[7]

As a church leader himself—the Mormon equivalent of a youth pastor in a Catholic diocese—Montague supported Boy Scouts of America troops as an activity arm for the kids. At weekly meetings, he witnessed the fallout from Pearce's legal onslaught. "I knew many of these kids on a personal level. Some of them were absolutely terrified. They lived in fear. This was a very real and harmful thing."

Montague even wrote to the politician, taking issue with legislation that made transporting an illegal alien a crime. "I said, 'Hey man, I'm a scout leader and I've got multiple illegal alien boys in my troop. And you're trying to make a criminal out of me and the kids.'"

Around 2010, Montague became a precinct committeeman for the Republican Party. He also met regularly with an informal group of politically active Mormons in Mesa, including local Stake President Jerry Lewis. Montague was particularly struck by hearing Lewis speak out against "the climate of hate that was being fostered by SB 1070." The damage to the LDS stake's Latino communities was a frequent topic, including discussions about the implications of Pearce's Mormon background. Many in the local Latino community knew the architect of SB 1070 was a Latter-day Saint, and that fact was hurting the LDS stake's Hispanic congregations. Instead of being a poster boy for a welcoming, nurturing church, Pearce had the opposite effect.

When Montague's group first learned about Randy Parraz's recall initiative, they figured it was a stunt. "No Senate president in United States history had ever been recalled," Montague said. "We just rolled our eyes and said, 'This is just a gesture. It's just sour grapes and we'll just have to get him next time.'"

Months later, when he learned those sour grapes had fermented and Parraz had forced a recall vote, Montague approached Jerry Lewis and suggested he run against Pearce in the recall. "Jerry was very well known in Mesa, not just as a stake president, but he'd been successful as a businessman and, at that time was working at four charter schools. So, he had some name recognition."

Lewis, who was coming to the end of his term as stake president, was lukewarm to that first approach, but Montague enlisted his father to appeal to their friend. "He and I both called Jerry and said, 'It's time we do something about this.'" A few days later, Lewis gathered with Montague and some friends. He said he'd spent time in reflection and prayer and talking with his family. He was in. "It was an electric moment," recalled Montague.

And so began a political baptism by fire for both Lewis and Montague. Now the *de facto* campaign manager/strategist, Montague reached out to Randy Parraz and invited him out for a meal. "I assumed he had someone in mind to run. Otherwise, why would you do a recall?" Montague remembered. And so he prepared to give the Democratic operative a hard sell.

"Listen," Montague said, "I've got a guy who could win this election. He's prepared to run, but only if we can win. And the way we win is that we've got to tag Pearce all the way to the far right of the spectrum. If we run somebody that's a little more centrist, we can count on all the Democratic votes and some of the Republicans, and then we can win—as long as we can isolate these two together in a race.

"That's great," Parraz said. "We don't have a candidate.'"

Montague was shocked. And elated. He told Parraz about Jerry Lewis.

"He was the perfect candidate," Parraz says, noting he was impressed by Mormon community's ability to engage in "old school organizing. A lot of folks don't have texts or emails. These folks had lists on their refrigerators of members and friends that they could call."

Parraz also believed the Mormon community was heavily invested in removing Pearce. He sensed that folks in the district were embarrassed by their senator. "Anyone who did research on the Mormon church knows that their fastest-growing population is the Latino, Spanish-speaking population around the world. So, the last thing they want is some Mormon leader in Arizona, talking about how he hates Latinos."

Jerry Lewis was the antithesis of Russell Pearce. He spoke fluent Spanish. He was a strong advocate for building bridges in the Latino community. He was, in part, the reason I had been directed to build Latino congregations in my ward. Several stake presidents like Jerry Lewis had been trying to better serve their Hispanic members. Randy Parraz never actually met with Lewis, but he didn't have to. He was absolutely right: the man was the perfect candidate.

ELECTION #1

Jerry Lewis's election campaign had one paid member on staff, two volunteers with any serious campaign experience, and a dedicated army of volunteers from all sides of the political spectrum. It was a rainbow Republican candidacy, with conservative and moderate Republicans, Democrats, hardcore lefties, Mormons, Catholics, Jews, and gay constituents. Montague worked as an unpaid consultant who wore several unofficial hats, from chief strategist to spokesperson to chief of staff, while his father Dea served as the campaign chairman.

The first thing Lewis did was make phone calls to prospective donors. Unseating the man widely regarded as the most powerful politician in the Arizona Senate, if not the state itself, would require money. The campaign eventually raised $118,000 with almost no donations from political action committees. This was not the case with Pearce. According to the Patriots for Pearce - Special Election filing, $80,631—almost one-third of the $251,924 raised—came from PACs. Meanwhile, the creation of 501(c)(4) groups allowed far-right donors to filter more money to Pearce while remaining anonymous.

Despite the impressive number of signatures gathered for the recall,

Pearce remained the favorite to keep his seat. Practically every established Republican in the state endorsed him over Lewis. Even with the advantages of a bigger war chest and the backing of the governor and other senior politicians, there were indications Pearce backers were nervous. Soon after announcing his candidacy, Lewis, an avid runner, was the victim of a bizarre drive-by attack—hit by a padlock launched from a car as he jogged his normal route in his neighborhood. The metal missile hit Lewis in the crotch and sent him sprawling to the ground. A police report was filed, but the lock-launcher remains unknown. Lewis for Senate signs began disappearing from lawns around Mesa, recalls Montague.

Pearce, meanwhile, was suffering from a self-inflicted wound. On May 13, 2011, *The Arizona Republic*, following up on a 276-page report issued by the board of directors of college football's Fiesta Bowl, documented thousands of dollars' worth of tickets that had been provided to Pearce between 2004 to 2009, including one package valued at more than $4,000—for an Ohio State and the University of Southern California game in L.A. The paper noted that "In 2005, Pearce pushed through legislation giving the Fiesta Bowl a public subsidy worth $263,000, as well as more control over operations during the 2007 national championship game at University of Phoenix Stadium."[8]

While Fiesta Bowl officials have disbursed tickets to other political figures, Pearce's gifts "stood out in the bowl's investigation because of the large amount of money spent," noted *the Republic*, which also reported that three Fiesta Bowl executives made $1,025 in Pearce campaign contributions. Pearce issued a detailed statement to *the Arizona Republic*, insisting he was in full compliance "as the law requires" and "accepted nothing that was not legally offered to every other member of the Legislature."[9] To be clear, he was never penalized or found criminally guilty of any wrongdoing—but the optics were potentially damaging, especially with Tea Party voters on the warpath over political privilege.

One other scandal took root in the run-up to the November election. A mysterious third candidate emerged on the ballot; a woman named Olivia Cortes. The press reported rumors that Pearce's organization had recruited Cortes—a charge she later denied—as an obvious ploy to split the anti-Pearce vote. The logic here was that a woman candidate with a Latino name might appeal to Hispanic voters and siphon off ballots that would otherwise be cast for Lewis. And when signs supporting Cortes began appearing written in Spanish—"Si, Se Puede" (or "Yes, it can be done")—it was hard to reach any other conclusion.

In an email interview published by the *Phoenix New Times*, Cortes gave short, low-key answers. She said she was running "to offer voters a choice" and that she was qualified to run because "I care for my community and my state." She was clearly a low-intensity candidate. She did not appear in the race's televised debate. She did not actively raise money. Yet she denied any implication that she was running to dilute Lewis support.[10]

In the end, it didn't matter. On Nov. 8, she received 227 votes, or 1.2 percent of the electorate, proving nothing but her irrelevance. Jerry Lewis captured 55.1 percent of the votes cast to Pearce's 43.5 percent. A margin of 2,691 votes separated the two men. For all the controversy and press, there were 7,000 fewer votes cast than the 2010 election. Evidently, a significant number of Pearce believers no longer believed.

DOWN BUT NOT OUT

There was still one person who believed very much in the disposed politician. That, of course, was Russell Pearce himself. After getting the boot, Pearce was appointed president of the Bar Amnesty Now anti-immigration group and was elected first vice chairman of the Arizona Republican Party. He also hosted a weekly radio show out of Phoenix. Despite this activity, he missed the legislature. In February 2012—less than three months after his recall loss, Pearce filed paperwork that would allow him to run for office in the GOP primary later in the year. According to Arizona politicos, Russell thought he was invincible in a Mesa GOP primary. As long as he would face Democrats and independents in the general election, he would win.

At first blush, the idea of Pearce running again after his sizable defeat might have seemed like an act of madness. But Russell Pearce had friends in high places and good timing.

In the wake of the 2010 Census, new voter districts were scheduled to go into effect. In Arizona, an independent redistricting commission handles this task. The commission is made up of four appointees from the Senate and House Republican and Democratic leaders. And those four members then pick a fifth member as the chairperson. When this quartet's new electoral map for Mesa arrived, it raised quite a few eyebrows. They drew a line putting Pearce and Jerry Lewis's home addresses in different voting districts. In other words, Lewis, the incumbent state senator now in District 26, had been gerrymandered out of running against Pearce, who was now in District 25.

When the new districting map came out and rumors swirled that Pearce would run again, Tyler Montague and his informal band of anti-Pearce advocates realized their work was not done.

Montague and his group scoured the community for the right candidate to take on Pearce. They had done it once and were determined to do it again. That's when he set his sights on me.

I've already shared my political origin story, so let me get to the race itself.

There was instant energy from the earliest moments of our campaign. It was like a huge shot of adrenaline had been administered to everyone around us. We worked all weekend getting the paperwork together. Tyler Montague had helped run Jerry Lewis, so he was extremely valuable. He may work in banking, but he has a marketer and strategist's instinct for generating publicity. Word had leaked that Russell Pearce would announce his campaign at 6 p.m. on the following Monday at a big Tea Party event. So, on Monday, March 19, 2012, at 9 a.m., we put out a press release announcing that I was running.

Instead of Pearce having all the headlines to himself as he had planned, we had taken over the spotlight. News trucks were parked in front of my home, and reporters shared what little they knew about me. I kept things broad and general in my interaction with the press, avoiding the issues—Pearce and his destructive agenda—that had spurred me to run. "Several business and civic leaders recently approached me and asked me to consider running for political office. I have never planned to run, but my wife and I wish to serve our community at this stage of our lives," I said. "Arizona faces many challenges, and I believe my past experience as an entrepreneur, a former CPA and cost-cutter, is exactly what we need in politics right now." When pressed for more, I asked the media to give me five days to get my campaign organized before they asked me any substantive questions.

That evening, my candidacy was every bit the story that Pearce's comeback bid was. We had beaten Pearce to the news cycle punch. Sure, he had a good story—controversial politician tries to jump-start his stalled career—but the media loves a new angle and a Cinderella story. And as a successful local businessman with zero political experience, I guess I was Cinderfella. Because of the timing of the press release, reporters were able to ask him about me, and why he thought I was running, he had no real answer. I was a wildcard, an unknown quantity. He didn't know me from Adam.

I admit it. When it came to running an election campaign, I was a complete novice and knew only slightly more about state politics. My opponent, however, was a twelve-year veteran of the process—of backbench deal-making, of dark money fund-raising, in total control of the local GOP apparatus and of getting out his base of true believers. In my mind, and I think for most of the state's power brokers, I was a long shot. One of the first things we did was conduct a name-recognition poll in Mesa. I scored a measly 15 percent to Pearce's 90 percent. So, I was in a deep hole right out of the gate. Nobody knew who I was and, as a rookie politician, I faced an enormous learning curve.

I had to figure out how to level the playing field, and I had to do it quickly. Early voting for the primary started at the beginning of August, and the election would be August 28. I had four months to get my act together and do the impossible.

ELECTION #2 – "ELEVATE MESA"

I made three decisions to guide my effort. The first was to run a positive campaign. This was fundamental to me and who I am. The negative energy and dirty tricks of politics had no appeal to me. I didn't want volunteers stealing my rival's signs. I wasn't going to spread negative rumors via negative polling questions. I decided I was running for office to "elevate" Mesa and to "elevate" our state. If I lost on this positive message, I didn't care; it was the only way I would run. When I talked about SB 1070 and its anti-immigrant sentiments, I was critical. I condemned the law because I thought it painted Arizona as an angry, vitriolic state. "That's not who we are and that's not the Republican Party I know," was the theme of my campaign refrain. I made it clear that the vast majority of our Latino neighbors were good people. They were hard-working men and women. They were innocent children. They were not the criminals that Pearce and Sheriff Joe Arpaio portrayed them to be. Extremism had taken over Pearce's agenda in the Senate. Mesa voters were embarrassed by his controversial political ideas.

The second thing I did was begin to study up on immigration. My rival had been beating the "illegal immigrants are evil" drum loudly and fervently for twelve years, plied with "data" from anti-immigrant organizations like FAIR, CIS and NumbersUSA. The talking points are now infamous, and it feels wrong just repeating them. However, here are common highlights of the false narratives that have been spread about immigrants: there is a non-stop parade of drug dealers, murderers, and rapists traipsing across the border; they come with bad habits (like "mordida" or bribing) from their own, inherently corrupt countries; their presence leads to increases in crime; they don't adopt American culture and language; they take away jobs from American citizens and keep wages low; they don't pay taxes; they drain our health and education infrastructure.

By looking into each of these assertions, I found out that none of them are true and were talking points of the anti-immigrant organizations.

While the U.S.-Mexico border does provide a way into America, the vast majority of illegal immigrants in our country arrive by legal means. They enter on tourist visas and don't leave. In 2017, 700,000 travelers to the United States overstayed their visas, according to the Department of Homeland Security. The Center for Migration Studies, a pro-migrant think tank, reports that from 2010 to 2017, illegal immigrant overstays have outnumbered border-crossers.[11]

What drives people to break the law and come here? The answers are pretty obvious once you discover a few facts, some of which I touched on in chapter one. It can take many years to legally obtain papers that would allow immigrants to work in the U.S. There are annual caps on the number legal immigrants allowed. And the Trump administration has been moving to shrink those caps. If you are a laborer with a family who earns $5 a day in Mexico and you learn there's a construction job waiting for you in Phoenix that pays $15 an hour, what are you going to do? You can't wait years. Your kids will be grown and gone. And so, the same things that brought so many of our ancestors—the promise of a better life for us and our children, of opportunity—becomes the impetus for crossing the border. And those who make it save their money and bring their families over, just like millions before them did with relatives from Italy, Ireland, Germany, England, and elsewhere.

A massive study conducted by four universities looked at immigration rates in 200 metropolitan areas throughout America and compared them with crime statistics. Crime was stable or fell in nearly 70 percent of the communities that had an increase in immigrant population between 1980 and 2016. And the ten areas with the biggest increases in immigrants in that time frame all saw drops in crime.[12]

The Cato Institute, a conservative, libertarian think tank initially founded with funds from billionaire industrialist Charles Koch, has gone a long way to debunking most of these myths, as well. They found very little correlation between immigrants and depressed wages and lower employment. The only segment they may impact negatively is the small proportion of Americans without a high school diploma.[13] There are many industries—farming, construction, livestock—which depend on migrants to function. We may not want to admit it, but anecdotal evidence from farmers suggests that there are some jobs that are difficult to fill with citizens, even at competitive wage rates.[14]

Having this understanding gave me the confidence to counter and refute Pearce's misleading assertions. It helped me discuss issues as I went door to door, introducing myself to voters, and when I debated Pearce. I also had an advantage that Pearce didn't have: my own campaign cash. My wife and I were fortunate that we have done well in business. We had significant assets and it was within our means to help fund the campaign. We had to. Most state Senate races are fairly low-budget affairs. If both candidates end up spending $100,000 in total, that would be on the high side of things. But Russell Pearce was amassing a war chest of over $250,000, thanks to his long-time supporters, private prisons, towing companies, dark money donors and out-of-state nativist fans. Together, our Senate primary battle was the costliest—at the time—in Arizona history.

So, I was able to develop my own platform—a positive, elevated, bridge-building, community-loving fiscal conservative. And I was able to spend on getting my message out via signage and targeted ads on social media. I felt like I was making headway in the recognition race with Pearce. And then, two complete and utter tragedies occurred—both reflecting poorly on my opponent.

On May 2, 2012, a woman made a 911 call from a home in Gilbert, Arizona. It was the address of a house that J.T. Ready shared with his girlfriend. During the call, the woman suddenly said: "Oh my God. He's got a gun. No!"

Two shots rang out.

When police arrived, they were greeted by a nightmarish scene of domestic violence.

Ready had shot and killed his girlfriend, Lisa Mederos, 47, who had made the call, her 23-year-old daughter Amber Mederos, her 15-month-old granddaughter Lilly, and Amber's boyfriend, Jim Hiott.

Then he turned the gun on himself. Police found Ready, who had been running for sheriff of Pinal County, at the blood-soaked scene wearing shorts and boots, lying on the floor, the murder weapon beside him.[15]

This was a tragedy. The final, senselessly brutal chapter of an unhinged, violent, white supremist figure who needed mental help, not guns. As you can imagine, old stories resurfaced in the media, examining the connection between Ready and Pearce, whom Ready regarded as a father figure. Stories of Ready's neo-Nazi doings appeared, too, including one that quoted him at a 2009 National Socialist Movement rally: "This is a white, European homeland. That's how it should be preserved if we want to keep it clean, safe, and pure."[16]

"Today's events have nothing to do with me and no connection to me," Pearce said in a statement, insisting he "worked to remove [Ready] from our Party," after "learning the truth about him."[17]

Pearce's connection to J.T. Ready, despite his flailing attempts to distance himself from his former pal, damaged him in the eyes of voters, according to our polling. Despite Pearce's disavowals, both men shared a fixation with immigrants. Sadly, Ready proved to be far more of a menace than the people he and Pearce had vowed to stop at the border.

Two months later, another horrifying mass murder ended up reflecting badly on Pearce. In the wake of the July 20, 2012 movie theater massacre that took place in Aurora, Colorado—when James Holmes marched to the front of a screening of *Batman: Dark Knight Rises* wearing a gas mask and opened fire, killing twelve people and injuring dozens more —law-and-order Russell Pearce posted a rant on Facebook, essentially blaming the audience for the carnage.

> What a heart breaking story. Had someone been prepared and
> armed they could have stopped this 'bad' man from most of this
> tragedy. He was two and three feet away from folks, I understand
> he had to stop and reload. Where were the men of flight 93????
> Someone should have stopped this man. Someone could have
> stopped this man.
>
> "Lives were lost because of a bad man, not because he had a
> weapon, but because noone [sic] was prepared to stop it. Had
> they been prepared to save their lives or lives of others, lives
> would have been saved. All that was needed is one Courages/
> Brave [sic] man prepared mentally or otherwise to stop this it
> could have been done.

Once again, the local and national press spilled ink, attacking Pearce for being insensitive, self-absorbed and essentially blaming the victims—who would have had barely a chance against a madman decked out in body armor and a gasmask, who stood amid the clouds of a smoke grenade during his killing spree. In a second post, Pearce tried to say his post was meant to blame gun control activists who want to ban guns. "All I did was lament that so many people should be left disarmed and vulnerable by anti-gun rules," he wrote, ignoring that fact he failed to mention any such thing in his initial post.

This last gaffe was perhaps the tipping point in our primary race. For anyone who wondered about Pearce's ability to be at all compassionate in a time of crisis—or to even just make logical sense—his words were self-indicting. It was clear that he would continue to make extreme comments at the worst possible time and further embarrass Mesa voters. The huge polling gap that existed between us at the early days of my campaign vanished. The race was now really a race, thanks to my gun-loving opponent shooting himself in the foot.

On August 28, Mesa's new District 25 voters cast their ballots. I got 17,200 votes to Russell Pearce's 13,534 to become the Republican nominee. I won the November general election against my Democratic rival with 66 percent of the vote. I was thrilled. I was also nervous about serving my constituents well. In the back of my mind, I thought about how in the next election season in just two years, I could pass the office to a new candidate who wanted to run and could go back to my old life.

But it turned out that leaving my new state Senate office was even harder than getting there.

Chapter Four

THE EDUCATION OF BOB WORSLEY

I WAS OFFICIALLY SWORN-IN AS a senator in January of 2013. I arrived at the Arizona Senate building feeling that I had already achieved something extremely important. I had removed the front man for legalizing policies that both cloaked and stoked abhorrent nativist ideologies that damaged Arizona's reputation. By defeating the figurehead of the movement, I felt like Arizona had finally put that element of the Tea Party on the defensive, at least with regard to its anti-immigration laws.

That said, I set out to be a peace-maker in the Senate, not a bomb-thrower. I believe in solving conflicts using the tools of collaboration and compromise as opposed to the sledgehammers of power brokers. I think I did that. I tried to lead by example. One of my campaign pledges was to introduce no more than ten bills into the Senate committees. This is because there is an utter log-jam of laws that are submitted each year. The year before I took office, the Arizona legislature introduced a record of more than 1,600 bills. Many of these bills were symbolic or designed to appeal to hot-button social issues (SB 1070, anyone?) that did little to improve Arizona, or our economy, and had flimsy legal standing. I believed legislators should introduce fewer bills, be more deliberative through the entire process, and pass bills that solidified Arizona's economy and job market. Republicans are vigorously against more regulations and laws, so why were Republican legislatures fond of submitting so many bills? Flooding the floor with measures made the body inefficient. I kept my word, presenting nine bills.

Only two of my bills saw the light of day. Part of that had to do with internal Republican Party politics, where the first lesson is "Honor thy party." That is putting it kindly. The real commandment is "Honor thy party leadership." As for the American Republic and the things that make it great—the Constitution, truth, justice, due process, Rule of Law—those are all secondary.

Over my six years of service, the most frightening lesson I learned in government was that might makes right. Common sense, genius, innovation, and ethics all take the back seat to power and control. And every time I witnessed leaders adopt a "my way or else" stance in the Senate, I had an old feeling sweep over me.

Back in 1977–1979, I worked for U.S. Steel's American Bridge Division at the Geneva Steel Mill in Provo, Utah, as a college student. I made an impression on the superintendent who thought I was a hard worker and asked me to join the union, which I did. I was a hod tender—someone who mixes and carries mortar for brick and stocks brick—for the masons who were relining the fire brick on the coke battery and the blast furnace for the steel mill. I was an eager, hardworking laborer who jumped to help my masons. I would move the scaffolding, planks, complex coded brick, and mud in anticipation of the next course of brick. I was hounded by the union bosses to slow down, never touch wood (planks) since that was Carpenter Union territory. Finally, I was told that if I didn't listen to them, I would be tossed in the furnace "accidentally." I never forgot the feeling that the union imposed on me—to do the wrong thing for the company in order to help the union. Those feelings rushed back into my life nearly forty years later in the Senate. Often, I found myself on the receiving end of veiled threats as certain colleagues urged me to do what the party wanted in spite of hurting the state or the population in general. Under Andy Biggs it was always loyalty first to party.

Andy Biggs was the Arizona Senate president my first four years in office. He was a Russell Pearce ally, to say the least. (Twenty-five years earlier, I had met Biggs when he was practicing law and renting space from my CPA firm. Not long after, he won $10 million in a Publishers Clearing House sweepstakes. The newly minted millionaire promptly retired from the practice of law and entered politics. His principles and policy framework was and is closely tied to the old John Birch Society belief systems which had been part of his family traditions.)

Suffice it to say, Biggs did not give me the warmest of welcomes. In our first meeting I made it very clear that while I couldn't force him to give me committee assignments that I wanted, I would really be a good member of his caucus unless he started running anti-immigrant bills like SB 1070, in which case I would be his worst nightmare. He heard me and stopped running Pearce-like bills.

I learned another lesson from my first term. I decided that the state leadership lacked the strategic planning processes that I had relied on for all my business efforts and startups. Starting with my time at Price Waterhouse, I had held many strategic planning retreats and then written detailed and comprehensive business plans. Why didn't government do the same? It seemed like a great place for me to add value as a sitting new state senator with a strong track record of running successful businesses. I did some homework and launched a new website called www.AZ2112. com, which still exists today. (2012 was the first 100-year birthday of Arizona and 2112 would be its 200th.) I looked high and low for any strategic plans or vision documents for the state. I discovered that 1979 was the last time a group of business leaders, the Phoenix 40, paid the Hudson Institute in New York to gaze into Arizona's future. The projections and conclusions were remarkable and accurate; providing vision for ground water protection (1980 Groundwater Act), future freeways (1980s passed a modest sales tax to build the best freeway system in the country) and in many other areas.

I asked Senate President Biggs if we could form a new committee, which I would chair, to put together a 100-year-plan for Arizona and to provide some sense of direction for where we were going. We were just going session to session with no plan or even session objectives. He rejected my ideas as a communistic command-and-control policy that was totally inappropriate for a republic like ours. Biggs said, "I have extensively studied world history and all governments of the past and any central planning of a government has been a disaster and communistic. You will never have my blessing to form any such committee nor do this work officially from the Senate."

I unofficially continued gathering and digitizing any visionary documents that I thought might be of use for critical planning that Arizona—and every state—needs. But from that point forward, I realized that any talent or experience I could lend to the state of Arizona would be blocked by the invisible hand of the far right in the party. I had committed an unpardonable sin: running against their golden child and beating him.

As it turned out, Biggs, who has gone on to become an ultra-right congressman and was named chair of the far-right Freedom Caucus in October 2019, also killed several of my bills which aimed to save money, improve lives, and make government more efficient. These nixed bills would have shared government savings with whistleblowers who exposed government waste; offered free college courses online; and allowed online voting to replace mail-in ballots—to save $12 million per year and reduce voter fraud. One nixed bill would have enforced penalties against any adult entering school grounds with intent to harm students.

Two bills I sponsored were signed into law. The first, SB 1384, broke the monopoly of taxi fleets in Arizona and allowed for fixed-fee app-based companies such as Uber and Lyft to operate in the state—something I thought might be better for consumers. The second was SB 1435, the tax relief bill for the cyber industry that was merged into the Omnibus Data

Center bill. The measure helped data centers move to Arizona, increasing our tax and job bases. Arizona's weather may be harsh, but it is also very stable. It's also land-locked and has little seismic activity. That makes the state the safest environment in the U.S. for data centers, provided we have cost-effective electricity to keep them cool.

I'm also proud that I collaborated across the aisle twice in my first term. My actions violated the unofficial First Commandment of the party. I did not care. I pledged to build bridges, not walls. So, I voted for a bi-partisan effort to expand Medicaid under the provisions of the Affordable Care Act. As economic and health policy, putting $10 billion from the federal government into Arizona's coffers made perfect sense to me. These funds could be used to help offset the costs of the indigent and undocumented immigrants who were allegedly taxing our health-care system, according to the likes of Russell Pearce. Ironically, the same year President Ronald Reagan passed his 1986 immigration reform bill, he also passed the Emergency Medical Treatment and Labor Act. EMTALA made it illegal for hospitals to do what was known as patient "wallet biopsies." In other words, they could no longer confirm ability to pay before treatment. All hospitals in the country were required to accept all patients and worry about payment later. This was a great law for our citizens, but it was basically an unfunded mandate on private hospitals. Thereafter, many hospitals carried up to 20 percent in bad debt from indigent folks showing up at the emergency rooms with no insurance and no savings or ability to pay. Medicaid expansion was a long overdue reimbursement of these costs by the federal government. I felt it was a fair and equitable solution. Senate President Biggs was livid that the newly-minted Senator Worsley, who beat his best friend Russell Pearce, sided with Democrats and moderate Republicans to deliver the legislation to Republican Governor Brewer who promoted the bill to the legislature. So, my first year wasn't exactly smooth, especially when I went on record with newspapers to say that "this was a no brainer vote."

The same politicians ranting about immigrants in the Arizona legislature were against Medicaid expansion. It was hard to understand their opposition other than possible objections to increasing federal spending. In my experience, the default solution of Tea Party Republicans, as opposed to more old school Republicans (like Eisenhower, Rockefeller, and George and Mitt Romney) is to shrink government. One of the few areas they are willing to abandon this principle involves policing immigrants, which means expanding enforcement and incarceration, extending legal powers, attacking individual rights, and increasing those governmental budgets.

I always want to ask die-hard budget shrinkers if they have ever thought about the hundreds of government-funded realities that have made America the amazing country it is. These include local roads and national highways, traffic lights and road signs, public schools and state and community colleges, high-tech research facilities, defense systems that guard us, safety regulations that keep us healthy, water systems that keep us alive and our farms green, passports that let us travel, and so much more. Budget shrinkers seem to take everything for granted. Maybe they hate paying taxes, but those taxes have provided a great deal over the last 250 years. They also hate regulation because, the thinking goes, it stifles growth and adds to costs. Sometimes it does, unquestionably. But would you rather have drug companies releasing unapproved drugs willy-nilly into the world? Would you like your next-door neighbors to be able to build a nuclear reactor in their backyard? Regulation isn't the problem. Irresponsible actors and actions are. Reasonable regulation is meant to enforce responsible behavior and reasonable taxes for infrastructure. Sadly, logic is not part of the purity test of extremist thinking.

In my first term, I learned the nuances of government. For instance, I knew lobbyists were a big part of the political process and that they could be instrumental in driving legislation. But now I saw the gears of government churning. It was not always a pretty sight. In fact, it was shocking. There are multi-million-dollar organizations that operate as legislative clearinghouses.

The American Legislative Exchange Council (ALEC), an organization whose roots date back to the 1970s, describes itself as "America's largest nonpartisan, voluntary membership organization of state legislators dedicated to the principles of limited government, free markets, and federalism." But that sidesteps the influence of the nearly 300 corporate or private foundation members. These groups send "experts"—from businesses, umbrella organizations, unions, and wealthy power-brokers—to draft policy in the form of "model legislation." They then find lawmakers they can influence in the state legislatures. When lobbyists find a match, you can guess what follows: they donate funds to their newfound legislative partners.

In 2008, the organization reportedly began to circulate drafts of proposed laws dubbed "No Sanctuary Cities for Illegal Immigrants Act" and a shorter "Immigration Law Enforcement Act,"[1] both of which contained similar elements to Russell Pearce's SB 1070. Who, you might ask, would have a vested interest in these laws or might benefit economically from this legislation? According to reports, the Corrections Corporation of America and the American Bail Coalition, composed of nine of the nation's top bail bond insurer/bounty hunter associations, were private sector members of ALEC's Public Safety and Elections Task Force. The private sector chair of the task force was the National Rifle Association (NRA). Russell Pearce was also a member of the committee.[2] (ALEC's anti-immigration policies are now barely visible on the organization's very robust website. This might have to do with the organization shuttering that very same Public Safety Task Force. It was closed after the "Stand Your Ground" legislation it advocated led to the death of Trayvon Martin and unleashed a torrent of negative press, leading to corporate donors pulling ties to the group.)[3]

I am not a cynical man by nature. But it isn't difficult to look at this list, evaluate the implications of SB 1070, and conclude these organizations and their members would all profit from laws that demonized the Latino population and allowed for the sweeping arrests of that population. Prison populations would increase. The need for bail would increase. And, as the population became fearful of an illegal alien invasion of criminals, gun sales would increase.

I know that money influencing politics is not big news. I even wrote about it before I took office in an op-ed piece I penned after the primary: "Winston Churchill said: 'Some see private enterprise as a predatory target to be shot, others as a cow to be milked, but few are those who see it as a sturdy horse pulling the wagon.' There are too many in elected office who view private enterprise as a cow to be milked."

Still, I was surprised how powerful, how organized, and how brazen ALEC was—basically funding anyone willing to sign on to the bills their business partners wanted passed. (Lest anyone think this is only a conservative phenomenon, in 2017, left-of-center lobbyists finally created their own organization to influence policy, the State Innovation Exchange.)

In Phoenix, lobbyists were everywhere. There are over 3,000 registered lobbyists peddling influence in the Copper State.[4] I'm sure certain sectors spend prominently in most states, but in Arizona some of the biggest check writers and law whisperers represent utilities, homebuilders, realtors, automobile and dealer associations, mining interests, trucking, universities, charter and religious schools, predatory lenders, cattlemen and ranchers, software vendors, and private prisons. Prominent Arizona lobbyists also include the NRA and related Second Amendment organizations, the Arizona Chamber of Commerce, the Arizona Tax Research Association, representing the state's biggest property and income taxpayers, and the evangelical Center for Arizona Policy.

I did not enter politics as a radical reformer. So, when lobbyists approached me with contributions, I had no problem taking their funds. I did not go looking for handouts or policy ideas from ALEC, and I was beholden to nobody beyond my constituents in Mesa. But I quickly discovered the way lobbyists work in Arizona—and probably in other states. It's quite simple: Lobbying money flows regularly to incumbents. (State law prohibits donations only during session, but the week before the 100-day legislative session starts and the week after it ends are the two big rainmaking weeks of the year.) These lobbyists have default funding settings. They have money to burn. They want to be able to pick up the phone and reach someone in a state senator's office. That means legislators can raise $100,000 without lifting a finger. Most of that money, symbolically enough, is funneled in the "Hell" week before the session starts, and the week after it ends. Then and now, it seems kind of sick.

RIP: SB 1070

As for the law that led to Russell Pearce's demise, it was still on the books but had been effectively neutralized by court challenges. One, brought by the Obama Administration, was quickly resolved on June 25, 2012—before I took office. The Supreme Court ruled that SB 1070 could not require anyone to carry "registration" papers provided by the federal government, or make it a crime for immigrants to work or solicit work without federal employment authorization, or give local police the power to arrest someone for previously committing a "removable" offense. The court did agree with one provision—that police should check the immigration status before releasing anyone they detained or arrested—but left open the possibility that it might be struck down.[5]

A second suit against the state of Arizona brought by ACLU, the Mexican-American Legal Defense and Education Fund and other advocacy groups also neutralized the law. Finally, in 2016, State Attorney General Mark Brnovich conceded that while state and local police officers can ask about immigration status during a traffic stop or criminal investigation, extending a stop or making an arrest to verify a person's immigration status is not permissible.[6] But these legal challenges did not deter Pearce or his followers.

My Senate seatmate was a doctor named Kelli Ward, the controversial Tea Party figure who later challenged (and lost to) Senator John McCain in the 2014 primary. Since then, she has distinguished herself with tone-deaf social media posts, especially during her 2018 primary run to replace Senator Jeff Flake, and again when the ailing Senator McCain announced he was stopping medical treatment for brain cancer. Ward, about to begin a final pre-primary bus tour, posted: "I think they wanted to have a particular narrative that they hope is negative to me." Hours later, McCain died. Two days later, the candidate was still playing politics, drawing more heat for tweeting, "Political correctness is like a cancer!"

Back in 2013, I figured Ward would be collegial. She was polite, courteous and friendly to my face. We were both Republicans, after all. I never suspected she was plotting my demise. But, as I found out later, she and Russell Pearce were grooming a candidate to replace me.

In theory, I had no problem being replaced. I would have gladly handed over the keys to the kingdom, so to speak, to anyone who wanted to act responsibly. I was thrilled when Ralph Heap, a well-known Mesa orthopedic surgeon, reached out to me in October 2013, saying he wanted to discuss the upcoming August 14 Republican primary. I didn't know much about him, but he lived less than two miles from my home, had a good professional reputation, and I assumed had money of his own to invest in an election. "He's gotta be like me," I thought.

Heap suggested we meet for lunch. I brought Christi because this was one doctor I really wanted to get a second opinion on. We sat down at a local Mexican restaurant and Heap informed us that he was going to run against me. At first, I thought about saying, "Don't even bother. I'll endorse you." I had run to keep Russell Pearce out of office and had no great desire to remain in the state Senate, especially with Senate President Biggs blocking any use of my talents and experience. But I wanted to find out more about him. It didn't take long to discern that he was regurgitating talking points as radical as Pearce's old platforms. Christi and I didn't even need to exchange looks. After a while, I said, "Your immigration views are inconsistent with mine. We didn't spend this time and money to see Mesa replace Pearce with a clone. So, I'm sorry, but I don't see how I can support you."

"You've been given fair warning," he said. "This is going to be very interesting for you."

Those words, which sounded like a veiled threat, pretty much marked the end of lunch—and the end of any idea that I would be able to turn over my seat to a reasonable replacement.

Heap was a much more formidable candidate than Russell Pearce. I believe he had ambitions of eventually serving in Congress. Like me, and unlike Pearce, he had no dirty laundry: no J.T. Ready, no Fiesta Bowl football ticket scandal, no political record. And he was something of a public figure in the community—a tall, handsome doctor who helped people, not just in Arizona, but in far-flung places like Papua, New Guinea, Bolivia, and Zimbabwe. He was a banjo-playing triathlete with lots of energy to knock on doors and shake hands on the campaign trail. The Heap name was also well-known in Mesa because of Ralph's nephew, Todd Heap, a local sports hero who played tight end for the local Mountain View High School, Arizona State, and for twelve years in the NFL for the Baltimore Ravens. So, while he didn't have the political name recognition of Russell Pearce, he wasn't toxic. Although he ranted against the Affordable Healthcare Act and my support for Medicaid—a program from which his own practice accepted funds—he wouldn't embarrass voters the same way that Pearce did. In addition, more conservative members of the Arizona Republican Party, like my seatmate Senator Kelli Ward, endorsed him.

I have to give Heap credit. He raised over $55,000 and "loaned" the campaign another $50,000, according to filings from August 14, 2014. I outraised him in both individual contributions and political action committees donations, which was to be expected since I was the incumbent. (In comparison, Russell Pearce raised almost $262,000 in his "Patriots for Pearce—Special Election" fund from November 23, 2010 to May 10, 2012 for his recall campaign. This included $80,000 from political committees and $169,000 from individual contributions. His "Pearce for Arizona" primary campaign against me raised an additional $83,000.)[7] But I also had deeper pockets. We spent nearly twice as much money on our second primary than we did on our first. And it was a much tougher race. We beat Heap by five percent of the vote, versus twelve percent against Pearce two years earlier. The general election against Democratic nominee Steven Zachary, a guy I liked, was far less stressful. I won on November 4, 2014, with 70 percent of the vote.

This was an unprecedented amount of money to spend on a primary in Arizona. I spent more than $1 million of my own on two primaries and three elections. That's $1 million for the right to serve my district and earn a salary of $26,000 per year—which I donated to charity. I had an *Arizona Republic* editorial board member musing in print that I should set my sights higher (Congress), since this was the kind of money typically spent to go to D.C., but a ridiculous amount to be spent defending a local state Senate seat.

I'm sure many people think my campaign expenditures point to an inequity in our electoral system. I absolutely agree. The campaign with the most money has an inherent advantage—usually. Michael Bloomberg spent nearly a billion dollars in pursuit of the 2020 Democratic presidential nomination and didn't move the needle.[8] Unfortunately, it is the system we have—a system thrown completely out of whack by the Supreme Court's Citizens United decision, giving businesses the right to spend unlimited funds backing candidates via political action committees. There was never a limit on what a candidate could spend of their own money, but Citizens United brought the entire investor class and corporate America into the political game everywhere. This decision has done incalculable damage to America's democracy. But the undue influence of money in politics and policy is a theme that will surface repeatedly in these pages. The anti-immigration movement has been funded for 100 years by people whose wealth dwarfs mine. So, in the end, I honestly feel the money I spent—not always strategically, in hindsight—was well worth it. We had no intention of letting extremists' ambitions take further root in Mesa or in Arizona as a whole. After three successful election cycles, my determination and my war chest evidently persuaded Pearce and his supporters to shift their efforts elsewhere.

PEARCE UPDATE

Although Russell Pearce no longer holds a legislative position in Arizona, his ability to generate negative headlines has remained undiminished. The law and order man—someone who accused immigrants of abusing the system and taxing Arizona's state services—drew plenty of criticism in 2017 after being promoted to chief deputy of the Maricopa County Treasurer's Office and getting a whopping $70,000 raise—while he was already collecting two pensions.[9]

The promotion and its giant salary boost generated whispers of patronage and cronyism. As columnist Laurie Roberts reported, Maricopa County's newly elected treasurer Royce Flora and Pearce were mutual fans. "With Flora's help, Pearce landed an $85,000-a-year job in the Treasurer's Office in 2014," Roberts revealed. In 2016, Pearce returned the favor, sending "around an e-mail urging Republican precinct committeemen to vote for Flora." Flora's rival, Democrat Joe Downs, had pledged to fire Pearce.[10]

Instead, with Flora's victory, Pearce wasn't out of job, he was in the money. As Roberts described it, "A gooey triple dip of taxpayer-supplied goodness for the guy who spent his political career calling for cuts to government waste and bureaucracy."

That Russell Pearce has a job in state government should defy logic. On September 6, 2014, while serving as the first vice chair of the Arizona Republican Party, Pearce reached a new personal low with regard to unfortunate comments. Given his many remarks about undocumented aliens and the shooting victims in Colorado, it should have been a career killer.

While discussing Arizona's public assistance programs on his weekly radio show, Pearce said: "You put me in charge of Medicaid, the first thing I'd do is get Norplant, birth-control implants, or tubal ligations." Not content to just suggest welfare mothers should undergo forced sterilization, Peace expanded on his demands.[11]

"Then we'll test for drugs and alcohol," he continued, before adding that those who want more children should "get a job."

When news broke that the first vice chair of the Arizona Republican Party was advocating sterilization of poor women to qualify for welfare benefits, the outcry was loud and clear. Critics may not have realized Pearce was voicing opinions shared by Nazi-sympathizers Madison Grant and Wycliffe Draper. Pearce may not have realized it either, but they knew eugenics when they heard it. "The poor must be made to stop breeding" was his message. That was also the dream of so many eugenicist reformers in the early twentieth century. And now, immigrant-targeting Russell Pearce was resurrecting this dangerous idea.

Pressure quickly mounted on Pearce and he resigned from his post with the party on September 14. As with his previous scandals, Pearce deflected any responsibility.

In a statement, Pearce claimed that there was an on-air "discussion about the abuses to our welfare system" and he "shared comments written by someone else and failed to attribute them to the author."[12]

"This was a mistake," he said, announcing he was stepping down from his role with the Party. "This mistake has been taken by the media and the left and used to hurt our Republican candidates."

I want to make two last points about the 2014 incident. First, the irony that Pearce was yammering about "the abuses to our welfare system" is impossible to miss, considering he is now earning three state-related pensions. The second is that, given Pearce's record of insulting, disingenuous, and insensitive comments, it is shocking that anyone would hire Russell Pearce for any public position.

THE PARTY IS OVER

When it came time to run in 2016, I ran essentially unopposed in the primary and the general election. While I was pleased with my local outcome, I cannot say the same for what was going on nationally. As a long-time Republican watching the Trump campaign, I felt a scary sense of *déjà vu* as I heard him beat the same ugly, anti-immigrant drum that Russell Pearce and Sheriff Joe Arpaio had sounded. Only this time, it was louder and with constant, national coverage, amplifying scare-tactic stories and plans to waste billions of dollars building a border wall. I will discuss Trump's anti-immigration visions in more depth later in this book. But I mention them here because, despite my success in Mesa and Arizona, I began to feel that the Horseshoe Virus, and related, insane political positions around illegal immigration, were continuing to devolve. I began to wonder if I could represent this party. Indeed, the inflammatory policies of Pearce and Trump have helped turn a once-solid red state purple.

Arizona law prevents legislators from serving more than four terms in the state senate, so I had only one possible run left. But whether or not I chose to serve it was actually a strategic chip—one I planned to use to protect the Senate seat from Russell Pearce's influence.

My decision was a perfect storm of events. I missed running our businesses, especially our renewable energy interests which I believe improved the health of our sick forested lands. I was also appalled by our President's behavior and it felt wrong representing voters of a party that seemed to be solidly in support of Trump. But as the 2018 election cycle approached, with no Pearce-wannabe in sight, I felt I could leave my seat and support an aspiring young candidate I admired and respected: Tyler Pace. As I wrote in a farewell column that ran in the *Arizona Republic*:

> Lack of civility in politics is not a confined phenomenon. It has bled into our neighborhoods. Increasingly, we associate only with those who share our opinions while viewing those who do not as bad actors.
>
> This is not only detrimental to the political process; it is harmful to our communities. On this issue, I agree with Sen. John McCain who recently said, "we are more alike than different."
>
> I ran my campaigns on one word: Elevate. It is the singular value that has guided my life. If a problem cannot be solved on the plane on which you stand, step higher. I still have great hope in a bright

> future for our state and our country. It has been my honor to serve
> for a season and now allow for others to have their season.[13]

I left the legislature, but I am still seeking to elevate. With more time and freedom to spend on my passions, I began to think about Russell Pearce, Joe Arpaio, Kris Kobach, Andy Biggs, and like-minded influencers. I had more time to study the history of the Federation for American Immigration Reform (FAIR) and the many other organizations started by John Tanton. I was able to read about Tanton, whose health was rapidly failing from Parkinson's. While Tanton had been responsible for the political strategies used to deny the entry of new immigrants to the U.S., he was not alone. I discovered that his handiwork was three centuries in the making.

My education continues, but now it's time to share what I have learned.

PART TWO

Chapter Five

THE ROOTS OF ANTI-IMMIGRATION

IN 2010, THERE WERE 308,745,538 people living in the United States. That precise number was determined by the 2010 U.S. Census.

At its core, the census functions as the official, state-by-state head-count, conducted every ten years to determine the proper allocation of seats in the U.S. House of Representatives, which is based on state population. But the census doesn't just count people; it gathers data about the people counted and allows us to parse our population in several ways—by sex, by residence, by age, by household composition (big families, small families, single-parent families, etc.), and by race and family origin. The responses help government agencies plan and fund age-related programs, such as child-care or elder-care, and they help monitor compliance with anti-discrimination laws, like the Voting Rights Act and the Civil Rights Act.

The census data also provides a mirror for our nation. If America is a melting pot, the census lists our ingredients. In 2010, we were 72 percent white (223.6 million) in total, with 64 percent of those non-Hispanic whites. We were 13 percent black (38.9 million). We were 5 percent Asian (14.7 million). We were less than 1 percent American Indian and Alaska Native alone (2.9 million) and only half a percent Native Hawaiian and Other Pacific Islander (0.5 million). Six percent of us (19.1 million) identified as "some other race."[1]

We were also 16 percent Hispanic (50.5 million). But that identifier is not a race.

"Hispanic origin can be viewed as the heritage, nationality, lineage, or country of birth of the person or the person's parents or ancestors before arriving in the United States," explains the Census website. "People who identify as Hispanic, Latino, or Spanish may be any race." The number of white non-Hispanics in the U.S. was 196.8 million or 64 percent. That percentage seems to set some people on edge.

More people than ever describe themselves as being multi-racial. Asians were the fastest-growing group, percentage-wise, from 2000 to 2010, increasing by 44 percent.

You can slice this raw data many ways and extrapolate all kinds of insight about who lives where. But what do those numbers really tell us? I have two takeaways. The first is that we are an incredibly diverse nation, one that will only become more diverse over time. The second is that the numbers remind me of the message I cited earlier, which first appeared on American coins in 1785 and, since 1935, has adorned the back of every dollar bill: *E Pluribus Unum*—Latin for "Out of Many, One."

WE THE PEOPLE VS THEY THE ENEMY

The vast majority of our ancestors came here from other countries to improve their station in life, often for their children, to start over, to not duplicate the lives they left behind. We did not come here because we shared a common heritage or ethnicity. We came to the New World to found a nation whose people would pursue happiness and liberty while bound together by a shared creed: a belief in and respect for a truly extraordinary and flexible document, the U.S. Constitution.

It is hard to quantify how ingenious this document is. Originally written on just four pages of parchment, it remains, 240 years later, a blueprint for governance by and for the people and the veritable bible for freedom and human rights. It's very first words resonate with the spirit of unity, inclusion, opportunity, and freedom:

> We the People of the United States, in Order to form a more perfect Union, establish Justice, insure domestic Tranquility, provide for the common defense, promote the general Welfare, and secure the Blessings of Liberty to ourselves and our Posterity, do ordain and establish this Constitution for the United States of America.

Abraham Lincoln echoed the core of the ideas that give this document such power in the Gettysburg Address. In his speech, given during the dedication of the Soldiers' National Cemetery, Lincoln expanded on some of the principles he enunciated earlier in the Emancipation Proclamation. But he also harkened back to both the Constitution and the Declaration of Independence.

Lincoln stated that our great nation was "conceived in liberty, and dedicated to the proposition that all men are created equal...that we here highly resolve that these dead shall not have died in vain—that this nation, under God, shall have a new birth of freedom—and that government of the people, by the people, and for the people, shall not perish from the earth."

The Civil War was not over when Lincoln shared these dramatic words, reaffirming the uniqueness of our union. In fact, this speech was the first time he referred to America as a "nation." His choice of words was telling. "Country" is a word tied to territory—an expanse of land. "Nation" implies commonality and unity, a shared culture. It is more synonymous with "tribe." Only months earlier, Gettysburg had been the scene of the war's bloodiest battle. But despite the terrible, bloody divide America was facing, Lincoln united the powerful guiding vision of our founders to his dream for the future, conjuring up a nation that would not be divided or stopped.

So how did our immigrant-built nation decide that immigrants—the core of "we the people" in the most prosperous and powerful nation in the world—are now "they the enemy"? And how did Americans with the tradition of liberty, which lured so many of their own ancestors to come and build a nation, start to pick winners or losers from the lines of immigrants based on color of skin or the language that they speak?

It is a long and complicated story. The leading roles were played by a few would-be aristocrats filled with a mixture of utopian dreams, high-minded ambition, fashionable but wrong-headed social theories, inaccurate science, vile racism, prejudice, enormous amounts of money, fear, and a thirst for power.

And that's just for starters.

GROWING PAINS

From the initial formation of our nation, American citizens were all immigrants on some level. The pilgrims arrived from England in 1620 and, while they get the spotlight at Thanksgiving, they were not the only new arrivals. The Dutch settled in New York. The Spanish in Florida. Swedish settlers launched a short-lived colony in Delaware. And not long after, thousands upon thousands of African slaves were forced here.

Although the rights of man are frequently discussed in the Declaration of Independence, citizenship wasn't clearly defined until the Naturalization Act of 1790 set out the first rules to becoming an "American."

> ...any alien, being a free white person, who shall have resided within the limits and under the jurisdiction of the United States for the term of two years, may become a citizen thereof.

The same year this intrinsically racist blueprint for citizenship was laid out, the first U.S. Census was taken. It counted the number of free white males of sixteen years and older in each household, including heads of families, free white males under sixteen years, free white females, all other free persons, slaves, and total inhabitants. Among the most interesting findings? Of the 3,893,635 people counted, 694,280 were slaves; that's nearly 18 percent of the population, which suggests the U.S. African-American population has decreased percentage-wise over the years. It's also worth mentioning that no count was made of the one demographic with the oldest claim to U.S. soil—Native Americans.

The Naturalization Act laws got bounced around in the early days of our nation. One short-lived bill dictated that newcomers had to wait fourteen years to become citizens, but the 1802 version of the law settled on a five-year residency requirement, automatically conferred citizenship on the children of naturalized citizens, and held that kids born abroad to U.S. citizens were also citizens. The 1802 Naturalization Act also decentralized the act of becoming a citizen. As long as they were white, anyone could appear at any court in any state or territory and declare their intention to become a citizen, support the Constitution, and renounce any allegience to "every foreign prince, potentate, state or sovereignty."[2]

The next major piece of immigrant legislation came five years later, as Haiti's successful anti-slavery and anti-colonial rebellion was coming to an end. Concerned that a sovereign nation of free black men and women now existed nearby, pro-slavery legislators pushed through a ban targeting "free" blacks. The penalty for a ship's captain allowing such entry was, "He shall forfeit and pay the sum of one thousand dollars for each and every negro, mulatto, or other person of colour."[3]

Four years later, for the record, the Act Prohibiting Importation of Slaves of 1807 passed. To its credit, the penalty for bringing in a slave was much more severe. Convicted slavers, the law decreed, would "suffer imprisonment for not more than ten years nor less than five years, and be fined not exceeding ten thousand dollars, nor less than one thousand dollars."[4]

At no time, however, were white people restricted from entering America. The flow of European immigrants to the promised land was steady. By 1840, the census counted 17,069,453 people in the U.S. Twenty years later, the population had nearly doubled to 31,443,322. The largest immigrant segments hailed from Ireland, where an estimated two million people fled the ravages of the potato famine in 1845, and from Germany. These arrivals boosted the Catholic presence in major cities.

The new, exploding population often arrived penniless, speaking a different language, cooking new cuisines, and practicing different faiths and customs. While many were eager to work, often for extremely low wages, significant numbers of newcomers were in no shape for physical labor. Worn out by famine at home, sickened and exhausted by their transatlantic journey, they arrived as broke, sick, starving refugees who came off the boat and soon entered "almshouses and lunatic hospitals as paupers soon after landing," according to the book *Expelling the Poor*.[5] But the point is that no one came here to continue to live in poverty. They left all that was familiar to start over here. In America.

Prejudice-fueled, anti-immigration fever continually misses this point. America is made up of self-selected, self-motivated optimists who want to make more of their lives. The lazy dross of other nation's societies stayed home, where they could continue to live lives without hope. I know this from my good friends from Argentina, Uruguay, Peru, Mexico, Venezuela, and pretty much every country in Central America. I have also met Uber and Lyft drivers from dozens of countries in Africa, Asia, and the Middle East, in whom I see the same common optimism that brought them to America, regardless of race, language, or customs. They get up every day to work in a gig economy or in many other hard jobs like framing, roofing, landscaping, farming in all its iterations, housekeeping, food services, and more. Why curse them? May God bless them.

Throughout our history, all-too familiar anti-immigrant sentiments swelled in sync to the rising number of new arrivals. Pamphlets, posters, cartoons, and news articles surfaced, spreading hate and calling for the deportation of so-called "leeches."

Seen through the lens of modern, post-Civil Rights Era America, the anti-immigrant rhetoric used throughout the nineteenth century is shocking. Today, many of the cartoons and posters of the day would be characterized as hate speech. But there was no such social sensitivity at the time. Patently offensive, incendiary depictions of Irishmen wearing beer barrels, stuffing ballot boxes, or posing with the Pope were printed and widely circulated.

Samuel Morse, an inventor of the telegraph, signaled the growing mistrust and suspicion in a book, *A Foreign Conspiracy Against the Liberties of the United States*. A Catholic-bashing bestseller, it described a papal plot to take over the country. Morse's book was followed by a salacious, bestselling tell-all by Maria Monk, who claimed to be a former nun from Canada. Her 1836 tale, *The Awful Disclosures of Maria Monk, or, The Hidden Secrets of a Nun's Life in a Convent Exposed*, recounted sordid tales of a nunnery in which priests had their way with women and murdered babies in basements. Monk, who was later exposed as a fraud, claimed to have escaped to save her baby and was rescued by a kind Protestant.

Various figures tried to weaponize the anti-Catholic sentiment to gain office. Morse ran for mayor of New York and lost. But in 1844, Monk's publisher, James Harper—whose company has evolved into the publishing giant HarperCollins—made a successful run at City Hall as the candidate of the American Republican Party (which later changed its name) to win a one-year term to run the city.

The demographic and social realities came to a head in the early 1850s, with the rise of America's first widespread, populist, anti-immigration movement. The Know-Nothing Party grew out of a secret society that formed in Manhattan known as the Order of the Star-Spangled Banner. Members pledged to have a pureblooded pedigree of Protestant, Anglo-Saxon stock and rejected membership of all "foreigners and Catholics in particular." According to lore, members were forbidden from talking about the group—which would seem to make recruitment a problem—and told to respond, "I know nothing," when asked about the group.[6]

In 1854 the Whig Party—formed 20 years earlier to oppose the demagogic behavior of President Andrew Jackson—fractured over internal divisions on slavery. The fissure famously led to the creation of the Republican Party. But it also gave the Know-Nothing Party, formally known as the America Party on the ballot, a brief moment to rise and rant. It did so with shocking efficiency, becoming arguably the most successful third party in American history, winning 43 seats in the 1854 congressional elections.[7]

Every movement needs a figurehead to stoke and manipulate public sentiment. The Know-Nothings had two New Yorkers beating the drums of social division: Thomas R. Whitney, a silversmith, the movement's brain or "theorist," and William "Bill the Butcher" Poole, its brawn or rabble-rouser. Does that sound familiar? The Horseshoe Virus relies on a combo of brain and brawn.

Whitney wrote what became the unofficial Know-Nothing bible, *A Defense of the American Policy*. The chapter titles say it all. In "Can a Papist be a Citizen of the American Republic?" Whitney essentially argues that the Pope is a civil authority who claims the ability to annul any and all oaths taken by his followers, which, by his logic, makes all Catholics untrustworthy American citizens. As for his chapter about the "'Effects of the Competition of Immigrant Labor on the Industrial Interests of the United States," the engraver hammered out a template that is still being used today. He blames the "superabundance of immigration from Europe" for "a train of evils." American mechanics, he writes, "have been alienated from their homes, their comforts, their ambition! How vast the number of those who have been driven from their employments to make room for the under-bidding competition of the foreign laborer!"[8]

Poole, however, became the movement's most famous figure. The leader of the Bowery Boys gang, a prizefighter and slaughter-house worker, Poole, who was portrayed by Daniel Day-Lewis in Martin Scorsese's 2002 film, *Gangs of New York*, was a beloved bad boy. On February 24, 1855, the Bowery Boy leader exchanged words, threats, and fisticuffs with Irish boxer John Morrisey, who headed the rival Dead Rabbits gang. Cops stopped the fighting at Stanwix Hall, a Manhattan saloon on Broadway. But that evening, Poole reappeared at the bar and was shot by Lewis Baker, a Welshman in Morrissey's entourage. He died two weeks later, with a quote made for and possibly by the newspapers of the day: "I think I am a goner. If I die, I die a true American; and what grieves me most is, thinking that I've been murdered by a set of Irish—by Morrissey in particular."[9]

A quarter of million people reportedly paid their respects to the gangster in March of 1855. Now the Know-Nothing Party had a martyr to go with its powerful platform, a significant voter bloc in Congress and eight governorships. But instead of growing, the movement was upended by another powerful social and political issue: slavery. When southern Know-Nothings called on the party to support slavery, the center did not hold. Many northern and midwestern Know-Nothings bolted to a new political group, the Republican Party. Its members included a former congressman from Illinois named Abe Lincoln. Doubtless, he was glad to see the populist party implode.

"I am not a Know-Nothing. That is certain. How could I be?" he wrote in a letter to his Springfield pal, Joshua Speed. "How can anyone who abhors the oppression of negroes, be in favor of degrading classes of white people?"[10]

Lincoln was hardly the only person to object to the nativist movement. Many publications of the time decried the movement. "We confidently look to see this 'Know-Nothing' party soon: No-Where!" wrote the editors of Virginia's *Cooper's Clarksburg Register*.[11]

"There is not a railroad or canal in the whole Union that has not been principally built with Irish labor," opined *The Daily Dispatch*, a Richmond, Virginia, paper. "As citizens they have shown themselves capable of appreciating the blessings of their lot in the New World." (Underscoring the nation's complicated conflicts with basic human rights, the same editorial goes on to praise the Irish for having "never, for a single moment, sympathized with abolition.")[12]

One other important event happened during the Know-Nothing's brief rise and flame-out in the new state of California, where a criminal law was passed in 1850 that codified racism:

> No black or mulatto person, or Indian, shall be permitted to give evidence in favor of, or against, any white person. Every person who shall have one eight part or more of Negro blood shall be deemed a mulatto, and every person who shall have one half of Indian blood shall be deemed an Indian.[13]

Four years later, the California Supreme Court issued a verdict in People v. Hall, a case in which a white man, George Hall, was convicted of murdering a Chinese miner. Hall argued that the Chinese witnesses' testimony against him should have been disallowed. The court agreed with him.[14] Chinese immigrants of California were now entirely disenfranchised.

In 1868, however, three years after the end of the Civil War, enfranchisement became, at least theoretically, the order of the day. With the Fourteenth Amendment ratified, all persons "born or naturalized" in the United States were now American citizens who were guaranteed due process under the law. This amendment was meant to clarify that blacks—both former slaves and those who lived in the North as free men—were now citizens with equal constitutional protections. History tells us this is not exactly what happened, as southern Jim Crow laws and northern prejudicial norms continued to frequently deny black empowerment for 100 years until the civil rights movement in the 1960s. And as the Black Lives Matter movement has shown, America still has not achieved full protection under the law for all.

THE MORMON WAR

There was a mostly white segment of America that repeatedly experienced disenfranchisement in the 1800s. My ancestors, the Mormons. In the 1830s, some of our great-great-great-great grandparents converted and faithfully followed the newly founded and now largest American-born religion called The Church of Jesus Christ of Latter-day Saints. Many followers of the new religion (including some in our own family) faced mob violence as they moved from one settlement to another, relocating from upstate New York to Kirtland, Ohio, to Independence, Missouri, to a town called Far West in the same state. In 1938, there were thousands of Mormons in Missouri, constituting a substantial and powerful voting bloc, which once again generated hostility. Various conflagrations, from the Gallatin County Election Day Battle to the Battle of Crooked River, led to an executive order from Governor Lilburn Boggs, who declared that "the Mormons must be treated as enemies, and must be exterminated or driven from the state if necessary for the public peace."

Issued on October 27, 1838, Boggs' Mormon Extermination Order, formally known as Missouri Executive Order 44, was a terrifying license to kill and was finally removed from the books in the 1970s. But it was effective. On November 1, 1838, Joseph Smith surrendered to authorities to stop the bloodshed and Missouri's short-lived Mormon War was over. More than 15,000 Latter Day Saints soon became immigrants within America, fleeing from Missouri to Illinois. There, the Mormon city of Nauvoo was erected. The ancestors of the Worsley family and my wife's family joined that migration to Nauvoo, relocating from Missouri and upstate New York, helping to build a city that was, at the time, larger than Chicago.

The Prophet was murdered in 1844, when an anti-Mormon mob stormed the Carthage, Illinois, jail where he was awaiting trial. (A little-known fact: Joseph Smith was running for president of the United States at the time, on a platform of the constitutional promise of liberty for all, regardless of religion.) Soon, his followers including both of our ancestors—over sixteen different ancestral lines were in Nauvoo from our two families—were on the move again, seeking sanctuary in the new Utah Territory.

Polygamy helped keep the Mormon faith on the America's unofficial list of minorities to be persecuted. Abraham Lincoln himself had two vices he wanted to tackle—the South's slavery and Mormon polygamy. He got to slavery and his successors tackled polygamy, using federal troops, asset seizures, and other pressure to force the Church to issue a Mormon Manifesto in 1890, abiding by the nation's new anti-polygamy laws.

Members of the Church of Jesus Christ of Latter-day Saints are not race or a nationality or an ethnic group. But the persecution our members endured underscores how easily prejudice metastasized in America. Like the xenophobic motivations that fueled the anti-Irish movement, a group was attacked on the grounds of its faith. That is no less horrendous than attacking some for their language or skin color.

TARGET PRACTICE

By 1880, the U.S. population was 50,189,209—a thirty percent increase in population in just ten years. Five years earlier, Congress passed its first targeted ban of a specific population with the Page Law, a piece of legislation that stopped the arrival of women from "China, Japan, or any Oriental country" who were "imported for the purposes of prostitution." But the broad and threatening wording of the statute, combined with daunting penalties that ship captains faced, effectively stopped the flow of Asian women to the U.S.[15]

What brought the focus on Asian women? While curbing prostitution was the stated intent, Asian men were another, perhaps indirect target. The law meant that arranged marriages and mail-order brides were effectively quashed, as ship captains could be liable if these women were deemed "prostitutes" on arrival. So, the law carried many quality-of-life implications for Chinese laborers that were in the U.S.

But why target that population?

China had experienced great upheaval in the mid-1800s. It was plagued by the Opium Wars with Britain, which left the country's economy in shambles. In 1852, the lure of the California Gold Rush and a crop failure at home resulted in more than 20,000 mostly Chinese immigrants arriving in San Francisco—18,000 more than the previous year. Visions of a promised land continued when, in the 1860s, as the Central Pacific Railroad recruited laborers to expand its lines. The new arrivals represented a tiny percentage of the U.S. population, but their existence was a threat to white workers—many of whom had struck out in the gold rush and resented competition for available employment.

The Page Law was followed by far more restrictive legislation. In 1882, Congress unleashed two major immigration statutes, the Chinese Exclusion Act, signed into law by President Chester A. Arthur in the spring, and the Immigration Act later that summer. The Exclusion Act expanded the targeting initiated by the Page Law by placing a ten-year ban on all Chinese workers coming to the U.S.—"both skilled and unskilled laborers and Chinese employed in mining." Non-laborers from China needed to produce credentials from the Chinese government to immigrate.[16] The number of Chinese immigrants was reduced to a trickle.

A second law issued the same year as the Exclusion Act, the Immigration Act of 1882, was the first recognition by Congress that the federal government should be responsible for the flow of migrants to the U.S. It called for the Treasury to begin actively monitoring the nation's ports. As far as traffic on America's northern and southern borders was concerned, it was still a free-for-all. But ports were now to be guarded. New arrivals were to be charged $0.50 as an entry tax to cover the cost of administration. The law also added a new class of people to be banned, in addition to felons and Chinese laborers:

[If] on examination there shall be found among such passengers

> any convict, lunatic, idiot, or any person unable to take care of himself or herself without becoming a charge... such persons shall not be permitted to land.[17]

Ten years later, the Exclusion Act was extended by a law written by California Representative Thomas Geary. The Geary Act of 1892 added a new twist to being a Chinese resident in America: a kind of resident permit needed to be carried at all times to prove that a Chinese person was here legally. Failure to produce a permit could result in a year in prison or expulsion from the country.

In 1902, the Exclusion Act was made permanent and stayed on the books until 1943—when the U.S. and China became allied against Japan in the middle of the World War II. A new law, the Magnuson Act, allowed Chinese residents, many of whom had been in the U.S. for generations, to become naturalized citizens. It seems clear that political expediency fueled our sudden compassion toward the descendants of the Chinese immigrants when we needed their assistance in World War II.

Congress continued to pick up steam on policing America's ports of entry, creating a new Treasury division in 1891, the Office of the Super-intendent of Immigration. One year later, the new agency opened Ellis Island in New York Harbor. The immigration station became the gateway to America for millions of arrivals. The facilities on the island included a hospital, hearing and detention rooms for exceptional cases, railroad ticket offices, and immigrant aid organizations to help new arrivals make their way. Other processing stations were opened in Boston and Philadelphia.

New arrivals at Ellis Island had many sights to take in: the silvery waters of the Hudson River, the evolving New York skyline and, not far off in the harbor, a dazzling, 305-foot high, neoclassical copper sculpture: the Statue of Liberty, a gift from France as post-Civil War salute the union's enduring triumph. The words on the statue's pedestal, written by Emma Lazarus as a poem entitled "The New Colossus," were too small to be read from Ellis Island, but they spoke to the new arrivals, articulating a welcoming dream of America:

> Give me your tired, your poor
> Your huddled masses yearning to breathe free
> The wretched refuse of your teeming shore
> Send these, the homeless, tempest-tost to me
> I lift my lamp beside the golden door!

With Ellis Island and other immigration centers, the federal government was clearly embracing an active role in monitoring its ports and its incoming population. The decentralized process of becoming a naturalized citizen that had existed for more than 100 years came to an end when Congress created the Basic Naturalization Act of 1906 and with it, the Bureau of Immigration and Naturalization, the direct forerunner of what is now the U.S. Citizenship and Immigration Service, which currently operates within the Department of Homeland Security.

THE NINETEENTH CENTURY BACKSTORIES

Looking back, it's clear that, in the development of U.S. immigration law, there was a constant tug-of-war. On one side was the liberty-loving political framework provided by the United States' foundational documents and an economy that required a growing population and workforce. On the other was the unbridled prejudice and racism of the times, underpinned by economic protectionism. Throw in the activist religious and moral thinkers who believed in the fellowship of man (and increasing their flocks) and the process has become combustible. And let's add in the *laissez-faire* attitude that comes with being a massive, ever-expanding, sovereign nation with a small population. America was a grand experiment—a country and an idea that had never happened before.

Speaking of new ideas, there were other movements shaping ideas about immigration.

The first of these, for the purposes of this book, came from the English intellectual Thomas Malthus. An economist, demographer, and professor of political economics, Malthus caused an academic and ideological upheaval in 1798 when he anonymously published *An Essay on the Principle of Population as It Affects the Future Improvement of Society.*

The work called for containing population growth. Malthus had a doomsday vision for humanity, fueled by the belief that the birth rate, if not checked, would lead to geometric population growth, outpacing food supplies and resulting in starvation and the stagnation of society. In his view, wars, famine, illness, and sexual abstinence—he called it "moral restraint"—would prevent what he saw as an inevitable crisis.

For many, Malthusian theories were as compelling as they were gloomy. Written in the shadow of European political and demographic upheaval, Malthus' work arrived at the end of revolutions in the U.S. and France and at the very beginning of the Industrial Revolution. Concerns of how society should function as a whole, and how it should address the over-breeding of the agricultural classes, were on his mind. The reception to his ideas was so great that the anonymous author quickly gave his name to a new book-length version of the essay, and subsequently issued six different editions of the book, each updated with Malthus' latest thoughts and rebuttals to critiques of his work.

More than 200 years after *The Principle of Population* was published, the world's population has increased many times over. Life expectancy has more than doubled and infant mortality has plummeted. While hunger remains an undeniable and troubling issue, its existence has more to do with poverty, distribution, and inequality than food supply. But Malthus' theories broke new ground, impacting economic and social policy and furthering the field of demographics.

Perhaps most important of all, however, was the strange, conflicted element of humanism that lay beneath the work. Beneath Malthus' thick layers of pessimism, Harvard professor Joyce E. Chaplin notes, was a moral philosopher who pondered "the criteria for human happiness." He was concerned about maintaining a well-functioning, well-fueled, sustainable society in which people were—something that social theorists rarely write about—content and fulfilled.[18] In his mind, sustaining human society meant limiting the number of humans. In hindsight, the world's elastic population and food supply have so far proven him wrong. But there was a resonant thread of idealism and social reform burbling within his work. Centuries later, it was a thread that would get pulled in a manipulative fashion.

Malthus was but one of many innovative nineteenth century figures interested in the development of mankind. In Belgium, a free-thinking mathematician and astronomer, Adolphe Quetelet, became an early sociological statistician—three centuries before anyone uttered the phrase "big data." Written in 1835, his book, *A Treatise on Man and the Development of His Faculties*, gathered data to study the events that "influence human development" and how these causes and effects "mutually modify each other." Digging into birth rates and crime statistics, he set about trying to establish what is "normal" within the human experience.

In France, anthropologist and surgeon Paul Broca conducted research that was, in hindsight, both brilliant and destructive. Broca was interested in brains. He was the first scientist to identify the left frontal region of the brain as the center for speech. But he also spent a lot of time measuring craniums and developing theories about different races. He believed that the shape and size of Europeans skulls proved that they were of superior intelligence to other races.[19] Although Broca was in other ways socially progressive for his time—he was against slavery and had no fixations about racial purity—his thoughts linking craniums and cognition would fuel future racist beliefs.

When Malthus died in 1834, Francis Galton was a twelve-year-old English boy with an older half-cousin, Charles Darwin. Galton, like his cousin, studied medicine, loved to travel (he was elected to the Royal Geographical Society), and became a multi-disciplinary genius. He was also astoundingly prolific, writing such disparate titles as *The Knapsack*

Guide for Travellers in Switzerland and *Decipherment of Blurred Finger Prints*. His most impactful studies, however, explored human intelligence and inheritance.

In 1859, Darwin published *The Origin of the Species*, the groundbreaking book that outlined ideas of evolution in which species arose from a process of natural selection in which adaptive traits that increase the likelihood survival are reproduced.

While Darwin was putting the finishing touches on his masterwork, a scientist and friar in Silesia (now the Czech Republic) named Gregor Mendel was studying pea plants and conducting breeding experiments with various groups of seeds. His botanical findings—tying certain recessive or dominant traits to different seed combinations—would not be widely known for years to come, but they marked the beginning of what would eventually be called the science of heredity and genetic studies: the way plants and animals pass physical development and behavior to the next generation.

Galton was interested in heredity—not so much in evolution from species to species, as Darwin was, but within one specific species: Homo Sapiens. Like Malthus, Galton was concerned at some level with improving human existence. But he was also writing at the height of the industrialization which had created a new urban underclass. The explosion of technology also came with attendant ideas about efficiency, progress, and science. Taken together, it's easy to see how Galton might try and harness those influences to address that underclass—or perhaps celebrate the ruling elite.

In 1869, expanding ideas he had shared in two magazine articles, Galton published *Hereditary Genius: An Inquiry into its Laws and Consequences*. Here is its opening salvo:

> I propose to show in this book that a man's natural capabilities are derived by inheritance, under exactly the same limitations as are the form and physical features of the whole organic world. Consequently, as it is easy, notwithstanding those limitations, to obtain by

> careful selection a permanent breed of dogs or horses gifted with
> peculiar powers of running, or of doing anything else, so it would
> be quite practicable to produce a highly-gifted race of men by
> judicious marriages during several consecutive generations.[20]

To answer what he calls the book's "primary issue—whether or no genius is hereditary," Galton concocted what he deemed "scientific studies" in which he aggregated and analyzed data on everything from math scores to chest measurements of Scottish military men. He also studied various segments of society—"Judges," "Oarsmen," "Literary Men," and "Men of Science"—to make his case that the geniuses among us benefit from good hereditary breeding. His study was widely praised by his contemporaries. Indeed, while genes as we know them had yet to be identified, the idea that heredity dictated human physical makeup gained traction. As enlightened as Galton was, the idea that nurture, not nature, can foster genius—that human character is also shaped by education, affluence, family, community, and other living conditions—did not factor into his studies.

The concepts of *Hereditary Genius* gestated with Galton—or perhaps I should say, bred—and grew. He took in the work of his cousin, Charles Darwin, and likely that of Quelet and Broca. Eventually, he came up with a new term for his vision of improved heredity: eugenics.

Galton introduced the term in his 1883 book, *Inquiries into Human Faculty and Its Development*. A footnote in the book explains the word is taken from the Greek word "eugenes," which he translates as "good in stock, hereditarily endowed with noble qualities." Galton says he wants a term to "to express the science of improving stock" that weighs the influences which "give to the more suitable races or strains of blood a better chance of prevailing speedily over the less suitable than they otherwise would have had. The word eugenics would sufficiently express the idea."[21]

That footnote has come to define Galton. It was the kernel of an idea, the genetic code if you will, that exploded. In a matter of decades, eugenics mutated, infiltrating the scientific world and spreading into social theory, reform movements, politics, and legislation for the first half of the twentieth century.

Eugenics—the idea that some "human stock" was fundamentally better, stronger, smarter, faster, and more "ideal" than other "human stock"— would be used to justify racism, fear, hate and crimes against humanity. In America, it was also a powerful weapon to wage war on immigrants. It is still being used today. But that's getting ahead of the story.

Chapter Six

THE MAINSTREAMING AND POLITICIZATION OF EUGENICS

GREGOR MENDEL'S EARLY RESEARCH INTO genetics took decades to get its due. While he printed and distributed one hundred copies of his 1865 paper, "Experiments on Plant Hybridization," the forty-eight-page work made little immediate impact. The author bears some responsibility for this; he didn't exactly trumpet his work as groundbreaking, and he left his biggest revelation until the end of the paper: "The behavior of each pair of differing traits in a hybrid association is independent of all other differences in the two parental plants," Mendel wrote. He italicized this line, but he probably should have worked it into his first paragraph. Instead, it took about thirty-five years before his work would be credited. Today, scientists view this quote as the Law of Independent Assortment, one of three insights known as Mendel's Laws.

An old proverb attributed to Alexander Pope declares, in effect, that a little bit of knowledge is a dangerous thing. Mendel's work on heredity had important, world-changing implications, but much of those were decades in the making. Not all of them were good.

DNA, the molecule that carries all genes, wasn't discovered until 1944. The double helix structure of DNA wasn't decoded until 1953, by James Watson and Francis Crick. In 2003, the sequencing and mapping of all human genes—the "genome"—was completed. Mendel had revealed basic laws, but at the turn of the twentieth century, genetics was imprecise. Questions abounded about how human qualities—intelligence, artistic capacity, musculature, dexterity—are passed down.

Despite the enormous lack of understanding about this new branch of science, several eugenics organizations sprung up to advance biological, social and political theories that sought to build on Mendel's breakthrough to make "better" humans. This same era was one where folks were susceptible to superstitions and huckster scams such as miracle tonics, cures, and lucky charms—and yes, I realize many are still susceptible today. Eugenics was the racist's miracle tonic, sold to the aristocracy around the world to make them feel special and well-bred versus the masses—the uneducated lower classes who were randomly mating.

The view of eugenicists, as J. P. Milum put it in his 1913 *London Quarterly Review* essay, "The Fallacy of Eugenics," was that natural selection had failed human life and therefore "must be replaced by conscious selection."[1] Social engineering ideas were all the rage, as were theories of racial superiority and its unavoidable corollary: racial inferiority. Eugenics supporters inhabited a similar bubble to the one occupied by many of Galton's admirers. In their view, genetics and race were the ultimate determinants of human behavior; class, wealth, poverty, opportunity, education, hygiene, family history—things we now take for granted as shaping our minds and lives—had nothing to do with how individuals and communities developed. Nature versus nurture was not well understood.

In 1903, the first annual meeting of the American Breeders Association (ABA) took place at the University of Missouri. The organization was formed to explore "the laws of breeding and to promote the improvement of plants and animals by the development of expert methods of breeding." That same year, Charles Benedict Davenport—a Harvard-educated scientist, former professor at the University of Chicago and ardent Mendel admirer—convinced the Carnegie Institute to fund The Station for Experimental Evolution in Cold Spring, a town in Long Island, NY. Three years later, Davenport approached the ABA and asked to form a Committee on Eugenics. Also, in 1906, the Race Betterment Foundation was founded in Battle Creek, Michigan, by John Harvey Kellogg, a doctor and the future inventor of Corn Flakes. In 1910, Davenport successfully wrangled the funds to launch the Eugenics Record Office to popularize eugenics. His benefactor was Mary Williamson Harriman, the widow of railroad magnate E.H. Harriman, who presided over a $100 million estate. She would not be the last millionaire to give Davenport money. The road to anti-immigrant targeting is paved with the money of some of America's richest citizens who were obsessed with putting eugenic theory into practice. In fact, geographic clusters of white supremacy, a sort of "birds of a feather" phenomenon developed, with brains and bounty festering in Michigan with the likes of Tanton and Kellogg, and in New York City with Carnegie, Mellon, and the Rockefellers.

By 1911, Davenport had written a textbook called *Heredity in Relation to Eugenics*—which he dedicated to Harriman. The book's preface couches Davenport's quests in careful terms: "A vast amount of investigation into the Laws of the inheritance of human traits will be required before it will be possible to give definite instruction as to fit marriage matings. Our social problems still remain problems. For a long time yet our watchword must be investigation."[2]

While the ultimate goal of human breeding is clearly on his mind, Davenport's opening salvo seems almost reasonable. He is adopting the long view, urging caution. The scientific grounding of the author, however, is thrown into doubt when you read further:

"It appears certain that, unless conditions change of themselves or are radically changed, the population of the United States will, on account of great influx of blood from southeastern Europe, rapidly become darker in pigmentation, smaller in stature, more mercurial, more attached to music and art and more given to crimes of larceny, kidnapping, assault, murder, rape and sex-immorality."[3]

Privately, Davenport's prejudices were even more unbridled. "Our ancestors drove Baptists from Massachusetts Bay into Rhode Island but we have no place to drive the Jews," he wrote in a letter to a fellow traveler with deep pockets and influential friends.

The recipient was Madison Grant.[4]

THE GODFATHER OF NAZISM

Born into a well-established, wealthy New York family, Grant attended Yale, got his law degree from Columbia University, and then spent a good deal of his immediate post-collegiate life hunting and hobnobbing. Confoundingly, Grant represents both the best and worst of America. He was a devoted conservationist who helped found New York's legendary Bronx Zoo and numerous national parks. He was also a devoted racist, who drove some of the country's most heinous legislation and crystallized the idea of a Nordic superior race that was later deployed by Nazism, which preferred the term Aryan.

In 1909, Grant became vice president of the Immigration Restriction League. Founded in 1895, the group's name spoke for itself. They favored literacy tests to stem the tide of immigrants from eastern and southern Europe. Attempts to get President Taft to back such a bill failed, but Grant was persistent. As a member of the American aristocracy, Grant knew people in high places. He was friendly with fellow nature lover Teddy Roosevelt and many other powerful figures, and lobbied them accordingly. Grant held executive positions for at least thirty-five organizations and associations, including the American Defense Society (trustee), American Eugenics Society (co-founder), American Prison

Society (vice president), Eugenics Committee of the U.S.A. (board of directors), Eugenics Research Association (president), and the Galton Society (co-founder).[5] Somehow, between all his committee meetings, Grant eventually put his ideas to paper, publishing *The Passing of the Great Race: Or, The Racial Basis of European History* in 1916.

The book is an abomination. A blatantly racist tract that promotes the theory of a master race, it lays down an argument for racial purity that is nascent Nazism. This is not hyperbole: years later, Leon Whitney of the American Eugenics Society recalled Grant showing him a letter from Adolph Hitler. The Nazi-in-chief had written to thank Grant for writing *The Passing of the Great Race* and called the book "my bible."[6]

"The Nordics are, all over the world, a race of soldiers, sailors, adventurers, and explorers, but above all, of rulers, organizers, and aristocrats," Grant gushed in one typical passage extolling northern Europeans and their descendants.[7]

In another section, he wrote, "To admit the unchangeable differentiation of race in its modern scientific meaning is to admit inevitably the existence of superiority in one race and of inferiority in another,"[8] It should come as no surprise, then, that Grant was horrified at the idea of members of different races and ethnicities having children together.

The Passing of the Great Race sold steadily and added to Grant's political clout, legitimizing eugenic pseudoscience among sections of the American aristocracy. Indeed, the book had built-in appeal to the people in power. Americans with Anglo-Saxon—Nordic—heritage comprised a great deal of the nation's ruling class.

PROGRESSIVE PROBLEMS

The title of Grant's *The Passing of the Great Race* strongly echoes an idea that had begun to flourish at the turn of the twentieth century in America, encapsulated in a powerful, ugly phrase: *race suicide.*

The term was coined by economist and sociology professor Edward A. Ross. A proponent of placing restrictions on immigrants, he used race suicide to describe what he envisioned as a looming cataclysmic crisis: the inevitable outcome when birth rates of Catholics and other immigrants outpaced Protestant Americans. For Ross, who often wielded a poison pen—he once described eastern European immigrants as "beaten members of beaten breeds"[9]—the influx of people who were not from white, Anglo-Saxon stock foretold a national disaster.

Ross wasn't alone in his thinking. In the 1890s, leading population scholar Francis Amasa Walker was another influential academic who believed immigrants from southern and eastern Europe were inferior and would degrade America's racial health. Add a slew of scientists falling under the trendy field of eugenics, and racial suicide was an idea that spread with alarming efficiency. In 1902, President Theodore Roosevelt wrote a letter to author Marie Van Horst, pronouncing "the question of race suicide" as the most important question in the country."[10]

Unlike the populist Know-Nothing rabble-rousers who spread fear and discontent fifty years earlier, race suicide's principal advocates were buttoned-up intellectuals.

Walker conducted two U.S. Censuses and went on to serve as the president of the Massachusetts Institute of Technology. Ross, who eventually disowned his incendiary work, went on to support the Bolshevik revolution, the New Deal, and spent a decade as the chairman of the American Civil Liberties Union.

Both men were exemplars of America's Progressive Era, the period from 1890 to 1920. This was an epoch of American expansion, coming as it did at the end of the Gilded Age when industrialization, urbanization, the spread of railroads, and enterprising investors created both explosive new wealth and social issues. To be progressive, then, was to be a reformer.

These progressives were in many ways a privileged class where poor idealists commingled with their wealthy counterparts. Yes, there were settlement house workers, labor union members, women's rights activists, muckraking and moralizing journalists, and temperance champions. But there were also politicians, big-thinking university social scientists, high-minded businessmen, and blue-blooded, nature-loving conservationists.[11]

"Progressives did not work in factories, they inspected them," Thomas Leonard writes in his book *Illiberal Reformers*. "Progressives did not drink in saloons; they tried to shutter them... Even when progressives idealized workers, they tended to patronize them, romanticizing a brotherhood they would never consider joining."[12]

In other words, many of those at the anti-immigration vanguard were what today's right-wing radio hosts and Fox broadcasters might sneeringly call the "left-wing media elite" or just the plain old elite. It was a fashionable, intellectual ideal, one that many of its adherents believed would benefit society.

As you can probably guess, a reformer's best intentions often collided with another trendy concept. This proved the case with eugenics and eugenicists. Some do-gooders believed that eugenics was based on pure scientific reason and might help reform. Meanwhile, some eugenicists believed reformers might help execute their visions of population control.

THE SANGER SNAG

One of the many do-good reformers who came under the grip of eugenics was Margaret Sanger, the woman who coined the phrase birth control and who founded the organization that evolved into Planned Parenthood. Sanger is a complicated figure and the organization that is her legacy is also complicated. On one hand, it has done tremendous work providing low-cost medical care for women throughout America. On the other hand, for foes of abortion, it is an object of scorn.

One of eleven children born to poor Catholic parents in upstate New York, Sanger became a nurse, married an architect, had three children, and moved to Manhattan's hotbed of left-leaning politics, Greenwich Village. There, she hobnobbed with the likes of future Literature Nobel

Prize winner Upton Sinclair, whose 1906 novel *The Jungle* exposed the brutal treatment of workers in the meatpacking industry, and anarchist Emma Goldman. Politicized, she joined the New York Socialist Party and began her journey to become one of the most important activists of the twentieth century.

Sanger sought to make birth control legal. She dreamed of a pill that could be taken to prevent pregnancy. She believed that "enforced motherhood is the most complete denial of a woman's right to life and liberty."[13] At one point, worried she would be arrested for violating obscenity laws for sending her writings through the mail, she fled to England.

There has been much debate about whether Sanger was an out-and-out eugenicist. But it seems clear that the eugenics movement presented a number of synergies with her own organization. In an essay entitled "The Eugenic Value of Birth Control Propaganda," she wonders if society's interest in eugenics can help promote her agenda, noting, "it is possible to use this interest as the foundation for education in prophylaxis, sexual hygiene, and infant welfare." In the same article, however, she does repeat a eugenic talking point: "the most urgent problem today is how to limit and discourage the over-fertility of the mentally and physically defective." She also writes this: "The campaign for birth control is not merely of eugenic value, but is practically identical with the final aims of eugenics."[14]

Among her copious writing, one sentence above all others has been used to portray her as a racist and eugenicist: "We do not want word to go out that we want to exterminate the Negro population, and the minister is the man who can straighten out that idea if it ever occurs to any of their more rebellious members," she wrote in a 1939 letter. At the time, Sanger was launching "The Negro Project," a plan to open clinics in the South. The letter described her plans to reach out to members of the religious community in the South to counter any rumors that might surface as clinics opened in the area.

Many scholars insist this was nothing more than an unfortunately worded sentence. Other critics, however, have pointed to it as proof Sanger and Planned Parenthood have eugenicist roots. In 2011, an anti-abortion group called Life Dynamics released "Racial Targeting and Population Control," a report written by the organization's president Mark Crutcher asserting that Planned Parenthood engaged in "racial targeting" by placing a disproportionate number of abortion clinics in areas where black residents exceed the average black population of the state.[15] According to Crutcher, this targeting policy had ties to eugenics proponents' beliefs that the "most effective way they could advance their agenda would be to concentrate population control facilities within the targeted communities." While other studies have challenged and refuted the "racial targeting" claim that Crutcher makes against Planned Parenthood and its alleged disproportionate distribution of clinics in America, a 2011 CDC study revealed the abortion rate of African-American women was four times higher than of white women.[16]

Another synergy between the women's health movement and eugenics at this time was less about Sanger's beliefs than those of eugenicists. Sanger's primary goals focused on providing women's healthcare and ensuring their access to birth control. She saw these as empowerment issues, not as race issues. Conversely, for many supporters of eugenics, birth control was an issue of paramount importance to stopping procreation of what they deemed inferior races—a central goal of the movement. At the Eugenics Record Office, founder Charles Davenport dreamed of a day when states could control reproduction by whole classes of people they deemed genetically inferior. Eugenicists by definition remain obsessed with breeding—what races, ethnicities, and types of people should and should not regenerate. While some eugenicists, like Davenport, worried that Sanger's work would promote promiscuity among "lower" races and lower the birth rate of intellectually "superior" classes who would practice birth control,[17] many other eugenicists supported her work. Birth control and abortions were tools of the movement.

A third synergy was money and power. The eugenics movement by the 1920s had gained traction in certain sectors of the aristocratic society. Some of these benefactors were true believers, but was there a "let them eat cake," out-of-touch nature to some arrogant and privileged members of the wealthy and intellectual class? Were they driven to justify their fortune, looking for science to affirm their position? Either way, money begets power and Washington, D.C. was under the grip of restrictive, racist immigration policies pushed by wealthy eugenicist Madison Grant and his pals. The ideas of the movement were now enshrined in academia, too, with more than 6,000 books written on the subject, according to the *Bibliography of Eugenics*, published in 1924.[18] If Sanger was looking for backers, she stood a good chance of finding them in a movement that was all about planning, or not planning, births.

She found a great deal of support at the American Eugenics Society (AES), which was launched in 1922 and incorporated by Madison Grant, millionaire Irving Fisher, and future Pioneer Fund board members Harry H. Laughlin and Henry Fairfield Osborn. In 1926, AES provided office space for Sanger's fledgling organization, the American Birth Control League. Her efforts drew the backing of a number of powerful members. Clarence C. Little, an avowed racist and president of the AES, was one of the board members of Sanger's League. AES member and Population Review Board founder Guy Burch served as the director of the American Birth Control. When that organization evolved into Planned Parenthood, General William Draper, a supporter of the Eugenics Congress, served as vice president of the federation.

General Draper figures in an event that captures the strange, discomforting intersection of progressive liberals and conservative eugenicists—the first ceremony held by the Planned Parenthood Federation of America to hand out the Margaret Sanger Award in 1966. Over the years, this award, bestowed each year to "recognize leadership, excellence, and outstanding contributions to the reproductive health and rights movement," has been given to Nancy Pelosi, Katherine Hepburn, and Supreme Court Justice Harry A. Blackmun, along with many doctors. That first year, however, the organization started off with a bang and handed out four awards—to President Lyndon Johnson, birth control researcher Dr. Carl G. Hartman, Martin Luther King Jr. and, yes, General William

Draper. America's greatest civil rights activist received the same honor as a former eugenics supporter who was also the cousin of Wycliffe Draper, one of America's most influential racists. Gen. Draper was on hand as Dr. King's wife Coretta accepted the award and delivered a speech. This is how entwined liberal causes and institutionalized eugenics were in our truly twisted nation.[19]

GRANT'S ASSAULT

Eugenics and anti-immigrant sentiment are recurring threads that frequently weave their way through progressive agendas—something I will examine in future chapters. But so is environmentalism and anti-immigration. Grant was something of an American idealist when it came to environmental causes. He believed in protecting and sharing the environment—a common progressive and inclusive democratic ideal. As for the people he wanted to enjoy these public spaces, his democratic ideals unwound. To him, the ideal people to inhabit the land were WASPs.

One year after Grant's book was published, the vision espoused by his beloved Immigration Restriction League—stemming the tide of immigrants—finally came to fruition. Congress overturned Woodrow Wilson's veto of restrictive new laws that included a literacy requirement. The resulting Immigration Act of 1917 was at the time the most restrictive immigration law in U.S. history.

The law, also called the Asiatic Barred Zone Act, levied an eight dollar tax on anyone over the age of sixteen entering the country and excluded from entry "[a]ll aliens over sixteen years of age, physically capable of reading, Illiterates, who can not read the English language, or some other language or dialect, including Hebrew or Yiddish." The test, by the way, would involve reading text "containing not less than thirty nor more than forty words." All Asian laborers, excluding Japanese and Filipinos, were banned from entering the country. The legislators, evidently under a eugenic-influenced distain for human frailty, took it upon themselves to list all other unacceptable entrants:

> All idiots, imbeciles, feeble-minded idiots, insane persons, epileptics, persons who have had one or more attacks of insanity at any time previously; persons of constitutional psychopathic inferiority; persons with chronic alcoholism; paupers; professional beggars; vagrants; persons afflicted with tuberculosis in any form or with a loathsome or dangerous contagious disease; persons not comprehended within any of the foregoing excluded classes who are found to be and are certified by the examining surgeon as being mentally or physically defective, such physical defect being of a nature which may affect the ability of such alien to earn a living: persons who have been convicted of or admit having committed a felony or other crime or misdemeanor involving moral turpitude; polygamists, or persons who practice polygamy or believe in or advocate the practice of polygamy; anarchists, or persons who believe in or advocate the overthrow by force or violence of the SIXTY-FOURTH CONGRESS.[20]

Given the modern anti-immigration movement's targeting of Latinos, it's worth noting that the immigration fee for Mexicans, who were already providing a huge labor force to the U.S., was eventually waived within a year.[21]

Madison Grant was not done with his exclusionary mission. In 1919, he targeted Albert Johnson, the Washington State congressman who headed the House Committee on Immigration and Naturalization. Grant took Johnson to New York's elite private clubs and introduced him to his eugenicist friends. Grant's wooing worked. Johnson got the 1921 Emergency Quota Act through Congress. Three years earlier, the 1918 Spanish Flu pandemic had killed millions around the world, including an estimated 675,000 Americans. Johnson reportedly feigned concern about a cholera epidemic in postwar Europe—along with charges of Bolshevik support among immigrants—to build an argument to support the bill's passage. The restriction—known as the Johnson Quota Act in some circles—was meant to deny entry to Jews and other immigrants from eastern Europe.[22] It limited the total annual amount of new immigrants to three percent of the number of residents from the same country that were already in the United States as of the 1910 census.

The restrictive policy was further refined and codified with the Immigration Act of 1924. This law reduced the percentage of immigrants to two percent of the total number of people of each nationality in the United States, while also carrying over the restrictions of the 1917 act. The new calculus reduced the number of immigrants flowing to the U.S. to an estimated 20 percent of the previous year.

This quota was in place as Hitler came to power in Germany and began his quest to establish a pure Aryan nation. While an estimated 180,000 to 220,000 European refugees arrived in the U.S. between 1933 and 1945— the annual number during that period were a fraction of the number that arrived annually before 1917. In fact, the U.S. State Department failed to issue the requisite number of visas to Jewish applicants from Germany, despite very sizable waiting lists and Hitler's targeting of Jews. An average of 18,000 visas went unissued between 1934 and 1937, despite as many as 80,000 applicants. By the end of the war, hundreds of thousands of Jews who had been on waiting lists were left to perish in the Holocaust.[23]

A NEW ALLY

Madison Grant and Charles Davenport had a partner in crime at the Eugenics Record Office, Harry Loughlin, whose influence within the American eugenics movement was enormous. When Grant was wooing Congressman Johnson, he introduced Loughlin to the D.C. insider. Johnson promptly made Laughlin the eugenics advisor to his committee.[24] Laughlin, a former school principal, was a master at making connections and parlayed an interest in eugenics into a life-long career dedicated to propagating the idea of a superior white race. In 1907, he wrote a letter to Davenport who, three years later, hired him as superintendent of Eugenics Record Office in Cold Spring, N.Y. He remained there for three decades.

In addition to working with Congress, Laughlin crafted other localized legislation regarding another beloved eugenics subject: enforced sterilization. Instead of trying to push through a national law targeting specific segments of the populace, eugenicists relied on state laws to unilaterally reduce the presence of an "undesirable" segment of the population. Indiana was the first state to pass a law approving sterilization in 1907. Loughlin leaped on this practice as a way for society to purge itself of "unworthy" populations, and eventually codified his arguments in his *Eugenical Sterilization in the United States*. This door-stopper of a book featured a chapter entitled "The Right of the State to Limit Human Reproduction in the Interests of Race Betterment," lists of sterilization options that included castration, and a "Model Eugenical Sterilization Law"—which Laughlin initially drafted in 1914—to make it easy for state lawmakers to adopt their own version. Ironically, Laughlin, who suffered from epilepsy, advocated culling the population of "socially inadequate classes," which included the "(1) Feebleminded; (2) Insane, (including the psychopathic); (3) Criminalistic (including the delinquent and wayward); (4) Epileptic; (5) Inebriate (including drug habitués); (6) Diseased (including the tuberculous, the syphilitic. the leprous, and others with chronic, infectious and legally segregable diseases); (7) Blind (including those with seriously impaired vision); (8) Deaf (including those with seriously impaired hearing); (9) Deformed (including the crippled); and (10) Dependent (including orphans, ne'er-do-wells, the homeless, tramps and paupers."[25]

In 1924, Virginia used Laughlin's model law to pass the Eugenical Sterilization Act. Aware the law might be challenged, the state found an "ideal" test case involving young Charlottesville woman, Carrie Buck, whose mother Emma had previously been charged with immorality, prostitution, and having syphilis. Carrie had given birth out of wedlock and her child was found to be feeble-minded at the age of six months.

The case arrived before the Supreme Court in 1927 and was upheld in a shocking eight to one decision. Justice Oliver Wendell Holmes delivered an infamously-worded decision:

> It is better for all the world, if instead of waiting to execute degenerate offspring for crime or to let them starve for their imbecility, society can prevent those who are manifestly unfit from continuing their kind...
>
> Three generations of imbeciles are enough.[26]

In hindsight, Holmes' words were chilling and misguided. Recent research has found that Buck was railroaded by her own defense counsel who conspired with the state to lose the case, that Buck herself was raped by the nephew of her foster parents, and that her daughter was later tested and found to be completely normal.[27]

THE SILENT PARTNER

In 1923, Charles Davenport received another letter from a stranger, Wickliffe Draper. The subject was "a bequest for the advancement of eugenics." For Davenport, who was a fundraiser and influence peddler, this was an immediate call to action. The men met the next day. William H. Tucker's exhaustive account of Draper and his financial support of eugenics research, *The Funding of Scientific Racism*, reports that Draper proposed a $1 million endowment (about $15 million, adjusted for inflation). But Davenport was ultimately flummoxed; the endowment was not immediately forthcoming.

The mysterious millionaire was more a strange bird than an easy touch.

Draper descended from a long line of New England bluebloods with deep colonial roots. The family made a fortune making textile manufacturing equipment. Despite a lackluster academic career at the coveted St.

Mark's prep school, Draper's pedigree opened doors at Harvard, where he established himself as an avid outdoorsman by the time he graduated in 1913. When World War I began, Draper enlisted in the British Royal Field Artillery until he suffered a shrapnel wound in his shoulder. Returning home, he became an instructor in the U.S. Army, which eventually promoted him to the rank of lieutenant colonel. The Colonel, as Draper liked to be called, split an inheritance worth $10.7 million with his sister Helen after their father's death in 1923. (When Helen died childless in 1933, Draper inherited her estate.) An avid hunter, he explored far-flung locales in Africa, Mongolia, and India. He funded anthropological digs in what is now Mali and was subsequently elected a fellow of the prestigious Royal Geographical Society.

Settling in New York City, Draper occupied a three-floor apartment with twenty-foot ceilings in a ritzy, East 57th Street apartment building. He never married and became a recluse who lived among his hunting trophies and substantial sword collection. One relative, William F. Draper, said the Colonel was so shy that he would "turn bright purple, as if he were reading pornography" at a simple greeting.[28] In his solitude, however, his mind was busy. As Tucker's book clearly documents, he spent a great deal of time thinking about racial superiority, the evils of miscegenation, and how to use his money to legitimize eugenics. Tucker summarized Draper's obsession: "Definitive scientific evidence for the importance of genetic influence, the intellectual inferiority of blacks or the disastrous effects of racial mixtures was only the preliminary step to the more important goal: a social policy based on that knowledge."[29]

Davenport eventually got some money. But any visions he may have had of blank checks wound up unfulfilled. Draper was very hands-on about his donations. He spent $10,000 on a study of miscegenation called *Race Crossing in Jamaica*. Predictably, the paper noted that, "The general impression made in this comparison of the three groups is that the Whites are relatively swift and accurate, the Blacks are slow but accurate, while the Browns are slow and inaccurate." Also, predictably, the study got a positive review in *Eugenical News*, which noted the report showed how in "many respects the native mental capacity of the Blacks and Whites differ." The paper, however, was criticized for containing data that failed to support these conclusions.[30] Draper, whose name was not tied to the report—he went through great lengths to maintain anonymity for most of his projects—was not pleased. Over the next few years, Draper thought up three essay contests for the Eugenics Research Association (ERA) to sponsor and put up $5,000 in prize money for each competition, which requested essays on the topics of the adaptability of blacks, the "fecundity in Nordic and non-Nordic peoples," and using family histories as predictive tools for being committed to a mental institution.

Davenport's associate Harry Laughlin would prove to have a more lucrative ERA connection with Draper. The editor and sterilization "expert" forged a much closer working relationship with the millionaire. It seems Nazism brought them together.

1933 was a dizzying year for Laughlin. Madison Grant published a second book, *The Conquest of a Continent*, which Laughlin helped prepare. The book, a racial history of the United States, is steeped in the racist, pseudo-scientific babble that Grant espoused in his earlier work. Laughlin is thanked in the book's preface. Meanwhile, in Germany, Hitler came to power and passed a measure near and dear to Laughlin's heart, the Law for the Prevention of Defective Progeny, allowing for the forced sterilization of the physically and mentally disabled, the mentally ill, inter-racial Germans and Roma/Gypsies. His effusive *Eugenics News* report on the new law said "nothing more could be desired" and praised Germany for being at the forefront of "great nations" that understood the "biological foundations of national character."[31] Laughlin's unabashed admiration is understandable. As the man who helped promote sterilization laws at a state level, the idea that Germans were nationalizing eugenical policy—becoming the world leaders in his life's work—must have made him elated but jealous.

Prior to the 1935 International Conference for the Scientific Investigation of Population Problems in Berlin, Laughlin asked the organization's president, the aptly-named German eugenicist Eugen Fischer, to invite Draper. The request was granted, and Draper attended. ERA President Clarence Campbell presented a paper of Laughlin's at the Berlin gathering. His appearance made international headlines, as he praised Hitler by name, lauding the Germans for constructing "a comprehensive racial policy of population development and improvement."[32]

A *Time* magazine article from the same event quoted Campbell saying: "The difference between the Jew and the Aryan are as unsurmountable (sic) as that between black and white."[33]

According to an authoritative law journal essay, "The American Breed," by Paul Lombardo, Draper wrote Laughlin from Berlin, thanking him for arranging his attendance. As Lombardo writes: "In Berlin, Campbell was the perfect proxy for Harry Laughlin and the ideal escort for Wickliffe Draper. All three men shared a rabid racism and thoroughgoing anti-Semitism founded on their interpretation of eugenic ideology. Laughlin must have known that applause for Hitler was music to the ears of Wickliffe Draper."[34]

When Draper returned to the U.S., Laughlin set up a meeting at the University of Virginia. Laughlin was evidently well-connected in the Old Dominion from his behind-the-scenes work establishing the state's sterilization law. His idea was to establish a university-based center for eugenics research, pitching it to Draper as "Institution of National Eugenics as a part of the University of Virginia." The proposal generated instant interest but never happened. During talks, however, University Dean Ivey Lewis suggested to Draper that he meet a man named Earnest Sevier Cox.

A fierce advocate of the Virginia Racial Integrity Act of 1924, which prohibited interracial marriage, and the author of a 1923 book called *White America*, Cox had several things in common with Draper. He was a colonel who served in France. He was an avid traveler who had toured extensively in Africa. And he was an obsessive racist who regarded "the negro problem" and the mixing of races—"mongrelization," as Cox would call it—as the greatest threat to America. In the view of *White America*, differing races were just incompatible. A subsequent booklet, *Let My People Go*, Cox proposed his ideal solution: all blacks in the United

States should be repatriated to Africa. He dedicated the work to Marcus Garvey, the black civil rights leader who led a back to Africa movement.[35]

Draper was intrigued. Laughlin brokered a meeting in 1936 and the two men who shared a vision of an all-white American nation formed a mutual admiration society that would last thirty years. Draper celebrated their instant connection by making bulk purchases of *White America* and sending copies to members of Congress and other important figures that Cox deemed strategically important. Cox then enlisted the support of Mississippi Senator Theodore Gilmore Bilbo, as virulent and outspoken a racist as has ever held office, who famously spiked his speech with epithets for blacks and Jews. The three men cooked up a repatriation bill in 1939 called "The Greater Liberia Act," which proposed to remove all blacks from the U.S. The bill never made it out of the committee that year. But Bilbo remained Cox and Draper's legislative proxy until his death in 1947. Bilbo failed to achieve his dream of vanquishing blacks from America, but he left behind his racial vision in a book published the last year of his life, *Take Your Choice, Separation or Mongrelization*, which remains in print today, along with texts from Grant and Cox.

With Bilbo out of the picture, Cox found another ally for his repatriation dream, North Dakota Senator William Langer. The senator, who represented a state with one of the sparsest populations of black Americans in the nation, introduced a Liberian repatriation bill in every session of Congress from 1949 to 1955. It never achieved any significant traction.[36]

Despite these legislative failures, Draper and Cox remained close and collaborated for years, working secretively to undo the integration changes heralded by Brown vs. Board of Education and other court decisions. Draper made donations to all-white schools. He funneled cash to the Coordinating Committee for Fundamental American Freedoms, which opposed civil rights reforms under review in Congress. He also gave millions to the Sovereignty Commission and Civil Rights Council, two Mississippi organizations dedicated to white supremacy. As Draper scholar William Tucker put it, "Draper clearly contributed millions of dollars to campaign against civil rights... With no immediate family members, the racist cause was the central concern of his life and he had the independent wealth to back his convictions."[37]

BACKLASH

In the late 1930s, as anti-German sentiment increased in America, eugenics finally became the true liability. A committee at the Carnegie Foundation evidently realized it was funding an organization—the Eugenics Research Office—that was in lock-step with Hitler's master race theories and took the ERO to task for pushing out "propaganda." Laughlin was forced to retire in 1939 and the ERO was shuttered the same year.[38]

In another five years, the full extent of Nazi Germany's horrifying efforts to exterminate Jews, gays, and other so-called inferior peoples would become widely known, essentially destroying the flimsy, racist pseudoscience of eugenics. But even before mankind was confronted with the mind-numbing, inconceivable cruelty of Holocaust atrocities, endless reams of empirical evidence flourished in popular American culture to disprove the concept of racial inferiority or superiority. In the melting pot of America, the land of opportunity, even the downtrodden were able to rise to show the glories of their humanity.

Black Americans, despite centuries of persecution and economic inequality, had time and again shown themselves to be their white counterparts equals in all aspects of society.

George Washington Carver, born into slavery, had become one of the world's leading botanists and inventors—although he only patented three of his groundbreaking processes. Garrett Morgan refined the sewing machine and developed a breathing machine that became the prototype for gas masks used in World War I. Black Americans created the music America danced to, jazz and all its many complex styles. The Harlem Renaissance of the 1920s heralded the arrival of powerful literary voices in Langston Hughes, Zora Neal Hurston, and Claude McKay.

Jesse Owens proved himself the fastest man alive in the 1936 Olympics. Jack Johnson in 1908 and Joe Louis in 1937 established themselves as the world's greatest heavyweight boxers, despite toiling in a business that wanted nothing more than to find "a great white hope."

The success of Jews, who encountered vast amounts of discrimination from schools and universities to social organizations, was also hard to miss. In 1921, while Madison Grant was pushing laws to cut Jewish immigrants to America, German Jew Albert Einstein won the Nobel Prize for Physics. One year later, Niels Bohr, born to a Jewish mother, repeated the feat. In the 1930s, Jewish sports included heavyweight champion Max Baer, baseball all-stars Hank Greenberg and Harry Danning, and the emergence of football legend Sid Luckman. In theater and film, Al Jolson, Eddie Cantor, George Burns, Jack Benny, and the Marx Brothers all became popular performers.

Similarly, America's Catholic population, which endured so much contempt from the mid-1800s onward, had many visible prominent representatives in mainstream America. Babe Ruth, raised in a Catholic orphanage, was the world's greatest baseball player. Gene Tunney was a heavyweight boxing champ. Al Smith became the four-term governor of New York, and vied with Franklin Roosevelt for the Democratic presidential nomination. California-born Amadeo Pietro Giannini headed and grew Bank of America. Hollywood's first family of acting, the Barrymores, were Catholics. So was George Delacorte, founder of Dell Publishing, not to mention popular writers like Joyce Kilmer ("I think that I shall never see / A poem lovely as a tree."), rabble-rousing journalist Heywood Broun, and F. Scott Fitzgerald.

By the way, *The Great Gatsby*, Fitzgerald's signature novel of the roaring twenties, actually contains a reference to Madison Grant's *The Passing of the White Race*, portraying the book's most arrogant, privileged character, Tom Buchanan, as a fan of a similar-sounding book. Here's the exchange with Gatsby narrator Nick Carraway:

> "Civilization's going to pieces," broke out Tom violently. "I've gotten to be a terrible pessimist about things. Have you read 'The Rise of the Colored Empires' by this man Goddard?"
>
> "Why, no," I answered, rather surprised by his tone.
>
> "Well, it's a fine book, and everybody ought to read it. The idea is if we don't look out the white race will be—will be utterly submerged. It's all scientific stuff; it's been proved."[39]

A FOUNDATION FOR THE FUTURE

In 1937, Wickliffe Draper decided to launch a charitable fund, naming Laughlin as the organization's president. According to papers filed with the state of New York, the new charity, the innocuously named Pioneer Fund, would have two purposes. First, it would provide for "the education of children of parents deemed to have such qualities and traits of character as to make such parents of unusual value as citizens." The certificate of incorporation specified that consideration would "especially be given to children who are deemed to be descended predominantly from white persons who settled in the original thirteen states." Second, it would fund the "study and research into the problems of heredity and eugenics in the human race." Additionally, it would also examine "the problems of race betterment with special reference to the people of the United States and for the advancement of knowledge and the dissemination of information with respect to any studies so made or in general with respect to heredity and eugenics."

Let's recap: As Nazism was on the rise in Europe, Wickliffe Draper created a unique charity for the offspring of "white persons" that was specifically formed to create and share information about eugenics. For race betterment. It was conceived, as Lombardo puts it, "as a reflection of the long-term aspirations of Laughlin and Draper to formalize a white supremacist agenda as the goal of eugenical science."[40]

It's easy to see the creation of the Pioneer Fund as a victory for Laughlin after so many years of coddling and planning with Draper. But given the historical context of the moment, it's also possible to view the Pioneer Fund as less a flowering for eugenicists than a secretive retrenching and a way for Draper to establish his legacy and keep his beloved dreams alive long after his death.

The first board of directors of the Pioneer Fund included Draper, his lawyer Malcolm Donald, Harry Laughlin, Frederick Osborn, a wealthy member of the American Eugenics Society, and John Marshall Harlan II, a lawyer and the son of a Supreme Court justice. Harlan remains an interesting figure in terms of his role with the Pioneer Fund. There has been some speculation he was drafted because of his expertise representing tax-exempt charities. But his presence also shows just how quietly the Pioneer Fund operated. When Harlan followed in his father's footsteps and was nominated to the Supreme Court in 1955, southern senators, concerned the northerner might support civil rights initiatives, grilled him. Evidently, they were unaware of the Pioneer Fund and its board of racists. He was confirmed by a 71–11 vote—nine of the naysayers were from the South. Although he was known as a conservative figure on the Warren Supreme Court, he did, in fact, vote in favor of a number of civil rights cases—votes that must have driven Draper and the other board members mad.

Over the last eight decades, the Pioneer Fund has been anything but an innocent charity. Laughlin's agenda for the very first board meeting detailed $50,000 worth of projects that included encouraging "high fertility by junior flying officers of especially superior heredity," developing educational films on eugenics, creating a questionnaire card for "population registration."

Research indicates the fund itself was something of a steering committee. Board members often put Draper in contact with a network of figures who shared his racist beliefs. Between 1954 and 1971, the Pioneer

Fund greatly reduced its official grants while Draper was busy making a slew of covert donations to fund anti-integration organizations in a desperate effort to block the civil rights movement.[41]

As Draper aged and then passed away in 1972, however, his fund became more proactive and slyly strategic when disbursing funds, choosing academics dedicated to uncovering racial differences that supported Pioneer's eugenics mission. These recipients were in many instances hereditarian scandal-mongers of the highest order. Among them:

- University of California Berkeley psychology professor Arthur Jensen, who received more than $1 million in Pioneer grants over three decades. In 1969, he published an infamous attack on the early education program Head Start in the *Harvard Education Review*, claiming that black children had an average IQ of only 85 and that no educational social engineering programs could improve that performance and suggested that welfare programs, "unaided by eugenic foresight, could lead to the genetic enslavement of a substantial segment of our population."[42]

- Nazi-loving English anthropologist and organizer Roger Pearson, an avowed racist who Draper scholar Tucker notes was, "in many ways, [Draper] reincarnate."[43] Pearson started the Northern League in the U.K. and launched *Mankind Quarterly* (a peer-reviewed journal whose peers largely shared racist views) and then migrated to the U.S. where he penned countless articles for the extreme-right. As editor of *The New Patriot*, he wrote or ran articles entitled "Zionists and the Plot Against South Africa," "Early Jews and the Rise of Jewish Money Power," and "Swindlers of the Crematoria." Various groups linked to Pearson received more than $1 million between 1975 and 1996.

- Conservative think tank wonk Charles Murray, the co-author of *The Bell Curve*, a 1994 book that regurgitated research asserting that black Americans had lower IQs than white Americans. The

Pioneer Fund recipient cited an uncanny seventeen sources whose work or editing had appeared in *Mankind Quarterly*—the controversial publication that had also received money from the Pioneer Fund. By backing Murray's work, the fund had created an echo chamber for previously specious research.[44]

Over the years, the Pioneer Fund has also reportedly given grants to Will Shockley, Ralph Scott and its own president, controversial Canadian professor J. Philippe Rushton, who received over $1 million for research that asserted genital size has an inverse relationship to brain size and that since blacks have larger genitals, well, you can try and do his math.

The Pioneer Fund also gave an estimated $1.5 million to two lobbying groups that continue to be extremely active in the anti-immigration movement, the Federation for American Immigration Reform (FAIR) and the American Immigration Control Foundation (AICF). Both groups were founded or co-founded by John Tanton, the godfather of the modern anti-immigration movement. While the Pioneer Fund was not the sole provider for these organizations—Tanton had other means of support—it is entirely fitting that Nazi-sympathizer Draper's well-funded, far-right foundation contributed to two funds that demonize immigrants.

If there was ever going to be a Mount Rushmore of American Racism, Grant, Laughlin, Cox and Draper would be on it.

So would John Tanton.

Chapter Seven

JOHN TANTON, THE PUPPET MASTER

VISIT THE WEBSITE JOHNTANTON.ORG AND a picture of a smiling, broad-shouldered, grey-haired, patrician gentleman appears on the homepage. Beside this affable image is the following text:

> **John Tanton:**
> **Visionary – Futurist**
> **Environmental Activist**
> **Pro-immigrant spokesperson for**
> **population stabilization**
> **and immigration reduction**[1]

The first three lines are hard to argue with, although the phrase "Visionary – Futurist" implies that Tanton's visions were laudable. While he did indeed have a vision for the future that evolved out of environmental concerns, it was, to be kind, elitist and exclusionary. At one point, that "vision" called for overturning a significant portion of the Fourteenth Amendment to the Constitution—the amendment passed after the Civil War defining citizenship rights and guaranteeing equal protection under the law.

The last three lines of this summary reveal the subtle, sinister nature of John Tanton and his body of work: "Pro-immigrant spokesperson for population stabilization and immigration reduction." That's an inherently contradictory statement. How can Tanton be "pro-immigrant" while advocating for "immigrant reduction?"—and yet it is presented with straight-faced sincerity as if it makes all the sense in the world. Six paragraphs down, the webpage copy qualifies the doublethink of Tanton's contradictory stance, explaining he was "pro immigrant and pro legal immigration—at environmentally sustainable immigration numbers."

In other words, he was only pro-immigrant as long as immigrants didn't tax America's resources. But in this instance, "environmentally sustainable" is a fungible phrase. Who determines what that is? This clarification also fails to tell the entire story. By the end of Tanton's life, the sustainability of natural resources, air, water, and land, wasn't his primary focus; sustainability of what he termed "European-American" culture, language, and power was. The passionate conservationist began to conflate stopping immigration with protecting American resources and redirected his efforts later in life toward anti-immigrant efforts. "He was pure as driven snow," laments his former close friend and FAIR co-founder Roger Conner, who also notes Tanton began "playing footsie with racists" in his single-minded pursuit of environmentalism.

Looking closely at the avalanche of papers, letters, and memos that Tanton left behind, his utter contempt for immigrants, particularly Latinos, becomes clear. The web of organizations he created precisely to stop the flow of newcomers to the United States has repeatedly spread false information about immigrants, tainting millions with a brush dipped in lies. In the following pages, I will share a number of documents that capture him engaging in activities that are unequivocally driven by a naked desire to stop immigrants—not to stop land development, not to preserve environmental resources, not to protect the air. His goal, by the end, was to cleanse America of the very people that helped build and continue to build this country: immigrants.

The larger takeaway from this webpage anecdote, however, is that Tanton was a shrewd manipulator of language and truth. He sought to influence laws and control the population of America by laundering false narratives. Chief among them was the idea that the anti-immigrant organizations he created were legitimate, non-partisan concerns that had arisen organically and had large memberships. In fact, his organizations were funded by a few, extremely wealthy ideologues and had surprisingly small numbers of supporters. The complex network of advocacy groups, think tanks, and lobbying organizations that John Tanton left in place when he died on July 16, 2019, at the age of 85, still are practicing his dark arts. He must have been a student of Draper and the Pioneer Fund—and not just because the fund supported Tanton's beloved FAIR. The Pioneer Fund sought to distribute money to pro-eugenics researchers to create the illusion of scientifically sanctioned racism. Tanton borrowed from and improved this model. He even found a bitter, childless, Draper-like benefactor to fund his work. Sadly, as the description on his webpage proves, many of the false narratives he has created—even about himself—remain firmly in place.

THE MAKING OF A LIBERAL

John Tanton, the mastermind of America's modern anti-immigrant movement, was born on February 23, 1934.

To an immigrant.

Tanton's father, also named John, was a Canadian chemical engineer who came to Detroit when work was scarce and married Hannah Koch. When Tanton was ten, the family moved to Sebewaing, Michigan, and farmed eighty acres of land. He attended Michigan State University, where he met Mary Lou Brow, who changed her name to Tanton when they married in 1958. He began medical school.

In 1964, John Tanton took a job as an ophthalmologist at the Burns Clinic in Petoskey, Michigan, a northern resort town with a sizable marina on Lake Michigan. The facility, modeled initially on the Mayo Clinic, was the leading medical center in the area. Tanton and his wife Mary Lou had both grown up on farms, and the rural environs outside of Petoskey appealed to them. A gushing biography, *Mary Lou & John Tanton: A Journey into American Conservation*, reports he wanted to keep bees, as he'd done as a teenager, garden, and chop his own wood.[2] Like Madison Grant and Wickliffe Draper, he was an environmentalist. That passion, like theirs, soon mutated into conservationism and obsessions about America's population.

That same biography, written by John Rohe, who had "a personal relationship spanning several decades" with its subjects, reports that in the 1950s John Tanton encountered the work of "the Population Reference Bureau (PRB), the oldest demographic organization in the world," and that those readings and Mary Lou's interest in Planned Parenthood inspired Tanton to work in a Denver family planning clinic during his medical internship. We don't know what Tanton read from the PRB—which is still in existence today and conducts, by all indications, legitimate studies. But it is worth noting that Guy Burch, who founded PRB in 1929, was a member the American Eugenics Society and a director of the American Birth Control League. According to *Reproductive Rights and Wrongs*, Burch said he supported birth control because he wanted "to prevent the American people from being replaced by alien or negro stock, whether it be by immigration or by overly high birth rates by others in this country." Burch also lobbied against admitting Jewish orphans, refugees from Hitler, to America, in 1939.[3]

Tanton began advocating for public policy changes in 1958 when he became secretary of the Michigan Natural Areas Council and led campaigns for the federal Wilderness Act, which was passed in 1964 to protect federal lands. His concerns about population, or rather, over-population, found outlets with the Sierra Club's Population Committee in the 1970s, and with Zero Population Growth (ZPG), an organization launched 1968 that proved Malthus' anxieties about sustainability were alive and well. The grassroots organization, now known as Population Connection, saw the soaring global population as a threat to the quality of life for people everywhere. Tanton eventually became the national chairman of the organization from 1975 to 1977.

If the ophthalmologist wanted supporting documentation to justify ZPG and its concerns, there was plenty of it in the zeitgeist. 1968 was also the year Stanford University professor Paul R. Ehrlich published *The Population Bomb*, a book that predicted impending disaster from overpopulation. It began with an alarmist, doomsday scenario: "The battle to feed all of humanity is over. In the 1970s and 1980s hundreds of millions of people will starve to death in spite of any crash programs embarked upon now."[4]

The book's dramatic title, as it happens, has distant ties to none other than Pioneer Fund founder Wickliffe Draper. It was coined by Draper's cousin. As Ehrlich recounts in his 2008 essay, "Population Bomb Revisited," his book's name "was taken (with permission) from General William H. Draper, founder of the Population Crisis Committee and a pamphlet issued in 1954 by the Hugh Moore Fund." William Draper had an interesting resume. He was a member of the Society of American Magicians, served as the undersecretary of the Army in the late 1940s, and vice chairman of the Planned Parenthood Federation. He also was also reportedly a sponsor of the 1932 International Eugenics Congress in New York[5]—a fact that fits in with Ehrlich's description of him as "most concerned with the control of the populations of dark-skinned people."[6]

The Population Bomb was not the only alarmist environmental bestseller. In 1972, *The Limits to Growth*, a report commissioned by the Club of Rome—a collective of business leaders and scientists concerned about the explosive impact of industrial growth—was published and quickly sold millions of copies worldwide. Soon after, worrying studies of the effects of acid rain were released, adding scientific proof that big business was hurting our planet and our future.

So Tanton was ahead of the curve. Or maybe he helped create the curve. As his biographer Rohe writes, while Mary Lou Tanton became involved in Planned Parenthood and family planning out of concern for the welfare of needy women and children, Tanton "was focused primarily on the competition of surging population over dwindling resources."[7] At some point in the early 1970s, Tanton began shifting his goals, moving away from his mission of slowing fertility rates. In 1965, women in the U.S. had an average of 2.5 kids during their lifetime. That number, however, had dropped to less than two by 1975. So, the zero-population growth dream, in terms of Americans having babies, was moving in the right direction from his perspective. (By the way, in 2018, the average lifetime number of births for women in the U.S. was 1.78.)[8]

In 1973, Tanton was voted onto the board of Zero Population Growth. He immediately began trying—unsuccessfully—to refocus the group from domestic birth control issues to immigration reform. Eventually, he was even appointed chair of an immigration study committee. Even after becoming ZPG president, he was unable to gather support for an ideological shift in the organization.

The first written evidence of Tanton targeting immigrants is from a letter he wrote in 1974 to James Greene, assistant commissioner at the Department of Immigration and Naturalization Service. The missive was part of a trove of Tanton documents donated to a University of Michigan library and later discovered by Heidi Beirich of the Southern Poverty Law Center. Her extensive reports on these documents shows the nascent strategist at work. Focusing on the language of the Fourteenth Amendment to the Constitution, he asks Greene, "Is there someone in your office that could provide me with a summary of the case and statutory law that has established that children born in this country to visitors and illegal aliens are automatically U.S. citizens?"[9]

If there is any doubt that Tanton was fishing for ways to prevent or undo the Fourteenth Amendment's citizenship provisions, they are completely vanquished by a letter he wrote a year later to Rutgers Law Professor Albert Blaustein, who helped draft the constitutions of Liberia, Zimbabwe, Bangladesh, and other nations.

"I'm still bothered," Tanton writes to the constitutional law expert, "by the provisions of the fourteenth amendment, which provide that children of illegal aliens born within the United States are automatically United States citizens. Looking to the future, this may become an undesirable situation."

He goes on: "What would the prospects be for changing the interpretation of this amendment, so that citizenship flowed from the parents, rather than the geographic area of one's birth?"

The answer Blaustein scrawled right beside Tanton's question was, "*!!!None*". He mailed the letter back, but not before adding a few brief comments that, read in 2020, may send chills down your spine: "No chance on the 14th amend. Forget it. Build an Iron Curtain. A Berlin Wall. That's the only hope."

At the bottom of the letter, Blaustein added: "*Everything* in Int'l law makes a person a citizen of the nation state in which he was born. Otherwise it would be too easy to deny one any citizenship at all."[10]

Looking at the questions and the concerns of the letter, it is clear that Tanton was searching for exclusionary policies for undocumented immigrants. His target at this time was immigrant children. More than forty years later, that target remains a major talking point of the modern anti-immigration movement. It has now been normalized among the far-right with a derogatory term, "anchor babies," a truly demeaning term to both immigrant parents and their children that implies the motive all immigrant mothers for having a child is to reap citizenship in the U.S. The use of this term by members of the far right who also claim to be pro-life is also offensive and hypocritical. When it comes to right-to-life issues, they adhere to the belief that every baby is innocent and worth saving. But if that baby's parents are undocumented, suddenly that baby is problematic and doesn't deserve to be here. Tanton, however, did not have any such conflict. He was a staunch supporter of birth control, abortion rights and stopping immigrants from coming to America and having children—so-called "anchor babies."

Around this time, Tanton was exploring the resurrection of the ugly cousin of population control: eugenics. Uncovered in his papers was an essay entitled "The Case for Passive Eugenics," dated April 24, 1975. Claiming that, "It is now beginning to appear, however, that the genetic character of individuals can be improved within families as well as between them," Tanton sets out to distinguish between "active eugenics"—that is, "identifying the 'fit,' 'superior' stock and encouraging its reproduction, while at the same time suppressing the reproduction of 'inferior' stock"— and "passive eugenics," which he describes as "working with natural forces to improve the genetic character of children within any specific family."[11]

Tanton was savvy enough to see "active" eugenics as problematic, but not savvy enough to realize the term was toxic. "There is serious question whether [positive or negative traits] are the products of genetics or the environment, or some mix thereof." The other liability, he notes, "is the question of who shall decide what the favored traits are, and who shall be allowed to or prohibited from reproducing. These problems have proved insuperable in the past, and there seems little likelihood that they will be resolved in the future."

Passive eugenics, he says, would embrace "restricting childbearing to the years of maximum reproductive efficiency, between the ages of 20 and 35" to reduce the chance of children born with Down syndrome (or "Mongolism"). It would also advocate for smaller family sizes, which he claims have been "shown to be positively correlated to intelligence."

Tanton's study is perplexing. Near the end of his essay, he says "active eugenics will deservedly continue to be rejected by most persons." Yet his advocacy of passive eugenics still trafficked in the same dangerous human engineering language that drove old school eugenicists—traits like intelligence or the idea of inferiority. The article is another early indication of Tanton's desire to become a master strategist who deploys language to carve out arguments that might seem nuanced and "ethical" but ultimately mask dubious and sinister goals.

One last point about this paper: it reveals a major block in Tanton's thought process—at least when he advocates for smaller families. This example of "passive" eugenics isn't eugenics at all; it is a form of family planning that can easily be categorized as "nurturing"—as in "nurture vs. nature." By pushing this point, he is unwittingly undermining the "nature/genetics" arguments of eugenics that he clearly supports.

These early attempts at strategic thinking were baby steps for Tanton. Dry runs. Experiments. They both failed. The idea of "passive eugenics" should have struck him as a non-starter. It was unsellable to the public at large or the scientific community. Eugenics was not a term anyone in their right mind would want to rehabilitate after the Nazis' wholehearted embrace of master race ideology and the slaughter of an estimated twenty million including six million Jews.[12] But John Tanton in his earliest strategic incarnation couldn't see what should have been obvious to even the most naive policy newcomer. He never fully let go of the discredited "science." Instead, he tried to rebrand it. More than two decades later, when he eventually got around to launching a group to study the subject of human traits, the deservedly tainted "E-word" was nowhere in sight—at least in public. In a 1996 memo discussing the formation of the short-lived Society for the Advancement of Genetics Education (SAGE), it's clearly on his mind: "As an example of the type of item we need to use, I enclose an article from *The Christian Science Monitor* (note the source—such considerations are important in gaining public acceptance). This piece can serve to highlight the two parts of eugenics."[13]

Another paper written by Tanton in the 1970s didn't result in failure; for the first time, his thoughts on immigration received a kind of affirmation. The paper was entitled "International Migration" and it won third place in an essay competition held by a conference devoted to the limits of growth sponsored by the University of Houston and the Mitchell Energy & Development Corporation. The paper, which was reprinted a year later in the *Ecologist* magazine, finds Tanton trying to sanitize the subject so near and dear to his heart:

An aversion to discussing immigration is also understandable in light of the seamy history surrounding past efforts to limit immigration. These were marked by xenophobia and racism, and gave rise to the likes of the Know-nothing political party, and the Ku Klux Klan. Other -isms of past debates that we seldom hear today include jingoism and nativism. The subject was often highly emotional and divisive. Any person who attempts discussion of immigration policy will soon learn as has the author that the situation is unchanged in this regard.

These difficulties must be overcome. In the inevitable stationary state to which man is consigned by the finiteness of our globe, the growth of both human numbers and material consumption must eventually end. ...

[I]nternational migration on its current scale is destined to end in the near future, owing to the same finiteness of the globe. As the principal countries currently receiving immigrants - the United States, Canada, Australia - reach or surpass the limits of population which they can support, they will likely move to curtail immigration.[14]

Like the faulty predictions of *The Population Bomb*, Tanton's vision has not happened. The United States continues to harvest and manufacture enormous amounts of surplus food. Our government sometimes pays farmers *not* to grow certain crops because there is an overabundance.[15] While the problems of global warming are serious and terrifying, they are largely the result of how we live, not how many of us there are. Industrial hyperactivity, off-the-charts energy usage, the prevalence of dangerous ozone-destroying chemicals, coal-burning, and wars—these are the threats to mankind. Immigrants? Some come from countries that burn coal. That is, to a large extent, their contribution to our current global environmental crisis.

ORGANIZATION MAN

Tanton's term as president of Zero Population Growth ended in 1977 and his passion policy project, reducing immigration, was still taboo for most board members. Not to be denied, he began actively thinking about a new entity that would focus solely on immigration issues. On January 2, 1979, like Draper before him, he launched his organization, the Federation for American Immigration Reform. There can be little doubt Tanton took pleasure—possibly *perverse* pleasure—in the group's acronym: FAIR.

FAIR, according to its first executive director and co-founder Roger Conner, was an outgrowth of two concerns. He summarizes Tanton's motivation this way: "Central to his thinking was how do you protect the environment? To protect the environment, you've got to stabilize the population. To stabilize the population, you have to do it one country at a time. If you're going to do it one country at a time, you can't let the prosperous countries that stabilize the population be swamped by the poor next door countries that give in to the Catholic church and refuse to stabilize their population."[16]

Conner, on the other hand, says he was not a true environmentalist and was drawn to create FAIR from a different angle. He and Tanton both exchanged ideas with Otis Graham Jr., a historian at UC Santa Barbara, where environmental extremist Garrett Hardin taught. Tanton and Conner would both come to admire Hardin, but it was Graham's writing, shaped in part by John Higham's 1955 book about American nativism, *Strangers in the Land*, that inspired Conner to start FAIR with Tanton. "There was new liberal logic for immigration reform, which was restricting immigration will increase opportunities for working class people," Conner recalled. "It will force the owners of financial capital to give up their racist attitudes towards blacks and will protect the environment and limit pupil population growth. It was a liberal logic for restriction."[17] Conner was a pleasure to interview and his views have not changed. A deeply religious man concerned about the poor on this side of the border, he believed that American minorities and blue-collar workers were the targeted benefactors of strict immigration restrictions. Not only would there be more jobs, but wages and living conditions would improve as the cost of business would naturally inflate for goods and services at a level to pay more salaries and wages. In other words, stemming the tide of cheap immigrant labor would help African-Americans and other communities plagued by lower income. Conner conceded to me that there was a flaw in his vision. He failed to recognize the destructive depths of racism in American society—a force not even labor shortages can easily overcome. FAIR set up shop in Washington, D.C., and its board of directors was made up of the wealthy, the connected, and the sympathetic. Financial backing came from Sydney Swensrud, former chairman of Gulf Oil Corporation. A sizable commitment from John "Jay" Harris, an environmental philanthropist and a descendant of Henry Flagler, who started Standard Oil with John D. Rockefeller, amounted to a half million dollars over five years.[18] Other early funding came from the Environmental Fund (now Population-Environmental Balance) and the Pioneer Fund. Although Wickliffe Draper died in 1972, the fund, headed by Draper's lawyer Harry Weyher Jr. from 1958 until 2002, donated $1.2 million to FAIR between 1985 and 1994.[19]

But the most important donor was Cordelia Scaife May, heiress to the enormous Mellon fortune. Tanton presented the multi-millionaire with Conner's proposal outlining the plans for the nascent organization. Cordy May, as she was known, studied it and decided to give $50,000. As Tanton would soon discover, she would give a great deal more, dwarfing the contributions of all the other donors in the history of FAIR and all of Tanton's projects.[20]

"John was a predator who got inside her perimeter wire and basically found a source of money to fund the immigration reform movement," Patrick Burns, an early employee of FAIR, told the *New York Times*. "John looked at Cordy as a buffalo to hunt and bone out for wealth."[21]

What did Cordy May initially think she was backing?

A group that planned "to make the restriction of immigration a legitimate position for thinking people," according to the Conner pitch.

That line also shows up in a version of the document sent to Zero Population Growth. It included a project budget for the first two years of operation and closed with a request for financial support. But the bulk of the document outlined the reasons for creating a dedicated immigration reform group and what the primary focus would be—creating an "organization on the restrictionist side around which the dominant public opinion can coalesce, providing the strength and visibility needed to push for change." Its tactics would be "the standard ones of grassroots organizing, research and writing, media work, direct mail, litigating, and finally lobbying."[22]

According to Tanton hagiographer Rohe, early on, the group sought to create "an organized system of classification, so its initial efforts focused on creating categories and terminology for describing and analyzing legal immigration, illegal immigration, immigration volume, optimum population, employment policies, and others. It soon became apparent that immigration issues could be distilled into three fundamental questions: How many people should be admitted? Who should be admitted? How should the rules be enforced?"[23]

Otis L. Graham Jr., wrote about his agenda for the organization, echoing Conner's vision for the organization: "A leading concern for me is to bring into FAIR strong representation from people in groups of liberal, progressive disposition."[24]

One year after FAIR launched, Tanton filed the paperwork for US Incorporated (US Inc), his tax-exempt, "educational" charity. Registered in his hometown of Petroiky, Tanton's new organization was even more shrewd than FAIR. While largely a lure for conservative funds, US Inc was also a political and ideological incubator fund. In today's investment world, incubators are investment funds that provide seed investments and support to launch start-up companies. In this sense, Tanton was nearly twenty years ahead of his time.

US Inc served as Tanton's ideological sandbox and piggy bank while he was alive, and it continues to operate. Since 1990, it has published *The Social Contract*, a quarterly journal devoted to its founder's favorite subjects: immigration, population, the sanctity of the English language, and the scourge of multiculturalism. Recent issues reveal the publication to be little more than a launchpad for fear-mongering and laundering hate literature, with articles like "Importing Diseases – The Toxic Threat of Infected Migrants" and "Immigration, Crime, and the Death of an American Paradise," and stoking anti-Muslim sentiment with alarmist pieces like "Limiting Muslim Immigration Is Reasonable and Pro-American" and "The Long-Term Consequences of Mass Muslim Migration."

The foundation also supported—and still supports—the Social Contract Press which hawks anti-immigrant tomes in its bookstore with titles such as *Alien Nation* and *America Extinguished.*

Tanton and his publishing house editor Wayne Lutton collaborated on *The Immigration Invasion*, published in 1994. In it, the authors made an alarming assertion: "Among illegal aliens, the incarceration rate is three times the U.S. average"[25]—a claim that continues to be regurgitated to this day by FAIR[26] and other groups, like the conservative Heritage Foundation.[27] In a hallmark of disingenuousness, Tanton and Lutton add, "These statistics do not imply that all or most immigrants are criminals. But under current immigration laws and procedures, frighteningly large numbers of newcomers see crime as their avenue to the American dream."[28] Canadian border authorities found the book so inflammatory in its attacks on immigrants, it was banned as hate literature.[29]

In 1994, Social Contract Press also published one of its most provocative books, an English translation of Jean Raspail's 1973 dystopian and racist novel, *The Camp of the Saints*, which depicts France overrun by "monstrous" and depraved immigrants who, by the novel's end, rape a young white woman to death. "Raspail's enemy is the entire non-white world. It tramples monks and white saviors alike in its invasion of France. His refugees are nameless caricatures, with no inner lives. He ascribes to them an almost supernatural combination of obstinance and depravity," wrote one critic.[30]

The unseemly content didn't bother Cordy May, who ponied up $5,000 to help distribute the book,[31] and it certainly didn't bother Tanton or his publishing organ, which touted the book this way: "The Social Contract Press is honored to be able to offer a reprint of this gripping novel, which envisions the overrunning of European civilization by burgeoning Third World populations."[32]

How connected is *The Social Contract* to Tanton's ultimate vision? In its summer 2010 issue, the journal ran an article entitled "Arizona Takes the Lead on Illegal Immigration Enforcement." The first paragraph immediately tried to distance SB 1070 from its obvious targets: "We in Arizona understand illegal is a crime, not a race." Its author was Russell Pearce.[33]

Ever the strategist, Tanton had more organizations to launch. In 1985, he worked with original FAIR board member Otis Graham Jr. to launch the Center for Immigration Studies (CIS), which describes itself as "an independent, non-partisan, non-profit, research organization." Like eugenics researchers of old, the new think tank fulfilled a major need, providing the arguments and data that would justify stemming the tide of immigrants into America. Over the years, the CIS methodology and reporting has been found to have major flaws by major media outlets and fact-checking sites like FactCheck, PolitiFact, and Snopes, as well as think tanks on both the left and right. Among CIS questionable reports: assertions that immigrants use more welfare resources than native households have been characterized as misleading and a claim that 81 percent of newly created jobs in Texas had gone to immigrants (both documented and undocumented) between 2007–2011 was widely denounced as flawed. More recently, a CIS report, citing data from a study by the National Academies of Sciences, Engineering, and Medicine, claimed a wall along the U.S.-Mexican border would "pay for itself"—but the authors of the study said CIS misused its data and that stopping illegal immigration might cost the government over time.[34]

NumbersUSA (NUSA) is another Tanton spinoff that bills itself as "non-profit, non-partisan," but to its credit, it is slightly more upfront about its mission: It admits to being an "immigration-reduction organization." For five years, the program was nested within Tanton's US Inc. Its ostensible leader is Tanton pal and US Inc/Social Contract employee Roy Beck. Tanton felt so comfortable with Beck, that in 1996 he shared the following trashing of Latino culture: "I have no doubt that individual minority persons can assimilate to the culture necessary to run an advanced society," he wrote in a letter to Beck, "but if through mass migration, the culture of the homeland is transplanted from Latin America to California, then my guess is we will see the same degree of success with governmental and social institutions that we have seen in Latin America."[35]

In addition to FAIR, US Inc, CIS, NUSA, SCP, and the Immigration Reform Law Institute, which employed Kris Kobach,[36] Tanton founded and funded Pro English and U.S. English. He also provided funds for American Immigration Control Foundation in 1983, American Patrol/ Voice of Citizens Together in 1992, the California Coalition for Immigration Reform in 1994, and Californians for Population Stabilization in 1996, according to the Southern Poverty Law Center, which also identified six of the organizations —AICF, APCCIR, FAIR, PE CPS—as hate groups.[37][38]

What was the point of creating so many separate institutions? Optics and strength in numbers. It might be more accurate to say *the appearance* of numbers to create an illusion of popular support. These multiple groups served to legitimize anti-immigrant narratives into mainstream media and America's legislative bodies, creating a mirage of a wide, strong social movement when in fact they all had the same puppet master and underwriter: Tanton. Furthermore, many of them were at the onset, if not shoe-string operations, quite humble in the non-governmental organization firmament. In its first eight years, FAIR, the organizational plum of Tanton's eye, raised $8.5 million—primarily through a handful of wealthy patrons. In 2000, 82 percent of US Inc's income came from five contributions, six donors accounted for 58 percent of all the contributions FAIR received, and fourteen donors made up 94 percent of the CIS's income.[39]

Digging into these organizations' tax filings and correlating them to these groups' membership fees, researchers at *The Intelligence Report* magazine published by the Southern Poverty Law Center concluded the organization's membership numbers were highly inflated. While FAIR claimed to have 75,000 members, the real membership was estimated to be about half that number. Meanwhile, the American Immigration Control Foundation, which US Inc helped fund, appeared to be even more inflated. "After subtracting the three major donations reported on AICF's 2000 tax forms, only $39,386 in income is left." The magazine noted, "If members pay $15 a year, as the AICF website says, then the group has at most 2,625 members—hardly the 250,000-plus that it claims."[40]

So, while none of Tanton's organizations arose out of mass social movements, he was determined to use wealthy donors to bankroll and manufacture one. Give him credit; Tanton was ahead of his time. His sprawling network of organizations focused on immigration reduction anticipated the echo-chamber effect that we now see generated on social media platforms.

Academics now have a term for the echo-chambers created using paid-for or entirely fake entities to influence public policy on social media. It is called "cyber-social warfare." Again, Tanton was ahead of his time.

There was one other reason Tanton diversified his ideological and strategic portfolio: taxes. Charitable organizations have to show they get one-third of their funding from the general public and don't just rely on a single donor—which was often appeared to be the case, thanks to Cordy May. Splintering his organizations was "critical in not just hiding the sources of funding, but it allowed his creations to meet the IRS's so-called public support test," Charles Kamasaki, a fellow at the Migration Policy Institute, told the *New York Times*. "Part of Tanton's genius, and it really was genius, was creating these multiple shells."[41]

THE REAL VISION

In 1986, Tanton wrote a memo addressing a group he had formed called the WITAN. As the Oxford English Dictionary explains, a witan is derived from the word witenagemot, which was—I can't emphasize this enough—*"the national council of Anglo-Saxon times."*[42]

Why in the world would the leaders of FAIR adopt a phrase that taps into the favorite bloodline of racist organizations like the Ku Klux Klan—white Anglo-Saxon Protestants? Were Tanton and his friends just showing off their profound knowledge of Olde English? Did they just draw the name out of hat?

Roger Conner attributed the name to Tanton's attempt at clever wordplay. "He didn't think of it as Anglo-Saxon and white. He thought of it as it was old wise people within a clan," he said, before admitting Tanton could also be completely clueless. "If you talk to people who knew him up in Michigan, they experienced him as widely read, a liberal progressive thinker who broadened their perspective about the world. But he was totally tone deaf when it came to issues of race and ethnicity."[43]

Not surprisingly, Tanton constantly disavowed any white supremacist motivations or sympathies over the course of his life. But it's hard to think of WITAN as anything other than a bigoted trope and one more unfortunate piece of evidence tying Tanton and his organization back to the racist political movements of the past.

Tanton's WITAN memos were printed in 1988 by the *Arizona Republic.* Their content, which actually touched on perceived threats to WASP culture, was even more disturbing than the group's moniker.

In the first memo, written sometime in 1986, Tanton lays out his strategic vision for the future. This includes infiltrating and taking over the Senate judiciary committee, working with other committees on targeted legislation to do things like deny earned income tax credits to illegal aliens, secure employer sanctions against those who hire undocumented aliens, emphasize better enforcement of laws already on the books, work on the state level to punish immigrants, and prevent undocumented aliens from receiving welfare and other benefits.[44]

A second memo, dated July 11, 1986, written by Roger Conner, echoes Tanton's vision and summarizes the group's long-term agenda into what he calls "The Five C's of Immigration reform."

> Cut the magnet of jobs which draws illegals here (employer sanctions)
>
> Control the border with technology and manpower
>
> Cap legal immigration, with the level periodically reviewed
>
> Close the loopholes which give illegals rights to welfare and lengthy bureaucratic procedural rights
>
> Contribute to population control and economic development in source countries.[45]

A third WITAN document from October 10, 1986 begins with Tanton admitting his work is "not highly polished," at the outset of the document. Evidently, he had a sense his writing was inherently offensive. Here are some lowlights:

"Will Latin American migrants bring with them the tradition of the *mordida* (bribe), the lack of involvement in public affairs, etc.?" he writes, packing two stereotypes in one sentence. Tanton resorts to the age-old prejudiced portrait of immigrants as sex-mad procreators, making what he thinks is a joke:

> On the demographic point: perhaps this is the first instance in which those with their pants up are going to get caught by those with their pants down!

Later, Tanton veers into eugenics territory while stereotyping two ethnicities, asking, "What are the differences in educability between

Hispanics (with their 50 percent dropout rate) and Asiatics (with their excellent school records and long tradition of scholarship)?"

He also suggests a concern that seems lifted from the Know-Nothing handbook— that the increase in Catholic Hispanic immigrants might affect American principles of church-state separation. Presumably, he thought the sheer number of Catholics—as opposed to Protestants— might somehow overrule constitutional law.

But perhaps the most alarming and telling question he asks is one that oozes with the kind of inherent race war rhetoric beloved by white supremacists: "As Whites see their power and control over their lives declining, will they simply go quietly into the night? Or will there be an explosion?"[46]

The embarrassing nature of these memos and their clear bias against Latinos and other groups had both long and short-term impact. "Tanton and the memos ruined my life," said Conner, who quit FAIR in 1989, and insists he was disgusted by the white nationalism that had taken over the organization ("I'd just want to take a shower when I got home"[47]). Linda Chavez, executive director of U.S. English, left the group over what she saw as Tanton's bigoted, anti-Latino bias. So did her fellow board member, legendary CBS newsman Walter Cronkite. The same day Chavez left, Tanton resigned as chairman of the organization.[48] But the organization, whose mission was to drive states to make English the official language—usually via amending the state constitutions—and require official government business be conducted solely in English, had already succeeded in getting measures placed on several state ballots. And, as I noted earlier, the measure passed in Arizona.

U.S. English is the only Tanton-initiated project over which he actually lost control. In a letter to Donna Panazzi, the program officer for his number one benefactor, Cordy May's family trust, he explains, "Things went rapidly downhill at that organization. I could detail the turmoil if you'd like, but the net result was that after several years, the board members who had been loyal to me were ejected from the board (Gerda Bikales, Robert Park, and Leo Sorensen) and the organization was taken over by Mauro Mujica, an immigrant from Chile. He had himself declared an executive director and chairman of the board—for life!—and authorized a salary for himself of $10,000 a month. (I have no idea what it is up to now.) Mr. Mujica saw FAIR not as a friend, but the enemy, and denied FAIR use of [U.S. English's] mailing list."[49]

In 1994, Tanton spun off a second language-lobbying group, ProEnglish, from within US Inc, housing it within NumbersUSA. It shared much of the same agenda as U.S. English and has been criticized for its "nativist agenda and xenophobic origins" by the Anti-Defamation League.

According to Roger Conner, the WITAN leak put John Tanton at crossroads. It exposed him as being caught in an ideological transition, shifting FAIR away from its economic agenda. "When you look at the mailing list for the WITAN society, it's [made up of] marginalized, racist people, and he was trying to stir up their interest in immigration. Why do you think, a few years later, he got the French book, *The Camp of the Saints*, translated into English? He decided that in order to get immigration control, he would have to stir up white fear and he wanted immigration control so badly, he was willing to do it even though he pledged earlier that he never would. But he was willing to violate the promises that he had made to himself and his family and other people because the issues that he was working on was so important to him.

"Once the memo was discovered and this great fall out happened, John had a profound decision to make. And that is, 'Do I confess error and change or do I say f*** you all?'

"And he chose 'F*** you all.' He said, 'Okay, I accept that I'm now marginalized, I'm no longer going to be talking to the likes of Warren Buffett. I'm going to be a marginalized figure and that's just fine.'"[50]

Tanton, having been caught stoking racist sentiment to fuel his single-issue cause, redoubled his efforts. He may have existed on the margins, but with Cordelia Sciafe May's money, he would create an empire on those margins, and conduct a guerilla policy war to infiltrate the mainstream.

THE LETTER MAN

Ten boxes of Tanton papers remain sealed, not to be opened until April 6, 2035, at Michigan State University's Bentley Historical Library, per his estate's donor agreement. In 2017, however, Virginia-based immigration attorney Hassan Ahmad filed a lawsuit charging that the papers were public records and should be unsealed. In July 2019, an appeals panel agreed with his argument and ruled it should be released under the Freedom of Information Act.[51] Based on the contents of the papers already made available to the public, it is abundantly clear that the justification and motivation behind Tanton's mission to stop immigration had little to do with environmental concerns. He was using terms like "immigrant" and "English only" as cloaks for his ultimate mission: ensure that European-American traditions—"White" culture—remain the dominant cultural currency of the nation.

In one communication after another, Tanton revealed his mission and motives, recalling the language and intent that motivated Madison Grant, Wickliffe Draper, and so many other white nationalists and eugenicists: ensuring the dominance of whites.

Tanton's anxiety was revealed in a 1997 letter to controversial Harvard political science professor Samuel P. Huntington—Kris Kobach's ideological godfather and the author of 2004 *Who Are We? The Challenges to America's National Identity*, a much-ridiculed work that the *New York Times* called "crotchety, overstuffed," and "alarmist." Tanton wrote:

> If for Europe one were to subtract out all of the births to the foreign born, the total fertility rate would likely fall to 1.4 or less (replacement is about 2.1). For the United States, the total fertility of the European-American component is about 1.7, and would be substantially less if we subtracted out pathological births (such as those to unmarried teens) subtracting out births to the foreign born, per document three above, would give us a total fertility rate well below replacement.

> The situation then is that the people who have been the carriers of Western Civilization are well on the way toward resigning their commission to carry the culture into the future.[52]

The irony of the former president of Zero Population Growth wringing his hands about a low birth rate should be impossible to miss. But the sustainability issue that Tanton was now obsessed with had nothing to do with the food chain, air quality, or land use. It was about sustaining "European-American"—white—culture. And ensuring that demographic had the numbers to stay in power.

Tanton's letters frequently show him reaching out to a *Who's Who* of extremely wealthy Americans. He dines with *Time* magazine owner Henry Luce. He woos Dr. John M. Templeton, the head of Templeton Foundation, a charity with a multi-billion-dollar endowment. In one 1984 memo, he spends five pages recounting a visit with Warren Buffett in which they discussed the FAIR agenda, U.S. English, fundraising, population control, and more.[53] It's not clear whether Buffett ever donated to Tanton's causes, but the file contains letters from Tanton, including an invitation for Buffett to join FAIR's WITAN meetings, up to 1989.

In letters to Charles Munger, Buffett's vice chairman at Berkshire Hathaway, Tanton made repeated requests for cash over three years from 1993 to 1996. When Tanton wasn't asking Munger for cash to print Social Contract books, he was thanking Munger for hosting him at L.A.'s exclusive California Club or sharing strategic insights, such as, "I know from reading the history of the 1924 Immigration Act, that garnering business community support was key to its Passage."[54] In another, bizarre letter, he tried to enlist Munger on what sounds very much like a eugenics project, asking if he can help ascertain the funding "abilities" of Robert K. Graham, a chemist "chap who started the 'genius' sperm bank, called The Repository for Germinal Choice." In addition to looking for inside information, Tanton was a painfully hokey over-sharer as he tried to ignite Munger's interest in the project. "Incidentally, Graham believes that the more able people should have larger families, and followed his own advice by having eight children!" The letters don't indicate whether Munger ever contributed funds to Tanton's projects. But it is an unwritten rule of successful fundraising that a confirmed donor will be targeted with repeated requests.

Graham was an obvious fundraising target. The maverick millionaire, who invented the plastic used for eyeglasses, solicited sperm donations from Nobel Prize winners and once set out to buy an island and start a sovereign nation of his own. Still, Tanton never seems to have gained traction with him. The two men worked on launching Society for the Advancement of Genetic Education (SAGE), but the correspondence suggests Tanton only got $5,000 out of the millionaire inventor for that project.[55] According to self-described eugenicist Marian Van Court, who attended the initial kick-off meeting of SAGE, "the organization was still-born because" Tanton "soon realized that if he got involved with eugenics, his anti-immigration work would suffer."[56]

THE BIG SCORE

John Tanton was a visionary. He was a strategist. He was relentless. But the success of his organizations and his mission, ultimately, comes down to one person who existed solely in the background: Cordelia Scaife May.

May was the right millionaire at the right time—a widow who never remarried after her second husband committed suicide in 1974. She had no children, but she did have causes. Like John Tanton, she shared environmental and population concerns. A huge admirer of Planned Parenthood founder Margaret Sanger, she sat on the board of the International Planned Parenthood Federation. She was also an environmentalist who loved wildlife. She joined the board of the Population Council, John D. Rockefeller III's foundation that promoted family planning to lower birth rates around the world.

As she got older, however, pregnancy prevention and family planning began to take a back seat to the population issue that had gripped Tanton. With the drop in birth rates and success of Planned Parenthood, her attention focused on another segment of the population that not yet been successfully stopped—immigration.

The first $50,000 that May staked FAIR was just chump change. Three Tanton letters in the 1990s and early 2000s thanked Donna Panazzi, Executive Director of the C.S. May Trust, for annual donations of $805,000[57] as well as extra donations of $175,000 and $50,000.[58] It is likely there were many others.

"Without Cordy May, there's no FAIR," said Roger Conner. "There was no money without her."[59] He could have added most of Tanton's organizations to that statement.

From 2005 to 2017, May's Colcom Foundation gave $180 million to Tanton's organizations, according to an examination of the foundation tax filings by the *New York Times*. Over that period, FAIR received $56.7 million, US Inc got $17.2 million, NumbersUSA got $58.2 million, and the Center for Immigration Studies netted $17.5 million.[60]

Those large amounts of cash should not be astounding to anyone, considering the vice president of philanthropy for the Colcom Foundation is John Rohe—the same man who wrote Tanton's fawning biography. But there's little doubt the funding was in keeping with May's wishes.

Tanton played the legacy card with May, according to Roger Conner. "John assured her what she believed in her life would carry on."[61]

May's money had been the tool that let Tanton expand his vision and his influence. It paid, in a sense, to stir up so much chaos in Arizona. This included the English-only ballot initiatives, which hurt all non-native students and created a hostile climate for any non-English speaker trying to navigate government offices. It also funded the legal strategies to pressure employers and penalize them for hiring undocumented workers, and the other elements of SB 1070.

Her legacy will resurface in the later chapters of this book. She was the rainmaker who enabled a so-called "visionary" whose principal vision was maintaining white majority in America.

In a letter to his friend and fellow provocateur, inflammatory environmentalist Garrett Hardin, Tanton revealed the primary driver behind all his work. An article in *Time* magazine, "III Cheers for the WASP" by conservative writer Richard Brookhiser, had caught his attention.[62] "I... was glad to see something kind said about the WASPs," he writes Hardin, "but I disagree quite strongly with the opening sentence of his penultimate paragraph:

"'The shrinkage of literal WASPs as a factor in the American mosaic is as inevitable as the multiplication tables, and of little moment.'"

Dismissing Brookhiser as part of a neo-conservative movement that opposed immigration control, he added: "They also have the idea that America is just an idea, and what particular people live here makes no difference." Then Tanton unloads what stands as one of his most infamous and telling quotes: "I've come to the point of view that for European-American society and culture to persist, requires a European-American majority, and a clear one at that. I doubt very much that our traditions will be carried on my (sic) other peoples—they have their own."[63]

John Tanton's concerns about the environmental impact of immigrants are nowhere to be seen in this letter. Instead, his anxious words about the persistence of "European-American" society reveal a man driven by the fears encapsulated in that ugly, paranoid phrase of the early 1900s—*race suicide*.

Chapter Eight

DECODING THE HORSESHOE VIRUS

THE POLITICAL SPECTRUM CANNOT ALWAYS be represented as a straight line, as a horizon spanning left and right. As I noted at the beginning of this book, where the anti-immigration movement is concerned, the political continuum looks more like a horseshoe—the far-right and the far-left have circled back toward each other to coalesce on anti-immigrant issues. The left-wing provided the brainpower in terms of legal and lobbying strategy and the right-wing provided the brawn by amplifying talking points, rallying and inciting voters, and stoking nativist emotions. To a conservative Republican like me, it has been shocking to discover that the left wing's radical element of extreme environmentalism and rabid support for abortion have provided the cooked data, legal guidance, and multiple organizations to influence not only far-right racists but also mainstream conservatives. Many middle-of-the-road voters and strident right-wingers who now automatically echo anti-immigrant arguments have been played. They have been poisoned by a virus as infectious as COVID-19. They have affiliated with people whose values—especially when it comes to abortion—are the absolute opposite of their pro-life beliefs.

How did this happen? John Tanton and Cordelia Scaif May, his benefactor and co-conspirator, are primarily responsible for the extreme liberal hoodwinking of mainstream conservatives. But their work hammering out the Horseshoe Virus has been aided and abetted by a number of other thinkers and political realities. What follows is my attempt to deconstruct how this infectious, sinister, hidden doctrine has been incubating.

HORSESHOE REALITIES

Over the years, the Republican Party, the party of Lincoln, my party, has moved further and further to the right. What was once a fiscally conservative party has become the hostage to the reactionary vision of the Tea Party. Sadly, the operating word of the Tea Party is not "unite" or "grow" or "prosper." It is "shrink." I touched on this earlier, but it is worth repeating. They want to shrink the federal government, shrink taxes, and shrink the national debt, and, of course, shrink the number of immigrants in this country.

The accountant in me wants to point out that at least two of the targets on this wish list—shrinking taxes and immigrants—will hurt efforts to shrink the debt. Taxes are a source of revenue to pay down the debt and many think tanks, including right-wing Cato Institute, believe shrinking immigration will hurt our economy.

The larger point in the context of this book is that one of the central tenets of today's Republican Party—that immigration is bad and that we must crack down on undocumented aliens and deport those who are here—is now a fundamental doctrine. And yet the right-wing, and the extreme far right (the neo-Nazis, the Minutemen, the Islamophobes, the Aryan Nation, and so many other hate groups) who believe this even more fervently, have no idea that the roots of their anti-immigrant ideology were developed by the very people—pro-choice elites—who are their complete opposites:

Progressives. Elites. Women's Rights Activists. Socialists, Environmentalists.

Liberals.

I've just cast a wide net there, but some of these people conspired to stoke anti-immigrant passions in the Republican Party. John Tanton was an environmentalist obsessed with sustainability, obsessed with stopping the damage to the land and the water. He joined Planned Parenthood. He didn't just believe in choice, *he believed in abortions.* He *wanted* women to have them. "When I met him, John was an ophthalmologist in northern Michigan, who quietly gave free work for the Native Americans in reservations living nearby and advocated for abortion in a conservative community where it made him a pariah," said Roger Conner, describing the figure he once admired. "I saw the side of John that was about as pure as driven snow. I mean, here was the guy who could be comfortably wealthy if he wanted to, but instead spent his time trying to get abortion and birth control for poor women and protect access to the Great Lakes for the public against developers."

Conner, a liberal and a Democrat at the time he co-founded FAIR, describes Tanton as a Rockefeller Republican—the term for moderate, social liberals within the party. But as a man who kept bees, raised his own food and even built a windmill and solar collectors to provide his own power, Tanton's real alliance was to the land.

"I think it is central to understanding John, that he was an introverted farm kid with a deep love of nature," says Conner. "And if it came down to nature versus humans, he would choose nature."

Conner also says he believes the former farm boy had contempt for the rich establishment. "His resentment of the Eastern Seaboard, upper-class elite was never far below the surface—although he didn't let it stop him from working with them."

And asking for their money.

Tanton's letters, however, tell something of a different story. His letters about meetings with Warren Buffett and other millionaires are filled with details about rich people's clubs and dining choices. But if Conner is correct, this attitude is remarkably similar to the anti-elite postures Donald Trump has assumed while beating his own nativist drum.

Eventually, convinced he needed a network to further his goals, Tanton began his political puppet master act, taking a page out of his hero Madison Grant's playbook on how to influence legislators to pass restrictive laws to stop new arrivals to America and Draper's playbook of funding multiple organizations to make the movement appear larger than it really was.

But first he needed benefactors and ideologies to help him launder and legitimize his ideas.

Who did he turn to? He prospected for any rich, white member of the aristocracy under the guise of discussing over-population—from Warren Buffet to Alistair Cooke. And yes, he hit up the eugenics-loving Pioneer Fund. But the real payday was connecting with Cordelia Scaife May, the old-money heiress whose estimated $800 million in holdings placed her at 383 on the Forbes list of wealthiest Americans when she died in 2005. She was a poster gal for progressive causes. She didn't just serve on the board of Planned Parenthood, she wrote fan letters to Margaret Sanger, her heroine. In one fawning missive from 1961, Cordy gushed: "Dear Mrs. Sanger, Thank you many times for sending me your photograph. It is one that I value highly, for, as you know, I have always admired and tried to take part in the work you started."[1]

Cordelia May's other work—and specifically, her money—boosted the anti-immigrant movement more than anyone not named Tanton. The movement for English Only? The doomsaying books that paint nightmare visions of America? Tanton, ever the strategist and the puppet master continually got Cordy Scaife May to pay for the puppets, the string, and the theater. Her foundation is still paying—providing an estimated $200 million and counting to Tanton's network, to shape public opinion, push laws that target immigrants, and fund reports and books that experts say fudge numbers and misinterpret data.

MISINFORMING AND MANIPULATING THE BASE

There are other puppet masters spreading the Horseshoe Virus. As I detail in chapter ten, by 2017, the virus infiltrated the White House and has become a centerpiece of Donald Trump's administration. One of the biggest advocates of incubating and releasing anti-immigrant vitriol is Steve Bannon, the millionaire and former Goldman Sachs vice president who founded the right-wing website *Breitbart News* before serving as Trump's chief political strategist.

Bannon, a former naval officer who reads military strategy books in his spare time, is an extremely agile analyst. He has leveraged the power of digital information to drive nativist narratives and shape political outcomes. Interestingly, one of his epiphanies came from a popular video game, *World of Warcraft*.

In 2005, Bannon invested in Internet Gaming Entertainment (IGE), a Hong Kong-based company that employed gamers to play *World of Warcraft* and earn virtual gold that is traded within the game for virtual goods. IGE would then sell the pretend gamer-gold to players for real cash. As *Wired* magazine put it, the company "sold imaginary goods in an imaginary world."[2] Die-hard *Warcraft* players hated the idea players were obtaining "game-gold" without actually earning it and started a campaign against harvesting. The online outcry worked. *Warcraft* owner Blizzard Entertainment closed accounts of gold farmers. "These guys, these rootless white males, had monster power... It was the pre-Reddit,"

Bannon said, referring to a popular discussion board which has been used to mobilize political campaigns.

For Bannon, the experience "provided a kind of conceptual framework that he would later draw on to build up the audience for *Breitbart News*, and then to help marshal the online armies of trolls and activists that overran national politicians and helped give rise to Donald Trump," wrote Joshua Green in *Devil's Bargain*, his 2017 book about Bannon and the Trump campaign.[3]

Bannon saw first-hand the speed with which an outraged community can mass, organize and disseminate information, telling Green, "You can activate that army. They come in through Gamergate or whatever and then get turned onto politics and Trump."[4]

Inflaming the predominantly male gamer audience with sensationalized news coverage on *Breitbart* became a major vector for the virus. The stories provided warped perspectives and skewed statistics—fodder for alt-right bulletin boards and other echo chambers of hate. They could make their way to Twitter and Facebook and other social media, creating a growing group of anti-immigration true believers, many of whom have no idea they had been fed "information" designed to create a cognitive bias. As long as these people remained in their digital echo chambers, they had no ability to recognize they were infected. John Tanton spent hefty amounts on direct mail campaigns to increase his audience and his message. In contrast, the unofficial network Bannon conceived of worked faster and reached more people and cost relatively little. It was a super-spreader.

THE ECO-EXTREMIST

Cordy May, John Tanton, and Roger Conner had another hero who also bore some responsibility for shaping their worldview and forging the horseshoe—Garrett Hardin. Once a respected ecologist and biologist at the University of California in Santa Barbara, Hardin ranked among the most outspoken and alarmist of the radical environmentalists. His 1968 Malthus-on-steroids article in *Science* magazine, "The Tragedy of the Commons," became a lynchpin for over-population paranoia. Offering a parable about villagers adding too many cows to their common pasture, Hardin's tale is a launching pad for attacks on over-breeding, resource depletion, the United Nations' Universal Declaration of Human Rights, the welfare state, and other concerns, all of which supposedly spell doom for planet Earth.

In Hardin's population-obsessed view, governments that care about the welfare of their citizens—including and especially children—were a problem. So was the idea of basic human rights, and the idea that family size is a personal choice.

Widely reprinted and anthologized, Hardin's article is still taught today as an example of environmental caution and the study of common property resources, although not without dissent. In her book, *Governing the Commons*, 2009 Nobel Economics Laureate Elinor Ostrom roundly dismantles Hardin's conclusion that social groups invariably screw up collective resources.[5] But for Tanton, May, and Conner, Hardin was a rock star ecologist who confirmed their greatest fears about immigrants and the destruction of the planet.

Hardin was so devoted to terminating pregnancies that he created an underground railroad in 1973, guiding 200 local women to get abortions in Mexico.[6] As he got older, however, Mexico was something he wanted to abort. In a letter to Cordy May, according to the *New York Times*, he complained of "the predominant Latinity of apprehended criminals" in California.[7]

He also wrote: "The hope of the future lies in the intelligent practice of discrimination."[8]

He wasn't kidding. "My position is that this idea of a multiethnic society is a disaster," he said in a 1997 interview with *The Social Contract*. "That's what we've got in Central Europe, and in Central Africa. A multiethnic society is insanity. I think we should restrict immigration for that reason."[9]

When I read these words, I wondered where people like Hardin and Tanton and May lived. Did they know any people of color? Did they know any Jews or Muslims or Latinos? As it turns out, Emmet County, where Tanton lived for more than fifty years, was 91 percent white as of 2019.[10] May, a rich recluse, essentially lived in an all-white society in Ligonier, Pennsylvania, which is 98.1 percent white. As for Hardin, in 1970, 3.3 percent of Santa Barbara's 70,000 population was black. No data on Hispanics was charted in the census, but 18 percent listed having a Spanish-speaking person in their background.[11] These anti-immigration backers, like Russell Pearce, were products of their environment. I spent time in the same community as Pearce, but he was a cop and I was their pastor. We all see the world from our own frame of reference, but we need to speak from facts, not our opinions and prejudices. I can think of few things that are more evil than making up facts and preaching them to suit our fantasy of a future nation or world.

In order to forge an ideological horseshoe, these population control agitators honed a narrative that appealed to radicalized right-wing anti-immigrant sentiments, economic fears, and social stigmas. Gradually, that narrative has slipped into mainstream political dialogues so that middle-of-the-road Republicans have also become infected with the virus. These are people who normally might say, "Wait a minute. My family were immigrants, too!" And who do these Republicans come face-to-face with? The people on the other side of the horseshoe—the living-in-a-bubble, elitist, progressive, pro-choice, single-issue environmentalists who have orchestrated a culture of hate and vitriol that is full of the virus.

This is not just a wild pet theory I hatched after Russell Pearce brought a cluster of the Horseshoe Virus to Arizona. At the time I was campaigning against Pearce, I had no idea he had been working with John Tanton's network. As I struggled to understand Pearce's legal assault on immigrants, and as I dug into the history that I have shared in these pages, it all became clearer.

THEORIES ABOUT A THEORY

When I mapped out the influences behind the anti-immigration move-ment, and the ideological perspectives and motivations of the central figures involved, I was struck by the prevalence of left- and right-wing thinkers. That out-and-out racists like Madison Grant and Wycliffe Draper would have connections with a liberal activist like Margaret Sanger. That Roger Conner's left-wing economic ideas would merge with John Tanton's radical environmentalism, which would then morph into thinly veiled tropes that allude to race suicide. The best visual metaphor I could come up with was a horseshoe.

For decades, others have documented the curious intersection of far-right and far-left. No doubt, the temporary alliance of Hitler and Stalin during the invasion of Poland boggled many minds. But politics and the quest for power can lead to surprising marriages of convenience. Michael Bloomberg has switched parties twice. Ivanka Trump was a registered Democrat until 2018. One of the earliest references to horseshoe politics came from a surprising source: Ronald Reagan. Our fortieth president may remain a conservative hero to many. But a note card from Reagan's papers from the 1966 California gubernatorial campaign suggests he was determined to seize the middle. According to the scholar who found it, the card "depicted a 'horseshoe' diagram of the political spectrum, in which the "extreme left" and the "extreme right" meet at the bottom of the graph, whereas the "moderate" is at home at the top."[12]

But the horseshoe theory, is generally attributed to the French phi-losopher Jean-Pierre Faye, whose 1996 book *Le siècle des idéologies* ("The Century of Ideologies"), expounded on the relationship between ide-ology and reality in political spheres and concluded that ultimately, both sides of the political spectrum—fascists and communists—end up embracing totalitarianism.

His dense book describes political and ideological events in history as an "arc of tremendous power" that "puts face to face two mirrors, which reflect each other inverse images of oneself towards the other."[13] That arc recalls a *fer à cheval*, French for horseshoe, a term Fay also used.[14]

This theory has failed to gain much traction or respect among political theorists, largely because there are exceptions to the rule. Both far-right and far-left adherents bristle at any hint of the horseshoe theory gaining traction. In France, for example, there are precious few, if any, instances of far-left parties or candidates throwing support to Marine Le Pen's right-wing National Front. The same can be said of elections in England, where fringe parties on opposite sides of the spectrum rarely agree. Here in the U.S., it's impossible to imagine the American Nazi Party would want to collaborate with the Communist Party USA. However, some of Bernie Sanders' and Trump's voters have been known to sympathize and even coalesce around the need for a "revolution" to address the so-called swamp in Washington, D.C.

Still, that both a radical philosopher and a Hollywood heart-throb-turned-politician hit on the same idea might suggest there is an intrinsic truth to the Horseshoe concept. I believe they were largely correct. Many authoritarian governments share similarities with communist and theocratic governments. They lack due process; they have command economies; civil rights are often non-existent; control is maintained by fear and repression; and an independent media is the enemy. Strange bedfellows exist everywhere you turn.

At any rate, I'm not offering the Horseshoe Virus as an absolute political law that applies to all political constructs and issues. My conclusion relates specifically to the anti-immigration movement. If it shares some of the same concepts of a political theory that isn't accurate 100 percent of the time, that in no way detracts from its accuracy and applicability to immigration. I came up with the name Horseshoe Virus because it accurately depicts an utterly unexpected set of relationships that have been forged specifically to control, define and exploit the anti-immigration movement in America.

There is one other, highly regarded model that foreshadowed the horseshoe theory. It was formulated by Seymour Lipset, one of the most influential sociologists of the twentieth century, who studied, among other things, the formation of voting blocs known as cleavages. Lipset's "Centrist/Extremist" theory echoes the metaphor of the horseshoe. In his view, extremist or populist movements threaten the democratic center of American politics. A vocal proponent of American democracy and the power of capitalism, Lipset was wary of the appeal and power of simple-yet-radical populist messages on the electorate. Like most political theories, his Centrist/Extremist view has critics—mostly from supporters of both left- and right-wing movements who accuse Lipset of lumping "together dissidents, populists of the left and right, supremacists and terrorists as an irrational lunatic fringe."[15] Of course those types will have strong opinions, but I agree with Lipset.

In the final stages of researching the book, as I pieced together the evolution and so many of the disturbing connections of the current war on immigration in America and tracing our national history of hating immigrants who weren't northern European, I discovered others had made connections similar to my own—including one person who surprised me.

CARLSON'S FAIR GAME

In 1997, journalist Tucker Carlson spent some time zooming in on FAIR and its leaders, specifically Garrett Hardin, the informal spiritual advisor and former board member of the organization, and Dan Stein, the executive director.

Writing in the *Wall Street Journal*, Carlson dug up some shocking Hardin quotes, recounting how Hardin praised abortion and infanticide to a five-months pregnant reporter: "In all societies practicing infanticide, the child is killed within minutes after birth, before bonding can occur," Hardin said. As for terminating pregnancies, he added: "A fetus is of so little value, there's no point in worrying about it."[16]

Since eliminating children is slightly problematic for pretty much the entire world, Hardin shifted his efforts elsewhere; Carlson reported that Hardin believed ending immigration was "the quickest, easiest and most effective form of population control in the U.S." and that his views fit comfortably within FAIR's ideological framework.

Then Tucker Carlson ripped into FAIR leader Dan Stein for supporting the stunning eugenicist musings Hardin made to *Omni* magazine.

> The problem, according to Mr. Hardin, is not simply that there are too many people in the world, but that there are too many of the wrong kind of people. As he put it: "It would be better to encourage the breeding of more intelligent people rather than the less intelligent." Asked to comment on Mr. Hardin's statement, Mr. Stein doesn't even pause. "Yeah, so what?" he replies. "What is your problem with that? Should we be subsidizing people with low IQs to have as many children as possible, and not subsidizing those with high ones?"

In another exchange, Stein said, "Certainly we would encourage people in other countries to have small families. Otherwise they'll all be coming here, because there's no room at the Vatican."

"There are reasonable critics of immigration, but Dan Stein is not one of them," Carlson wrote, disturbed that "a number of otherwise sober-minded conservatives seem to be making common cause with Mr. Stein and FAIR." He ended his article wondering if "conservatives who embrace FAIR know all they should" about the organization. This question, as you might have noticed, underscores the main purpose of this book. FAIR, Tanton, and all the supporting organizations that the far right embrace are not what they seem, and they are playing you. The Horseshoe Virus is a conscious coming together of the far left and far right.

In case you are wondering, the Tucker Carlson who wrote this article criticizing FAIR is the same conservative Tucker Carlson who now appears nightly on Fox News supporting the anti-immigration policies which were first conceived of and promoted by FAIR and have been adopted by Donald Trump and Stephen Miller. I suspect ratings, money, and power have all factored into Carlson's about-face and embrace of the far right's side of the horseshoe, despite knowing who is behind the progressive side of the same movement. But exactly when and why he picked up the virus—the virus he once tried to expose as an unusual combination of Planned Parenthood and Nazi sympathizers—are questions only he can answer.

I will note, however, that Dan Stein does make one factual statement in the article: "Immigration's weird. It has weird politics."

Which is exactly my case with the Horseshoe Virus.

CORROBORATING TESTIMONY

Carlson isn't the only one to pick up on the sinister virus embedded in FAIR's strategic DNA. Author Mario Lopez blows the whistle louder and harder in his essay "Hijacking Immigration."

"The evidence shows that the primary leaders and funders of the anti-immigration movement were drawn to it because they were also active organizers and supporters of, and contributors to, the population-control movement in the United States. This should give pause to pro-life Republican advocates who might consider collaborating with groups such as FAIR, CIS, and NumbersUSA on the issue of immigration," Lopez wrote. Lopez distilled the essence and inherent contradiction of the Horseshoe Virus movement—that its leaders do not share the values of its right-wing base:

> Once one scratches the surface, the whitewashing, rebranding, and slight refocusing of the most radical side of the green movement—advocates of population control, abortion, and family planning—is striking, and stands diametrically opposed to the pro-life cause.[17]

For Roger Conner, Tanton's single-minded vision mutated in dangerous ways. "You will misunderstand the moral of Tanton's life if you say that this guy was a racist from day one trying to preserve white power. His story is that of a profoundly decent, progressive person who succumbs to the danger of single-issue advocacy. The danger of picking one issue, that one string you could pull so that everything falls down—that one thing that changes everything. He was willing to do anything to pull that string. That was his Achilles heel." Tanton embraced the hard-right Nazi and racist rabble rousers not because he shared their roots, although he had come to share their race suicide paranoia. He used them just like he used Cordy May's money. He was hunting for resources for his passion to reduce immigration. On the other hand, Conner maintained his original vision and walked away from FAIR in 1989, when it was clear Tanton was hellbent to prostitute FAIR to get his anti-immigrant policies implemented.

Political scientist Elizabeth Cohen charged Tanton with engaging in "overpopulation hysteria." This allowed him to refine a tactic she called "'greenwashing': cloaking one set of motives in the language of environmental concerns." By the mid-1990s, Tanton was greenwashing legal immigration policy in devious ways, wrangling his pals at the Sierra Club to co-publish a book with CIS called *How Many Americans? Population, Immigration and the Environment.* The book suggested denying due process rights to immigrants as well as stopping almost all legal immigration to the U.S.[18]

Those ideas, floated twenty-five years ago, were at the hidden core of Arizona's SB 1070 law. But they are no longer hidden. The Horseshoe Virus has now metastasized in America. Tanton initially spread it by channeling the same fears that once drove race suicide anxieties more than one hundred years ago. Now it is spread in large part by men with direct and indirect ties to Tanton's network. After their initial success in Arizona, which we were able to fight off, they have found the ideal messenger nationally for their hate-driven agenda, Donald J. Trump.

PART THREE

Chapter Nine

DIVIDED WE STAND

THE AMERICAN ANTI-IMMIGRATION MOVEMENT HAS not grown in a vacuum. John Tanton may have started his journey fixated on the social and economic damage that population growth and accompanying environmental disaster would rain down on the world. But he shifted his doomsday narrative—painting immigrants as the major cause of America's economic and social woes.

This vision is misguided and misleading. Since the end of the Cold War, our political and financial leaders have fostered the rise of economic globalization. Globalization for America translates into the idea that inter-connected international trade will generate efficiencies and profits for stockholders by creating new markets and exploiting cheap labor around the world. Proponents of globalization believe societies will benefit from the proliferation and exchange of commerce and goods. Critics, however, point to two disturbing trends: the number of jobs in

America has decreased over the last few decades[1] and, when it comes to the distribution of wealth, the chasm between rich and poor in our nation has grown wider.[2]

This book is not a takedown of globalization. In fact, I support many aspects of international trade policy, especially when it proves mutually beneficial for all parties—workers, consumers, and manufacturers. I do business globally. But globalization has played into the hands of the American anti-immigration movement. Tanton's initiative benefited from the economic realities—particularly the reduction in blue collar jobs—that are tied to the way goods and money now move around the world. With so many more now having so much less, the economy and job security have become major issues. Tanton's organizations seized on these concerns. FAIR, as noted earlier, got off the ground in part because co-founder Roger Conner believed shrinking the supply of immigrants would benefit America's poor minorities, improving employment opportunities and wages. Forty years later, the research director of FAIR spin-off CIS, Steven Camarota was repeating that unproven tenet to the *New York Times*, which reported that he "believes that wages would rise and motivate many chronically unemployed Americans to get back to work" if undocumented workers suddenly vanished.[3]

FAIR, CIS, and NumbersUSA have spent decades and hundreds of millions of dollars stoking anxiety among the electorate, issuing papers, articles and talking points that target immigrants as a threat to working Americans and blaming undocumented immigrants for depressing wages and taking jobs from our citizens.

Tanton even crafted a policy to politicize immigration in the minds of all Republican Party members. In a letter to Fred Stanback Jr., the heir to a headache powder fortune who had donated more than a half million dollars to FAIR by 1994,[4] Tanton laid out his strategy:

> "The goal is to change Republicans' perception of immigration so that when they encounter the word "immigrant," their reaction is "Democrat."

But Tanton used his organizations to spread his cynical vision without party-lines, too.

In 1998, CIS published "The Wages of Immigration" by the organization's then "resident scholar," Camarota. The article finds him making a loaded assertion based on a Current Population Survey from the U.S. Census, yet couching the argument in extremely qualified wording choices: "The findings indicate that immigration is likely to have contributed significantly to the decline in wages for workers with only a high school degree or less in the last two decades."[5] *Indicate that immigration is likely to have?* That's hardly decisive or conclusive wording. By 2007, Camarota was back again, this time as CIS director of research penning, "Immigration Is Hurting the U.S. Worker," once again recycling arguments that "the disproportionate flow of undereducated immigrants to the U.S. has also depressed wages for native-born workers on the lower rungs of the economic ladder."

The alarmist also introduces another line of assault: the sheer number of newcomers. "The U.S. has never confronted an immigrant population that has grown this much, this fast," he writes, citing the census as he claims "1.6 million legal and illegal immigrants settle in the country each year."[6] This wording is meant to imply there is an unprecedented flood of immigrants into this country. That was and is not the case, according to the Department of Homeland Security's 2014 Yearbook, which tracked the number of annual legal immigrants from 1820 to 2014.

In terms of sheer numbers, no year saw more traffic than 1991, when 1,826,595 immigrants arrived. The total U.S. population was about 250 million at that time, so the new arrivals increased our current population by 0.7 percent. In 1882, when America was populated by about 50 million people, 788,000 immigrants arrived—accounting for a 1.5 percent boost in population.[7] As far as a percentage increase of our current population, Camarota's research was more spin than fact. (We will address more problematic work from this researcher in chapter ten.)

In 2018, CIS was still at it. Despite the draconian measures instituted by the Trump administration, CIS put up an article entitled "Immigration

Continues to Surge." It buried the slowdown deep in the article and led with data from 2016, noting 1.75 million immigrants "(legal and illegal)" arrived in the U.S. The article also zeros in on arrivals from Latin America. The author says, "Half of the increase in new arrivals (legal and illegal) since 2011 has been from Latin America." Why that is important is not made clear in the article, but given Tanton's obsession with European-Americans, it's hard not to think there's a subtext involved: *Warning: Latin Americans generally speak Spanish and are brown-skinned.*[8]

As recently as July 2019, FAIR was ranting about immigrants stealing jobs from American citizens. An article titled "Illegal Aliens Taking U.S. Jobs" claimed, "The advocates of open borders and cheap-labor business lobbyists would have Americans believe that the U.S. economy would suddenly collapse without illegal immigration and cheap foreign labor. This is a classic scare tactic. It is also implicitly based on the false and outright insulting claim that native-born Americans are somehow averse to hard work."[9]

Having talked to business leaders and farmers in Arizona, however, I know this is no "scare tactic." For lettuce farmers on the Arizona greenbelt, having foreign labor available—people who will work in 110-degree weather—is a life or death matter. If they don't have the staff to pick their crops during the short, intense harvest period, they will be out of business. And if they had to leave crops unpicked, prices for produce would rise across the country.

As a businessman, I can also tell you that the mantra of lower wages is misleading on another level. The best organizations do not nickel-and-dime their staff. Every business owner, large or small, that is worth his or her salt would rather pay more for excellent, productive workers, than pay less for undependable employees. I have no doubt there are exploitative business owners. I have heard the nightmare stories. They exist. But by and large, successful businesses want to foster positive cultures that promote stability and productivity because it works long-term.

I'm not alone in challenging the Tanton organization's three essential talking points—immigrants take jobs away, they lower wages, especially for the poorest Americans, and they are flooding America like never before. Other think tanks and scholars with impartial backgrounds agree with me. The National Academies of Sciences, Engineering and Medicine 2016 Immigration Report, "one of the most comprehensive studies yet on the topic," according to the *Wall Street Journal*,[10] refuted the default economic anti-immigrant arguments, citing data collected from 1994 to 2013.

"Second-generation adults—the children of immigrants—had, on average, a more favorable net fiscal impact for all government levels combined than either first-generation immigrants or the rest of the native-born population," the immigration report noted. "Reflecting their slightly higher educational achievement, as well as their higher wages and salaries, the second generation contributed more in taxes on a per capita basis during working ages than did their parents or other native-born Americans."

The National Academies' research also concluded that immigration has an overall positive impact on long-run economic growth in the U.S. "Waves of immigrants coming into the U.S. in recent decades have helped the economy over the long haul and had little lasting impact on the wages or employment levels of native-born Americans," was how *the Journal* summarized the paper.

Other organizations and think tanks, like the CATO Institute, have also dismantled CIS and FAIR's economic attacks on immigrants, both legal and undocumented. But Tanton's strategy was diverse. It issued other refrains to stoke anti-immigrant sentiment. CIS sponsored a lengthy research paper advising labor unions to stop embracing immigrants[11]—something that has run counter to most organized labor policy for decades. Articles appeared about the number of households where languages other than English are spoken—as if that was a bad thing. For anyone who has lived in an ethnically diverse city, like New York or Houston or Los Angeles, this comment will probably merit a "so what?" But for nativists and white nationalists in rural areas and the heartland who shared Tanton's paranoid fears of the evaporation of what he called "European-American society and culture," this is a rallying call to action.

POLICY TUG OF WAR

We can argue about the implications of immigration, whether it hurts or helps the American economy. Whether it benefits newcomers at the expense of the underclass already here. Whether it is just a continuum that is part and parcel of America, from earliest English, Dutch, Swedish, Spanish, French settlers to the Irish, Italians, and Germans of the 1800s to the Jews and eastern Europeans of the early 1900s to the Asian and Latinos who make up most of our nation's recent additions. But it serves no purpose to say that immigration is not an issue. It is. And over the last fifty years the U.S. government has shifted radically in how it treats the issue, often taking a step in one direction and then veering three steps the other way.

Until the 1965 Immigration Act was passed, the U.S. had quotas in place for the national origins of immigrants coming to America. These quotas, dating back to the 1924 Immigration Act, overwhelmingly favored people from northern European countries and discriminated against eastern and southern Europeans. "The law was just unbelievable in its clarity of racism," said Stephen Klineberg, sociologist at Rice University in a 2006 interview. You can hear the work of Madison Grant and Wickliffe Draper's eugenics-boosting pals in Klineberg's description: "It declared that Northern Europeans are a superior subspecies of the white race. The Nordics were superior to the Alpines, who in turn were superior to the Mediterraneans, and all of them were superior to the Jews and the Asians."[12]

With the 1965 law, the invisible gate that kept out Latin Americans, Africans and Asians was lifted to some degree. 120,000 immigrants from the Western Hemisphere were now set to get visas.

Those measures stayed in place until 1986, when President Ronald Reagan signed the Immigration Reform and Control Act (IRCA), granting citizenship to an estimated 2.7 million undocumented immigrants in America. While Tanton and his small band of immigration restrictionists were critical of the amnesty, they looked upon the bill as a partial victory. It was the first measure to pressure the business community to stop hiring illegal aliens, instituting fines for employers with more than three workers, who knowingly hired undocumented workers. This tactic was clearly spelled out in FAIR's WITAN documents, which phrased the goal this way: "Cut the magnet of jobs which draws illegals here (employer sanctions)." FAIR's Gerry Mackie spun it as a glass-half-full law: "In order to get the employer sanctions to turn off the job magnet that draws illegal aliens here, we had to drag along the baggage of amnesty."[13]

Conner confirmed he too considered this a victory at the time. But the *realpolitik* that so often drives Washington, D.C. interfered. The Democrats were seized by "the progressive liberal orthodoxy that we shouldn't control immigration," he said, and "employers had control of the Republicans. Enforcement of employer sanctions was sabotaged, and with it, any chance for controlling illegal immigration. Immigrants came in, they married, they got jobs, they bought houses and became church members. The notion that you're going to round them up and send them away was fatuous." Indeed, the lobbyists of the powerful Chamber of Commerce—at both state and federal levels—are mighty advocates for a constant immigrant labor pool.

At around this time, "Tanton, with this singular focus on restricting immigration, was playing footsie with the racists," said Conner, and "began constructing a parallel movement outside of FAIR with U.S. English and through his WITAN society."[14]

The small victory was fleeting. When George H.W. Bush signed the 1990 Immigration Act, he boosted the number of visas handed out each year from 270,000 to a total of 675,000. The law assigned different categories and numbers to newcomers: 480,000 family-sponsored visas; 140,000 employment-based visas, and 55,000 diversity visas. Immediate relatives of U.S. citizens were exempt from these numerical limits.[15] Still, there was a potential silver lining in the law for restrictionists. The law established the creation of something called the U.S. Commission on Immigration Reform, mandated to issue four reports on U.S. immigration and make recommendations to Congress. This served to clarify an important issue for Tanton's groups. The lobbyists now knew who they had to lobby.

That said, by 1994, the population concerns that may have initially stoked John Tanton's interest in targeting immigrants had lost traction. In a letter to FAIR leadership, Tanton wrote that the issues "to which we should hitch our wagon" were "crime, health care, and welfare reform." What happened to Tanton's foundational issues—population and environmental damage caused by overpopulation? Here's his answer: "No population group (save Population/Environment Balance and NPG) will say that immigration is a US population problem; nor will any of the environmental groups. We're on our own. My conclusion: while we can still and should make the population and environment arguments since many individuals buy them, we shouldn't hang our organization hat on them, as other organizations won't validate our arguments."[16]

This admission was shocking. Tanton was abandoning the group's entire reason for being. Instead, he was advocating the group focus solely on hot button nativist issues—tying immigration to crime and the taxing of America's health and welfare systems—that FAIR continues to push today.

A CONFUSING TURN

The U.S. Commission on Immigration Reform was chaired by former civil rights activist Barbara Jordan, the first woman elected to Congress from Texas and the first southern black female ever elected to the House. Jordan, a charismatic orator, described the agenda of her committee very succinctly: "To support legal immigration in the national interest."

When the commission released its report, Jordan distilled this enormous issue down to four key recommendations. The first called for improving border management: "A strategy to prevent illegal entry and facilitate legal ones in the national interest. It is far better to deter illegal immigration than to play the cat and mouse game that results from apprehensions followed by return followed by re-entry."

The second was to reduce the magnet that jobs currently present for illegal immigration. Jordan expressed enthusiasm for a computerized system to verify Social Security Numbers.

The third focused on public benefits. The committee felt "that illegal aliens should be eligible for no public benefits other than those of an emergency nature, when such aid is in the public health and safety interest, and when it is constitutionally protected." Legal immigrants, Jordan made clear, should be eligible for safety net programs. "That does not mean that the Commission wants to see legal immigrants in our public benefit programs... However, the bottom line is that circumstances can and do change: deaths occur, illnesses, accidents. When there is need for help, and no sponsor is able to provide it, legal immigrants should be able to call upon the broader society for assistance."

The causes of illegal migration were the commission's fourth major issue. Jordan reported that "we are convinced that the U.S. government can only go so far unilaterally in controlling illegal movements into our country. We can help eliminate some of the pull factors in the United States, but bilateral and multilateral action is needed to reduce the push factors in source countries. A great deal of lip service has been paid over the years to this concept, but we have seen more talk than action...trade and investment present the best opportunities in the long run for reducing the economic differentials that cause migration."[17]

It is hard to read Jordan's words and not wonder how much FAIR and CIS and NumbersUSA influenced the commission. These recommendations clearly echo many of the concerns on FAIR's agenda. The *New York Times* reported that Republican restrictionists' platform "was strengthened when Ms. Jordan's panel, in its second report, recommended in June 1995 that legal immigration be gradually reduced by one-third, to about 550,000 immigrants a year."[18] Clinton, never one to be out-flanked by Republicans, met briefly with Jordan and embraced many of the panel's proposals, including the cuts in legal immigration.

In recent years, Tanton's organizations have lionized Jordan as a pioneering restrictionist. NumbersUSA boasts a website calling her work "part of the inspiration for NumbersUSA's founding."[19] CIS has a profile that claims "One of Jordan's goals was to reduce legal immigration by eliminating the right for citizens and legal immigrants to sponsor the immigration of siblings."[20]

Bruce Morrison, who served on the commission, called this a blatant mischaracterization of the groups' recommendations. Infuriated by a report that NumbersUSA regarded Jordan as its "spiritual godmother," the former Connecticut congressman denied Jordan was a restrictionist, writing that NumbersUSA "seeks to claim she advocated for cuts in legal immigration that neither she nor the commission supported."

Morrison went on to stress that the commission recommended "a reallocation of existing numbers of immigrants with an emphasis on the children and spouses of green card holders who were waiting in long lines... It was a priority setting, not an overall reduction in legal immigration."[21]

By echoing some of the far-right's concerns, the commission's report did, arguably, help set the stage for the 1996 Illegal Immigration Reform and Immigrant Responsibility Act. The legislation, signed by Bill Clinton, represented a significant shift on immigration. It was a crackdown, a tough-on-crime move made by a shrewd politician whose party had just been shellacked in the 1994 midterm elections, losing control of both the House and the Senate.

The 1996 act introduced laws that allowed undocumented immigrants to be deported for misdemeanor or felony crimes. It also introduced penalties for racketeering, alien smuggling, and using or making phony immigration-related documents. But perhaps the most chilling clauses were ones that obstructed the pathways to citizenship for undocumented aliens. Now, unauthorized immigrants who had married a U.S. citizen or qualified for a Green Card through a relative were unable to apply for papers directly. The new law reversed a number of long-held policies that allowed immigrants to obtain legal status if they faced extreme hardship at home and had been in the U.S. for seven years. It capped one hardship program at 3,000 when, previously, there had been no restrictions.[22]

THE RULE OF FLAW

There is a perception that Rule of Law is the bedrock of America. In many ways, it is. We have legislative branches of federal and local government. We have federal, state, and local law enforcement agencies. We have the wonderful Bill of Rights that affords citizens due process and protects against the abuse of our rights. But anyone who tells you our system is infallible or that truth and justice always prevail is either lying or not paying attention.

Drafting laws and enforcing them are two different things. Our litigious system often creates conditions for what might best be termed "lawfare," a form of battle where those with the best and brightest lawyers and the deepest pockets can influence outcomes in their favor. There is also willful institutional blindness—especially when local economies benefit by ignoring laws. Since Ronald Reagan signed the Immigration and Control Act, prohibiting employers from hiring unauthorized workers, a black market for the creation and sale of fake documents has blossomed. Fake Social Security cards, green cards, and driver's licenses are offered for sale in urban centers that attract immigrant populations. The doctored documents generally cost anywhere from $50 to $200, depending on their quality and market demand. These documents—known as "Mica" cards in the Latino migrant community—were only part of the story.

The fact is that most of Main Street and Wall Street didn't want to banish immigrants; they needed them. Labor shortages are a problem in some business sectors. Hard-working, eager migrant workers are a solution. And so, employers blindly accepted whatever documents they were offered. For many employers, there is also a sense of helping down-and-out immigrants who are profoundly grateful for employment and work very hard—an attitude that is the exact opposite of the entitlement mentality of many of our citizens. Removing the legal question for a moment, what employer would not make this choice? What business owner wouldn't want a labor force full of eager, grateful employees? I really don't agree that obtaining cheaper labor is the ultimate motivation for employers. Immigrant workers are often stellar employees, and wise employers should pay them the same wages, if not more.

Business owners weren't the only ones who benefited from the additional, undocumented workforce. As noted earlier, local, state and federal governments accepted the Social Security, unemployment insurance and tax contributions these workers paid into the system using their bogus IDs, donating hundreds of millions of dollars annually that they would never claim.

Everybody won in this setup, although the undocumented workers got the short end of the stick, as their path to citizenship, legal status or benefits remained in doubt. But even Tantonists won—they still had something to complain about.

The 1996 Immigration Act saw reduced numbers of immigrants crossing the borders for about three years, with legal arrivals averaging around 700,000 between 1997 and 1999. It also soon doubled the number of ordered deportations and caused an increase of undocumented immigrants who were returned to their home countries without a court order. But the flow of immigrants, thanks to the many promises of America and the low wage options in their home countries, never stopped. From 2001 to 2012, an average of more than one million legal immigrants entered the U.S. annually. In 2012, 417,000 were ordered deported and another 230,000 were returned.[23] President Obama, having campaigned on immigration reform, hired Arizona Governor Janet Napolitano to run Homeland Security. As we will discuss in a future chapter, Arizona's role in bringing this issue to the floor of the U.S. Senate was a direct result of SB 1070 and my election battle. Both of Arizona's senators served with six of their colleagues from both sides of the aisle to finally address our broken immigration system. In 2013, this bipartisan group of senators, dubbed "the gang of eight," issued a proposal for the Border Security, Economic Opportunity, and Immigration Modernization Act of 2013. The law, sponsored by Republicans Jeff Flake (AZ), Lindsey Graham (SC), John McCain (AZ), Marco Rubio (FL), and Democrats Dick Durbin (IL), Michael Bennet (CO), Bob Menendez (NJ), and Chuck Schumer (NY), promised a major increase in border patrol enforcement, but it also included a path to citizenship for millions of undocumented workers. The Senate passed the bill over the objections of a vociferous critic, Alabama senator Jeff Sessions, who dispatched his manically anti-immigration spokesman Stephen Miller to attend hearings and to craft all-out criticisms of the bill. Miller crafted a twenty-three-page guide to stopping the deal, which galvanized support among organizations like FAIR and generated pressure on Congress.[24] The negative campaign paid off. While Democrats held the majority in the Senate, the Republicans controlled the House, where leaders refused to take up the bill.

Sessions and Miller, it would turn out, were just getting started.

Chapter Ten

"OUR COUNTRY IS FULL"

ON JUNE 16, 2015, DONALD Trump appeared at Trump Tower in New York City, to announce he was running to become president of the United States. In his maiden campaign speech, he called Mexican immigrants "rapists." At this point, he was essentially operating a bare-bones, long-shot campaign. His primary goal, according to several sources, was to simply market the Trump name, not to actually win the Republican nomination, never mind the presidency. His former lawyer, Michael Cohen, told Congress Trump viewed his run at the Oval Office as the "greatest infomercial in political history."[1] But in that first appearance, Trump displayed some impressive skills as a candidate. Most notably, he had a gift—if you can call it that—for spewing offensive, frequently inaccurate statements that tapped into the perceived grievances of the American working class using xenophobic, racist language. These statements ultimately generated headlines with machine-like efficiency.

For a candidate seeking maximum exposure at minimal cost, this was a true gift. In campaign politics, it's called "earned media," basically free promotion or exposure that you didn't pay for—free advertising. Trump had used earned media extensively in New York with his real estate empire. He even posed as his own PR guy and bragged about himself in 3rd person to unwitting reporters.[2] The more bombastic and outrageous he was, the more he played the media, the more they gave him free ink.

> When do we beat Mexico at the border? They're laughing at us, at our stupidity. And now they are beating us economically. The U.S. has become a dumping ground for everybody else's problems... When Mexico sends its people, they're not sending their best... They're sending people that have lots of problems, and they're bringing those problems with us. They're bringing drugs. They're bringing crime. They're rapists. And some, I assume, are good people.[3]

The themes Trump struck were not entirely new for him. In 2013, Trump appeared at the Conservative Political Action Committee conference in Washington and declared the country "a total mess." He raised the specter of eleven million illegal aliens becoming citizens; he railed against China and the lack of jobs. His words resonated with burgeoning conservative strategist and agitator Steve Bannon, the chairman of the new hard-right *Breitbart News* website. Months before, Bannon had begun looking for a candidate who could take a populist message to the American people that focused on trade and immigration. Bannon hosted a dinner-and-strategy session with Alabama Senator Jeff Sessions, a staunch opponent of immigration who, in 2010, echoed the agenda of John Tanton by calling for hearings to discuss amending the Fourteenth Amendment deny birthright citizenship to children of undocumented immigrants.[4] Also in attendance was Session's trusted spokesman, Stephen Miller, who shared his boss' anti-immigrant passions. At one point during the evening, Bannon turned to the senator and declared, "We have to run you for president." Sessions demurred, however, citing concerns that previous allegations that he had used racist language would likely cripple a national campaign. Sessions' checkered, racist history played well in Alabama but not nationally.[5]

The meeting, however, served to distill this trio's dream candidate: a populist who would galvanize white middle- and lower-class voters by focusing on the influx of immigrants and blame new arrivals for America's economic and social problems.[6]

When Bannon heard Trump's 2013 speech in D.C., he was intrigued. So were his anti-immigration compatriots. Miller, who had fed a steady stream of bile-filled immigration stories to Bannon and his *Breitbart* staff, even began telling people he hoped Trump would run for president. The New York businessman was talking their language.

MILLER'S TALE

In January of 2016, however, Trump began talking Miller's language. The gaunt Sessions spokesman with a close-cropped, balding pate left his gig with the Alabama senator to become a Trump campaign policy adviser. That title didn't quite encapsulate Miller's broader job description. He didn't just advise, he wrote speeches, he floated stories and badgered reporters, and he exhibited his unrivaled sycophantic nature by volunteering to be Trump's warm-up act on the campaign trail. "Pacing the stage with a relaxed smile, he resembled an insult comic, leading chants of 'Build the wall,'" wrote Jonathan Blitzer in an eviscerating *New Yorker* profile on Miller. "He'd flash a peace sign and make way for Trump."[7]

Miller has been very careful not to claim credit for shaping Trump's anti-immigrant message—and, clearly, Trump has a gift for making incendiary comments and attacking immigrants—but numerous sources have credited Miller with spearheading the president's restrictive, draconian immigration policies and selling them to Trump.

After Trump shocked the political establishment by winning primaries in New Hampshire, South Carolina, and Nevada, Sessions became the first senator to endorse the nativist candidate in late February. By the end of March, Sessions had become one of Trump's most trusted associates. At an infamous March 31 meeting of campaign advisors at the Trump International Hotel in D.C.—where George Papadopoulos famously suggested setting up a meeting with Russia—Trump asked Sessions for his opinions on various issues, according to a source who was in the room, who noted Miller was there too, always lurking in the shadows.

What was Miller doing in the Trump campaign's shadows? He was sharpening the attacks he'd begun working on as a reactionary student in Santa Monica, California. Miller was the son of Jewish Democrats, but at Santa Monica High School, he projected a staunch conservative and contrarian persona, writing pieces supporting the Iraq War, complaining about school announcements made in Spanish at Santa Monica High School,[8] and delivering a speech in which he said, "Am I the only one who is sick and tired of being told to pick up my trash when we have plenty of janitors who are paid to do it for us?"[9] Attending Duke University, his commitment to conservative causes deepened. He organized "Islamo-Fascism Awareness Week." He wrote for the school paper and ranted against diversity. "America without her culture is like a body without a soul," he wrote in one column. "Yet many of today's youth see America as nothing but a meeting point for the cultures of other nations." He also met and befriended white nationalist Richard Spencer, who was attending graduate school in Durham. Spencer, if you are not familiar with him, has admitted he supports "the creation of a White Ethno-State on the North American continent" and "peaceful ethnic cleansing."[10]

After Duke, Miller worked as the spokesman for Minnesota Congresswoman Michele Bachmann, a Tea Party zealot who, during a 2008 debate, described illegal immigrants as "bringing in diseases, bringing in drugs, bringing in violence."[11] Eight years later, on the campaign trail, Miller had a new vessel to repeat these slurs and draw the biggest headlines imaginable.

What else was Miller doing behind the scenes on the Trump team?

While Miller now "rarely puts anything in writing, eschewing email in favor of phone calls," according to the *Washington Post*,[12] that wasn't always the case. Hundreds of emails Miller sent former *Breitbart* editor Katie McHugh from March 4, 2015, to June 27, 2016, reveal Miller's unrelenting efforts to shape anti-immigrant sentiment and his admiration for white nationalists. McHugh, who was fired from *Breitbart* after posting an anti-Muslim tweet, has renounced the far right. By sharing the Miller-penned emails, she has exposed how the president's future advisor sought to integrate extreme anti-immigrant sentiment and float conspiracy theories into *Breitbart* coverage.

As with so many aspects of the modern anti-immigrant movement, Miller's behavior often melds with and echoes the talking points established and promoted by John Tanton's organizations. On September 6, 2015, while still on Jeff Sessions' payroll, Miller pushed a story angle promoting *Camp of the Saints*, a book beloved by white nationalists for its racist portrayal of "white genocide" that was translated and published by Tanton's Social Contract Press. "… you see the Pope saying west must, in effect, get rid of borders." Miller wrote McHugh, reinterpreting Pope Francis' compassionate words urging aid for Syrian and Iraqi refugees arriving in Europe. "Someone should point out the parallels to *Camp of the Saints*." Less than three weeks later, McHugh's *Breitbart* colleague Julia Hahn wrote, "'Camp of the Saints' Seen Mirrored in Pope's Message," treating an over-the-top, paranoid work of fiction to a four thousand-word tribute that claims, "All around the world, events seem to be lining up with the predictions of the book."[13]

The same month Miller joined the Trump team, he painted immigrants as marauding criminals to McHugh. "It has never been easier in American history for illegal aliens to commit crimes of violence against Americans," he wrote in an email titled "off-the-record observation."[14]

At the time of this email, Miller was well aware that respected conservative researchers had found ample evidence showing immigrants were *less likely to commit criminal acts*. He was reacting to a *Wall Street Journal* op-ed piece by Jason L. Riley, of the conservative Manhattan Institute for

Policy Research, who wrote: "A new report from the Immigration Policy Center notes that while the illegal immigrant population in the U.S. more than tripled between 1990 and 2013 to more than 11.2 million, 'FBI data indicate that the violent crime rate declined 48 percent—which included falling rates of aggravated assault, robbery, rape, and murder. Likewise, the property crime rate fell 41 percent, including declining rates of motor vehicle theft, larceny/robbery, and burglary.'"[15]

Miller dismissed the article as being "more lies about new [A]merica," which is hardly surprising. In email after email to McHugh, he linked immigrants to crime and terror. In one exchange he claims the arrival of Muslims is "creating huge pockets of radicalization," but offers little to no proof. He calls out lone-wolf terror attacks in the U.S. whenever there is a Muslim angle. Somehow, though, he fails to ever make that connection when it comes to mass murders and hate crimes in America, the vast majority are committed by white men.[16]

Perhaps the most disturbing of the many paranoid and prejudicial comments unearthed in this trove of Miller emails appeared in his dismissal of a July 7, 2015 *Salon* article that dismantled arguments linking immigration and crime.[17] "Don't believe your lying eyes and those liars in law enforcement," Miller wrote. Confronted with statistics provided by government institutions, the president's future immigration guru fired up the ultimate conspiracy excuse: law enforcement is lying; it's all a deep-state plot.

Miller's strategy to highlight any crime anywhere in the U.S. that involves an undocumented immigrant—sorry, they refer to these people only as "illegal aliens"—has been replicated and mimicked outside of *Breitbart*. Fox News and other conservative outlets have consciously started to use similar clickbait, as do Tanton's organizations. Early on in his presidency, as part of his deluge of executive orders, Trump, likely spurred on by Miller, opened a new office in the White House to collect as many negative stories as possible and distribute them. The acronym for the new Victims of Immigration Crime Engagement, VOICE, is one that would make John Tanton proud. As a division of the U.S. Immigration and Customs Enforcement agency, VOICE employs twenty-four community relations officers, two program management analysts, one deputy assistant director, and one acting assistant director, as well as six contractors who work the hotline. Its mission:

1. Use a victim-centered approach to acknowledge and support immigration crime victims and their families.

2. Promote awareness of rights and services available to immigration crime victims.

3. Build collaborative partnerships with community stakeholders assisting immigration crime victims.

4. Provide quarterly reports studying the effects of the victimization by criminal aliens present in the United States.[18]

Not surprisingly, VOICE hasn't had a lot to do because, contrary to the false narrative promoted by anti-immigration forces, immigrants generally are law abiding people. Over a six-month period in 2017, the office received 4,602 calls of which more than half (2,515) were classified as "unrelated" or "commentary." Some 244 callers requested victim services and only 127 of those callers wanted social service referrals. Another 254 asked about the status of a case and 600 others were referred to ICE divisional offices. So much for gathering damaging data about "criminal aliens present in the United States."[19] Talk about government waste!

But, sadly, that is the Miller-method: highlight news that suits the lack of statistics but builds the anecdotal story line that all illegals are rapists, murderers, criminals. *Forget the stats, we will take any story nationally and blow it up, sensationalizing the tawdriest elements to scare and energize voters.* I witnessed Arizona State Senator Steve Smith deploy this strategy when he was making a congressional run. A convenience store clerk, Grant Ronnebeck, was gunned down by an undocumented Latino with special needs in my Mesa district. Senator Smith, who obviously didn't represent my district, used the far-right media to publicize the story and promote a law called "Grant's Bill," which would tie immigration status to stricter prison sentences. The law never passed, and Smith's congressional run failed as well. When you don't have compelling facts, tell horrific stories of isolated cases that make your point. Fortunately, voters saw through Smith's calculated, polarizing spin. Miller has practiced the same dark art. His emails to McHugh are obsessive and alarmist. It is hard to read Miller's words and not wonder if he is unhinged. Muslims loom as future terrorists; lawmen are liars; immigrants are potential crooks, rapists, and murderers. His efforts to substantiate his claims, when he bothers to provide them, are so selective that they often seem an exercise in bias confirmation. That stands to reason. Confirmation bias is what the "official" anti-immigration movement has excelled at for decades.

INFLUENCE AND CONSEQUENCE

When Trump won the 2016 election, Miller didn't want to be a cabinet member or chief of staff. He wanted one thing and one thing only: to be the administration's immigration policy advisor. He headed the White House's Domestic Policy Council, a position that kept him close to the president and shielded him from congressional scrutiny. (A Senate confirmation process would have forced him to answer some tough questions about his background.) There, he became the unofficial immigration policy czar, drafting executive orders for Trump to sign. Aside from Jared Kushner, Miller remains Trump's longest-serving advisor. In an administration plagued by a revolving door of fired and scandal-plagued staffers, it is a notable accomplishment. Miller honed his skills after watching Bannon and Sessions both get booted from the administration by the president—Bannon for getting too much credit for Trump's victory and Sessions for recusing himself from the RussiaGate inquiries. The lessons were clear: don't upset the president; don't seek the limelight;

defend the president's actions and words; and always project absolute fealty because sycophancy is the way to survive and thrive. He kept a low profile. He rarely, if ever, disagreed with the president in group settings. But for those covering the White House, an inescapable consensus has emerged. When it comes to immigration, the spokesman Miller and the president's roles have reversed to a certain extent. Trump has been speaking Miller's words, signing Miller's policies, repeating Miller's falsehoods, and defending Miller's racist vision. Fans of the president insist they are in lockstep. This includes Miller, who sent this ingratiatingly canned quote to a reporter: "It is the single greatest honor of my life to work for President Trump and to support his incredible agenda." But for many White House insiders and the reporters who cover them, there seems little question regarding who is the architect of this "incredible agenda" and who is the guy who goes out and does the sales pitch.

Miller wasted little time launching his xenophobic, anti-immigrant portion of that agenda. In his first week in office, Trump signed three executive orders designed to curb the flow of both legal and undocumented immigrants. His "Enhancing Public Safety in the Interior of the United States" order stripped federal grant money to sanctuary cities—areas that vowed not to target undocumented workers. But it also instituted a section of Russell Pearce's SB 1070 Arizona law that was struck down by the Supreme Court—empowering local and state police to detain or apprehend people in the United States illegally. It also ordered the Secretary of Homeland Security to hire 10,000 more immigration officers and, in a move that certainly sounds near and dear to Miller's heart, collate a weekly list of crimes committed by undocumented immigrants.[20]

The "Border Security and Immigration Enforcement Improvements" order directed that federal funds be used to construct a wall, hire 5,000 Border Patrol agents, construct holding facilities along the border for undocumented aliens, and stop the "catch-and-release" policy for undocumented immigrants so they would now be detained while awaiting court hearings.[21] While that declaration arguably had some basis in law-and-order protocol, the third immigration order was the most incendiary. Titled "Protecting the Nation From Foreign Terrorist Entry Into the United States," it stopped the entry of immigrants from seven predominantly Muslim countries—Syria, Iran, Iraq, Libya, Sudan, Yemen, and Somalia—for ninety days. It also placed a 120-day moratorium on all refugees entering the country and banned Syrian refugees indefinitely. It also suspended the 2012 Visa Interview Waiver Program that let frequent U.S. tourists skip the visa interview process.[22]

This order provoked national protests, numerous lawsuits, and was ultimately blocked by a federal judge. Miller went on the offensive, appearing on *Face the Nation* where he attacked the judiciary and seemed to say the president had the divine right to enact laws: "Our opponents, the media and the whole world will soon see, as we begin to take further actions, that the powers of the president to protect our country are very substantial and will not be questioned."

Miller went back to the drawing board and Trump signed a new proclamation on March 6, 2017. The new version focused on banning citizens from six Muslim countries—Iraq was now off the list—from entering the U.S. for ninety days. It, too, was challenged on multiple grounds, including discriminating against Muslims, and suspended. The administration rewrote the order a third time, putting forth the new, more expansive and more expansively titled "Presidential Proclamation Enhancing Vetting Capabilities and Processes for Detecting Attempted Entry Into the United States by Terrorists or Other Public-Safety Threats." This order, written with previous challenges in mind, was also contested and made its way to the Supreme Court, which narrowly ruled 5–4 in its favor. It took eighteen months, but Miller had gotten a Muslim ban—a narrower one than he initially sought—presumably keeping America one step away from *The Camp of the Saints* fantasy that kept him and John Tanton awake at night.

Miller and Trump did not stop with these three executive orders.

In September 2017, after relentless lobbying from Miller and others, Trump announced he was ending the Deferred Action for Childhood

Arrivals (DACA) program, which was put in place as a path to citizenship for unauthorized immigrants who had arrived here as children—the so-called DREAMers of Obama's Dreamer Act. Instead of naturalizing these young people who lived and worked here and, like so many of the people I knew in my church in Arizona, paid taxes and aspired to be law-abiding Americans, Trump, urged on by Miller, wanted to arrest them and evict them. All of them.

The Dreamer Act was not a lax, come-one, come-all program. To qualify for DACA, applicants had to have arrived in the U.S. before 2007, meet age restrictions, have a clean criminal record, and be enrolled in high school or have a high school degree.

Once again, the administration's assault on immigrants wound up in court, and successful challenges have shielded over half a million unauthorized immigrants from deportation. On June 18, 2020, Chief Justice John Roberts provided the swing vote preventing the dismantling of the program, holding that the Trump administration had failed to prove adequate justifications to shutter DACA. For the DREAMers, this is only a temporary reprieve; Trump and Miller can renew their assault on the program by making new arguments in lower courts. But that may change in November if Trump loses the 2020 election.

The same month plans to dismantle DACA were announced, Miller also pushed through a reduction in the number of refugees, getting Trump to cap the program, part of the 1980 Refugee Act, at 45,000, down from 110,000. The State Department, the Defense Department, the Office of the Vice President, and the Office of Management and Budget objected to the lower number. Miller wanted it to be even lower. So, 45,000 was a compromise.[23] In the run-up to this decision, the White House requested that the Department of Health and Human Services study the costs of refugee resettlement. The resulting report found the revenue generated by refugees in the form of local, state, and federal taxes over a ten-year period exceeded the costs of resettling them by sixty-three billion dollars. Miller then suppressed a part of the study, ensuring only the costs—not the benefits—were included in the report, according to the *New York Times*.[24]

Miller "was obsessed with the idea of consequences," a top D.H.S. official told the *New Yorker*. "He'd always say to us, 'They are breaking the law, and the only way we'll change that is if there's a consequence.'" His solution was both stunning and numbing. He advocated inflicting "consequences" on children, pushing ICE to separate parents and children once they reached the border.[25]

"Miller made clear to us that, if you start to treat children badly enough, you'll be able to convince other parents to stop trying to come with theirs," the DHS source said.

While Trump has repeatedly blamed the Obama White House for initiating a policy of separating children from their parents, multiple news organizations have reported this is a false statement. Separating children from adults occurred only in suspected child-trafficking cases or when false claims of parentage were made.

FAIR TRADE

While Miller has established himself as the ultimate survivor on Trump Island, he is also surrounded by many anti-immigration true believers. His old *Breitbart* editor pal Julia Hahn became a Special Assistant to President Donald Trump in January 2017. Many other allies of Tanton's network, and others with ties to white nationalist groups, have also joined the administration. Kellyanne Conway, counselor to President Trump, who arrived to head the Trump campaign with Steve Bannon, was a pollster for FAIR, CIS, and NumbersUSA. Robert Law, a senior policy adviser to the Department of Homeland Security's U.S. Citizenship and Immigration Services bureau (USCIS) was the lobbying director for FAIR. He is joined at USCIS by another former FAIR lobbyist, Elizabeth Jacobs, who is also a policy adviser. Jon Feere, a longtime policy analyst at CIS, was hired as a senior advisor at ICE. FAIR Board of Advisors member Lou Barletta was a member of Trump's transition team. Julie Kirchner, FAIR's former executive director, was the ombudsman of the U.S. Citizenship and Immigration Services at the Department of Homeland Security. Ian M. Smith, an investigative associate with the Immigration Reform Law Institute, became an immigration policy analyst for the Department of Homeland Security until he resigned in August 2018—just before the *Atlantic* reported that he had ties to white nationalists, including Richard Spencer and Jared Taylor, the founder of the white nationalist publication *American Renaissance*.[26]

For anyone who might think these hires and connections are coincidental, the ties between groups like FAIR and CIS and the Trump team are tight. Stephen Miller was the keynote speaker at a 2015 CIS conference. His speech was filled with effusive praise for CIS staffers, including Jessica Vaughan, Director for Policy Studies and Steven Camarota, Director of Research for the Center. Miller hailed Camarota for knowing "more about immigration numbers, history, demography, the economy than anyone I've ever worked with" and called their conversations "one of the great pleasures of my professional life."[27] Three years after those laudatory words, a federal judge offered a much different opinion of Camarota, repeatedly calling him "not qualified." The scathing rebuke came over Camarota's research on a voter registration issue. Kansas Secretary of State Kris Kobach—he'd progressed since helping sculpt SB 1070 for Russell Pearce—had hired Camarota to see if a state requirement to provide documentary proof of citizenship in order to register to vote was a burden to Kansans. Not surprisingly, Camarota issued a report saying the proof of citizenship was no trouble. The judge ruled against Kobach and ripped into Camarota, assailing his data collection methodology and his background. "Camarota is not qualified to explain the reasons for the change in data… or to insert assumptions into the record based on studies or academic literature regarding voter registration and turnout… he is not qualified as an expert in voter registration, voting trends, or election issues, so he is not qualified to opine on issues of causation."[28]

Meanwhile, the talking points and policy visions of FAIR, CIS, and NumbersUSA have crept into Trump's speeches and immigration vision. On March 2, 2019, Trump appeared at the CPAC convention and delivered a speech repeating the same claim that John Tanton first made in his 1994 book, *The Immigration Invasion*. "All the nonsense you hear about 'the people that come in illegally are far better than the people we have,'" said Trump, without citing exactly where "the nonsense" was heard. "It's not true, folks. Okay? It's false. It's false propaganda. Right? One recent study from FAIR—F-A-I-R—found that illegal aliens are incarcerated at three times the rate of legal residents. Those are the numbers."[29]

Except that those aren't the numbers. There is no national database that compares crimes committed by people with legal or illegal immigrant status to those committed by American citizens. For the record, Texas is the only state that tracks the immigration status of convicted criminals. As mentioned earlier, available studies show overall, crime rates are lower among immigrant groups than they are among native-born Americans. And a report from the conservative Cato Institute that used Texas data gathered from January 1, 2011 to November 15, 2017, found that native-born Americans represented 83 percent of the population but accounted for 90 percent of the murder convictions in the state. In other words, legal or undocumented immigrants were less likely to be murderers in comparison to American citizens.[30]

Those are the numbers, at least in the only state they are kept: Texas.

MILLER'S CROSSING

Dr. David S. Glosser, a retired neuropsychologist and the brother of Stephen Miller's mother, Miriam, exposed his nephew as "an immigration hypocrite" in an essay published by *Politico*. Glosser recounted how Miller's great-great-grandfather, Wolf-Leib Glosser, left an impoverished village that had been plagued by anti-Jewish attacks in what is now Belarus and arrived on Ellis Island in 1903 with eight bucks in his pocket. One of his sons arrived soon after. The men saved money and eventually sent for the rest of the family to join them in America. The family prospered, building a chain of discount stores and supermarkets that employed thousands of people and was eventually listed on the stock exchange. The story of how the Glosser family got here and rose from rags to riches, notes Glosser, is the essence of what Miller and Trump and other anti-immigration zealots rail against: chain migration—even though family ties have driven the movement of people around the world for thousands of years.[31]

"I have watched with dismay and increasing horror as my nephew, an educated man who is well aware of his heritage, has become the architect of immigration policies that repudiate the very foundation of our family's life in this country," Glosser wrote.

Miller's uncle also noted his forefathers arrived a few years before the enactment of the 1924 Immigration Reform Act, which had been designed to stop Jewish, Italian and other non-northern Europeans from entering the U.S.

"Had Wolf-Leib waited, his family likely would have been murdered by the Nazis along with all but seven of the 2,000 Jews" in his hometown, Glosser adds.

"These facts are important not only for their grim historical irony but because vulnerable people are being hurt. They are real people, not the ghoulish caricatures portrayed by Trump."

It is easy to see why Miller's uncle is horrified. His nephew's policies echo those of eugenicists and anti-Semites like Wickliffe Draper and *White America* author Earnest Sevier Cox—who hated African-Americans, Jews and other non-Aryans. They are in a direct line to these privileged white supremacists, including Madison Grant, the man who bragged about penning Adolph Hitler's "bible" and pushed through the 1924 Immigration Act. That Miller chooses to ignore these connections—and often seems to actively embrace them—is, as his uncle notes, hypocritical. It is also historic. While this book has shown America has indeed battled restrictive, racist nativist immigration instincts for centuries, it has never completely succumbed to them. Under Miller's direction and Trump's quest for power, we the people are in danger of doing just that.

There is one more aspect of Trump administration policies that carries equally disturbing implications and echoes of the past. The separation of families arrested at the border and held by ICE officers has conjured terrifying and tragic images of the Holocaust, where so many Jewish families were divided, sent to death camps and subjected to inhumane conditions and extermination. The separation policy officially went into effect on May 5, 2018 as part of a "zero tolerance" edict. Over 2,000 children, including infants and toddlers, were taken from their parents and incarcerated in large, chain-link fenced, cage-like rooms. Reports later surfaced that as many as 1,768 were separated from their parents between October 2016 and February 2018 in what an official termed a "pilot program."[32] Images and reports of tearful mothers and confused, frightened children predictably sparked outrage and horror. Trump was forced to sign an executive order ending the practice on June 20, 2018.[33] Anyone wondering how this shocking, inhumane practice was ever implemented can look to Miller. Evidently, this fit with his idea of "consequences."

A BIG NEW LIE

Donald Trump hit on a new sound bite in 2019. The man who reused Ronald Reagan's 1980 "Let's Make America Great Again" campaign slogan, was at an April 5, 2019 meeting at the U.S. Border Patrol Station in Calexico, Ca., when a new quip popped out of his mouth. Twice.

"Can't take you anymore. Can't take you. Our country is full. Our area is full, the sector is full," said the president, apparently directing his words to theoretical immigrants. "Can't take you anymore. I'm sorry. So turn around. That's the way it is."

It took two more days for Trump to regurgitate his "country is full" line on Twitter.

"More apprehensions (captures) at the Southern Border than in many years. Border Patrol amazing! Country is FULL! System has been broken for many years. Democrats in Congress must agree to fix loopholes - No Open Borders (Crimes & Drugs). Will Close Southern Border If necessary..."

Eighteen minutes later, he was at it again:

"...Mexico must apprehend all illegals and not let them make the long march up to the United States, or we will have no other choice than to Close the Border and/or institute Tariffs. Our Country is FULL!"[34]

At this time, John Tanton was in the last months of his life; he would pass away after a long battle with Parkinson's Disease on July 16. But if he heard those words, he must have rejoiced. It's easy to imagine Madison Grant cheering in his grave in Sleepy Hollow, New York, too. The president of the United States was parroting the policy Tanton had envisioned for fifty years and Grant espoused one hundred years ago. The most powerful man in America had gone to the border and declared there was no room at the inn.

Despite Trump's vehemence and repetition, farmers, economists, demographic experts, think tanks, and small businesses begged to differ. There were plenty of vacancies. While Trump was beating the drum for restrictions, another branch of his government was telling a much different tale. The Labor Department's Office of Foreign Labor Certification reported that it granted 242,762 H-2A temporary visas for foreign agricultural workers in 2018, an increase of 16 percent over the prior year.[35] And in 2019, the administration granted 96,000 H-2B visas for non-agricultural jobs (landscaping, hotel work, etc.), the most since 2007.[36]

In other words, the president—who ranted on and on about immigrants "stealing" American jobs and declared the country full—was actually doing something else. His administration was giving jobs away. "It's ironic that Trump is demagoguing and railing against a so-called dangerous and scary flood of migrants and caravans from Mexico and Central America, and even threatening to shut down the border, while at the same time using his legal authority to grow a guest worker program," said Daniel Costa of the Economic Policy Institute.[37]

Why was Trump talking out of both sides of his mouth? The answer is complicated.

For all Stephen Miller's and Trump's talk of a migration crisis, the number of arrests at the southwest border during Trump's tenure do not approach the border arrest record of 1.6 million in 2000 or the annual, million-plus busts that occurred during the Bush administration.[38] The Obama years, which saw a spike in immigrant traffic due to vast social unrest and instability in Central America, also had more deportations. During Trump's first three years in office, the Border Patrol made 415,000, 521,000 and 977,000 apprehensions, respectively.[39]

Did Trump's hardball rhetoric deter immigrants from coming in 2017 and 2018? Did the huge jump in apprehensions in 2019 occur because of improved surveillance at the border? Or did the arrests increase because Trump's legal assault created a sense of urgency for Latinos who had been weighing the chances of getting through? If there was a wall, if there was no chance of having an asylum hearing, then it's likely that the approaching reality of the border being sealed caused an increase in traffic.

This has always been a quandary with the Border Patrol. Authorities can only count the number they catch. It is much more difficult to ascertain the number of immigrants that got past them.

Speaking of sneaking, in the last weeks of February 2020, the lies and sinister goals of Trump's and Miller's war on immigrants broke into public view from within the administration. On February 19, Acting White House Chief of Staff Mick Mulvaney committed a shocking act— he told the truth.

Our country was not full.

According to Mulvaney, America needed more immigrants, not less!

"We are desperate—desperate—for more people," Mulvaney said in a candid interview in England. "We are running out of people to fuel the economic growth that we've had in our nation over the last four years. We need more immigrants."[40]

Speaking at the Oxford Union debating society in England, Mulvaney said the United States needed "more immigrants" but wanted them in a "legal" fashion.

Mulvaney also addressed the wall that has been so central to Miller and Trump and jettisoned any idea that it was the must-have solution to stopping illegal immigration. "Does it solve the problem? No, it doesn't," he said. "Does it slow it down? Yes, it does."[41]

These heretical admissions from the administration member who sat at the president's right hand—at least when Trump's two designated hitters, Jared Kushner and Stephen Miller, were not there—are stunning in their frankness. Immigration experts, economists, and prominent think tanks, however, have raised this issue for years.

In a normal universe, the Trump administration's continued advancement of its anti-immigrant narrative should leave the president hamstrung. As the cheerleader-in-chief for the stock market—which he confuses with the economy (only half of America's working population has access to 401(k) retirement plans and a fraction of that number own individual stocks)—the president needs a steady, incoming population. This means not just skilled labor but immigrants who arrive with and earn cash to spend here. By cracking down and placing strict quotas, the revenue generated by new labor and by wealthy foreigners will not make up for the shortfall to sustain Social Security and other programs.

Anyone hoping that Mulvaney's admission might signal an awakening within the Trump administration was out of luck. The chief of staff was replaced less than three weeks after his comments crossed the Atlantic Ocean and the administration signaled that its hardline was going to grow even harder. The Department of Justice announced the formation of the "Denaturalization Section"—a section within the Civil Division's Office of Immigration Litigation—to strip immigrants of their citizenship if they are found to have violated naturalization laws.

The new division was announced with an appeal to law and order—just like so many anti-immigrant legislative moves, à la Russell Pearce. "When a terrorist or sex offender becomes a U.S. citizen under false pretenses, it is an affront to our system—and it is especially offensive to those who fall victim to these criminals," said Assistant Attorney General Jody Hunt. "The Denaturalization Section will further the Department's efforts to pursue those who unlawfully obtained citizenship status and ensure that they are held accountable for their fraudulent conduct."

It remains to be seen just how narrow the new department's focus will be in identifying naturalized Americans who "unlawfully obtained" papers and stripping them of their citizenship.

There will be few if any objections to bouncing murderers and rapists. But the fact is that the law powering the Denaturalization Section (Revocation of Naturalization, Title 8, Section 1451 of the U.S. Code) is disturbingly broad. It states that citizenship can be revoked if it was "procured by concealment of a material fact or by willful misrepresentation."

In other words, if a citizen made a single mistake on an application, it could be used as an excuse to take away citizenship.

"This is frightening," a friend of mine told me after hearing of the new enforcement team. "My grandfather had beaten tuberculosis years before he arrived at Ellis Island. He was completely healthy. When officials asked if he had ever had T.B., he answered 'no.' He didn't want to give immigration officers a single reason to send him back to Europe and Adolph Hitler. He always wondered what could happen if he was found out. Now there is a division specifically geared to unmasking people." I suspect that, like VOICE, this will be a waste of money and time for the government and is only symbolic.

Ever since Stephen Miller and Steve Bannon convinced Donald Trump to run a campaign that appealed to white voters by blaming and demonizing immigrants, an unanswered question has loomed over America. If he succeeds, what happens next? Immigrants serve a purpose for Trump as a campaign issue—they can be blamed, as FAIR and CIS and so many other discredited organizations have tried to do, for America's economic woes, for lower wages, for unemployment, and for taxing our social services. But if there are no undocumented immigrants, what happens next? Who will be demonized by hate-mongers?

The Denaturalization Section offers a potential answer, providing a way for Trump to continue his assault on a vital segment of the American population—immigrants who are here legally but may now be subject to scrutiny—and demonization and expulsion—because of paperwork.

THE NUMBERS DON'T WORK

Let's return to Mulvaney's shocking admission that America actually needs immigrants—that we are, in fact, "desperate" for them. Earlier, we touched on the increase in temporary visas for laborers under the Trump administration. We need them to pick crops and to work in service industries. But there's another, critical reason we need new bodies in this country.

We need them because our country isn't economically sustainable without them.

Of all the bitter truths, this is one John Tanton and his legion of anti-immigration extremists either ignored or never saw coming, and it needs to be stressed.

Two social programs vital to our citizens' well-being—Social Security and Medicare—are largely financed with funds paid by current workers for the benefit of those not working or retired. These contributions are then transferred to cover the costs of current recipients/retirees. Viewed another way, the new money coming in pays the distributions of the previous contributors since there are no endowments built up from prior contributions.

For decades, the ratio of retirement-age Americans and our working-age population remained fairly constant—about nineteen retirees for every hundred Americans between ages eighteen and sixty-four. Recently, this "dependency ratio" started to rise, going from twenty-one to twenty-five retirees for every hundred Americans from 2010 to 2017, according to the U.S. Census. Projections for 2030 put the ratio at thirty-five retirees for every hundred working people. So as population declines, there are fewer paying workers to pay for the benefits our elderly population expected when they paid their contributions years ago.[42]

The lower fertility rates that Tanton, Hardin, and May once pined for were achieved in America in the 1970s. Population experts estimate the U.S. needs a fertility rate—the average number of births each woman is expected to have over her lifetime—of 2.1 to sustain our population levels. Around 1975, the rate fell under two, however, in 2018, it dropped to an all-time low of 1.72. (For comparison, in the post-war baby boom years, the birth rate was 3.77.) The decline resulted in the lowest number of births in the U.S. in thirty-two years.[43]

These numbers, from non-partisan government agencies, point to the truth behind Chief of Staff Mick Mulvaney's declaration. Even if the birth rate suddenly exploded this minute, our nation needs more working-age people immediately, to contribute to the safety net that has been in place for eighty-five years.

This, tragically, is where John Tanton's information warfare, his fabrication of facts, and his campaign to legitimize inherently prejudiced arguments has led us. Divided we stand—led by a president who disregards facts and delegates paranoid contrarian Stephen Miller to craft immigration policy based on white nationalist propaganda designed to provoke fear and hatred and energize a disenfranchised base. These policies don't improve the lives of that base. They threaten the base's well-being, putting unnecessary stress on the economy and on Social Security benefits. This seems likely to create a cycle of right-wing, agenda-fulfilling prophecies: Immigration is stopped, hurting production and creating a downturn that will stoke more frustration and provide more ammunition for hate-mongers, who will continue to blame immigrants. The very immigrants that are maligned are those who contribute to the Social Security checks the far-right racists will expect after they retire. But without the immigrants, our natural childbirth rates will bankrupt the nation's pension plan and Trump's supporters will take to the streets protesting their lack of Social Security. Oh, the irony. Trump followers walk both of Tanton's planks to plunge and drown in debts caused by lower birth rates and no legal or illegal immigration.

We need a different approach. One grounded in unity, respect, and productivity—not fear, contempt, and isolationism. It's time to discuss new options, to re-fire, re-forge, and straighten the collapsing horseshoe. It's time to find a vaccine for this virus before it kills us.

Chapter Eleven
A SANE SOLUTION

STATES ARE OFTEN SAID TO be the great laboratory of our democracy. I agree, as would America's leading anti-immigration strategists. John Tanton, Kris Kobach, Russell Pearce, and others in the FAIR orbit have tried to launch an onslaught of state legal "experiments"—although I think "assaults" may be the more accurate word—against immigrants through state legislatures. The problem with laboratory experiments, though, is sometimes they backfire. Pearce's SB 1070 represented the most dangerous of these initiatives and, in terms of hurting immigrant communities, the most "successful."

Until it wasn't.

The new law didn't just take its wrath out on immigrants, it hurt the Arizona economy. It also severely damaged the brand and identity of Arizona. Six million media stories—in newspapers, on TV, radio and the Internet—exported news of this "experiment." The coverage was far from laudatory. A slew of boycotts and cancelations were announced, in a replay of the backlash that Arizona experienced over the controversy over honoring Martin Luther King Jr. Arizona's Hotel and Lodging Association reported a combined loss of $15 million in revenue due to meeting cancellations just four months after the bill was passed. Factoring in vanishing revenue from food, entertainment, transportation, and retail sales, a Washington think tank study estimated the total loss of business from conference cancelations at $141 million.[1]

Once the governor signed this horrific bill, Arizona was transformed into the modern equivalent of Alabama under anti-integration Governor George Wallace in the sixties—a racist society with backward laws.

There was a lot of hand-wringing at first, but two remarkable women, Denise D. Resnik and Lisa Urias, spearheaded a bipartisan group called the Real Arizona Coalition (RAC). More than fifty civic and community groups, faith-based organizations, corporations, and public figures such as former Supreme Court Justice Sandra Day O'Connor, came together.

The initial goals were simple: First, stop the state-led immigration enforcement-only laws that hurt our economy and communities. Second, encourage Congress and the White House to take the lead in federal immigration reform.[2]

The RAC picked up steam during my campaign. When I entered the race, I had zero name recognition in my Mesa district, with only three months to get my name out before early voting started. Nobody thought I had a chance, but I had to do it. I had seen the damage inflicted by SB 1070. I saw no upside. And the stories of all the wonderful people who were forced to flee, who were arrested, and who lived each day in fear, convinced me that I had to at least try and do what I could.

So, I was busy door knocking and attending grassroots meetings while RAC was getting off the ground. But like RAC, I thought Mesa and Arizona had a branding problem. "Mesa is better than this," I would insist on the stump. "*We* are better than this." My entire goal was to elevate the community, elevate the state Senate and elevate Arizona as a whole. Russell Pearce and the FAIR strategists were playing to the lowest common denominator known to politicians and demagogues everywhere, instilling fear, tapping into tribalism and stoking hatred.

I wanted to appeal to the opposite of that. I wanted to celebrate the diverse people who came to Arizona to make a better life. I honestly believe, in my head and my heart, that the vast majority of people are really good, caring people. I tried to elevate the discourse with that perspective. Arizona was having its one hundredth birthday on February 14, 2012—and that was definitely worth celebrating! It is a great place with wonderful people, churches, businesses, natural resources, and don't forget one of the seven natural wonders of the world—the Grand Canyon! Sit on the south rim and contemplate our small space in this world. Think about the millions of years that the Colorado River was digging its way to a mile below the rim. We are not the nasty place filled with bigots—a reputation earned by a few, misguided, power-hungry, rabble rouser politicians.

When we achieved the impossible, upsetting Russell Pearce, I quickly became more involved with RAC, particularly with an offshoot of the collaborative group dedicated to honing a bipartisan immigration policy we called SANE. It was made up of Republicans, Democrats, independents, but SANE really wasn't about political parties. It was truly a cooperative effort: bright problem solvers and strategic thinkers trying to come up with solutions—real Arizonans with goodwill and kind hearts.

Our goal was one of show and tell. We didn't have any illusions that our work would be immediately enacted. Instead, we wanted to create a bi-partisan policy that codified baseline issues and could be used as a launching point for Congress. Immigration was a federal issue. It needed to be addressed by Congress and the president. Not Russell Pearce and Joe Arpaio.

I'll resist the temptation to share the entire SANE Immigration Platform, but here's the framework:

> It is based on our state and national business and labor needs, a respect and acknowledgement of the contributions of immigrants, and comes with the understanding that many of us, from the hotel and tourism industry to the farming and construction industry,

have relied heavily on immigrant labor since our inception. We must be honest about our complicit participation in the issue and the benefits received.

SANE distilled the issues to four key policy concepts.

- **S**ecure our sovereign borders—How are we going to police the vast boundaries we share with Mexico and Canada?

- **A**ccount for those here without lawful authority—Allow for the 11 million undocumented immigrants to come out of the shadows, undergo a background check, and live and work here legally. Our group never addressed the thorny issue of eligibility for citizenship. I am philosophically flexible on this point. I know Republicans are nervous about legalizing 11 million democratic voters but that is shadow boxing. Many Latinos are very conservative people and could be wooed into the Republican Party if there were less vitriol against Hispanics.

- e**N**act necessary bureaucratic reform—Our visa system is broken. How can we welcome those we want and need efficiently and securely? How can we provide for those who need us, as well?

- **E**ngage all levels of government—A national program needs to be embraced by local and state governments, law enforcement, businesses and neighboring governments. We cannot engage in the same dysfunctional immigration behavior over and over again which has allowed for and supported illegal immigration.

Our work on the SANE platform was largely done by the end of 2012, and we got it into the hands of the federal representatives of the state. It was no coincidence that, the following year, two Arizona senators, John McCain and Jeff Flake, became part of the so-called "Gang of Eight" who drew up and passed the bipartisan Security, Economic Opportunity, and Immigration Modernization Act of 2013. This bill, which the

Republican-controlled House refused to address, embraced many of our SANE proposals and sought to answer the issues we wanted addressed.

Notably, several congressional representatives from Arizona who opposed the measure are Russell Pearce pals—Andy Briggs, Debbie Lesko, and David Schweikert. They are part of a bad hangover from their days in the state legislature or in Maricopa County politics when SB 1070 was passed. As members of the Tea Party and Freedom Caucus—who are actively fed talking points by FAIR and other Tanton groups, and are sympathetic to Steven Miller's White House cabal—they will outright obstruct any reasonable compromise on immigration reform. It is my understanding that as the Gang of Eight made progress in the Senate, the anti-immigration lobby from FAIR martialed forces to flood Senate Minority Leader McConnell and others with calls to oppose the bill. They succeeded.

In my opinion, the third part of SANE—"eNact necessary bureaucratic reform"—is the most important thing we need in order to fix this glaring gap in our immigration policy. It should also be the least controversial. Our processing of immigrants is a joke. We have arcane limits and regulations. Our laws see-saw back and forth, restricting numbers one year, loosening them, and restricting them again.

Canada, by comparison, has a much more focused and organized system. True, our northern neighbors are further removed from the enormous influx of people coming from Central America, but for years Canada has been embracing immigrants instead of moaning about them. "New Canadians," as they are called, are part of a growth plan for a country with a low national birth rate. Canada accepts about 300,000 permanent residents each year. That's close to one percent of its population, a ratio that experts say may have to rise for Canada to maintain its standard of living—an issue that mirrors America's required ratio of workers to retirees to keep Social Security viable. Application of that same ratio for the U.S. would mean a full 3.5 million new immigrants per year. That's a far cry from Steven Miller's numbers—which include accepting only 18,000 refugees annually—calculated to maintain a WASP majority in America, even though restricting immigrants will put our economy in peril. I would much rather support Social Security and Medicaid by bringing in new Americans. Culture changes. Powdered wigs used to be a thing, so did slavery. Change can be great; we need to just get used to it.

"The biggest contrast between the U.S. and Canada is that we have reformed our immigration system continuously, intensively, for a decade at a time when the U.S. has been facing gridlock," said Chris Alexander, a former Canadian minister of Immigration, Refugees and Citizenship. "The consensus in Canada that immigration is part of our economic future and that part of our identity has never been stronger."[3]

Unlike the U.S., which has traditionally issued green cards on the basis of family connections and chaotic lotteries, Canada has been focused on how it determines who will get residency. Its express entry system assigns points to those applying for papers. Among the criteria that creates an applicant's score, which includes their skills and experience; their spouse's skills, such as their language skills and education; skill transferability, including education and work experience; whether they have a Canadian degree, diploma or certificates, a valid job offer, and a brother or sister living in Canada who is a citizen or permanent resident. There are ten other categories for entry.[4] In the U.S., there are at least three dozen categories for visas[5] and green card applications.[6] Meanwhile, the difference in the average wait time for skilled workers to receive a Canadian Permanent Resident Cards versus a U.S. green card is embarrassing—six months or less in Canada; seven months to eleven years in the U.S., according to immigration experts.[7]

If there are ways to simplify the process, to ensure newcomers have been screened while in their home country, and to have them go to a U.S. embassy to get their visa, then they can fly, sail, or drive a car here. With such a process in place, they can walk across the border or even have an extreme Sonoran Desert crossing experience. It doesn't matter.

We also need to secure our borders, and there are simple ways to do this. I am a proponent of using digital technology to track movement in our remote border areas. Spending billions of dollars on a physical fence is absurd. If I put a duffel bag full of cash on one side of a wall, and no one was around watching it, would you figure out a way to get it? Most people would, using tunnels, ladders, climbing equipment, or drones. Desperation and need are great motivators of human ingenuity. So is the enormous amount of money flowing across the border as the result of drug trafficking. That's why constructing physical barriers or establishing patrols to physically monitor every foot of our southern border is insanity. The costs would be enormous.

Digital sensors, however, make sense. In 2014, I witnessed a drug bust that was the result of a test program. Sixty-five sensors had been deployed in the desert at cost of $250,000. The day I was there, forty-seven of the sensors were triggered and officers busted a drug mule—a carrier crossing the border—with 140 pounds of Mexican weed. Those censors increased drug busts tenfold year-over-year in the area they were deployed. I proposed building an Arizona Virtual Fence in 2014. The plan called for 300 mobile sensor towers spaced at just over one-mile intervals along the border. My focus was on using the towers to locate drug traffickers and relay images and location information to law enforcement agents. But there is little doubt this technology could be used to identify immigrants crossing the desert.

The other part of bureaucratic reform is a shared responsibility between the public and private sector. If the government is going to up its game by streamlining entry to the U.S., helping ensure our business community gets the workers it needs, then our business community will have to get with the program. It is not tremendously onerous for employers to know who they are employing; they can use E-Verify, a Web-based system built specifically for this purpose. Nearly every white-collar business in America asks for ID paperwork and conducts background checks on employees. There is no reason it can't be done across the country. The U.S. Chamber of Commerce (USCC), however, has been extremely good at lobbying to loosen requirements. Like Tea Party true believers, members of the USCC sometimes operate under the belief that any regulation is bad regulation. To them, passing laws that put pressure on business is to be avoided at all times. The USCC is a powerful lobby, but it is not all-powerful, and it must evolve if our society is to improve.

That brings us to the last element of the SANE vision for immigration policy: engagement at all levels. This applies not only to local, state and federal government, law enforcement and business, but also to the governments, their law enforcement agencies, and businesses in nations spawning immigrants. It also must include sanctuary cities. As our statement spelled out, unified action is essential. "We cannot engage in the same dysfunctional immigration behavior over and over again which has allowed for and supported illegal immigration. We need clear identification for all those who are here legally. We need to know what rights and responsibilities are associated with legal immigrants. And we need to support and enforce laws that prohibit illegal immigration." Our statement addressed this as a safety and national security issue, noting that collaborative synergies would free up "resources for our Border Patrol, ICE, and other law enforcement to truly tackle the growing criminal element along the border, drug and human traffickers who must be detained" and, perhaps most chillingly of all, "prevent terrorist crossings."[8]

This has to be a package deal. Americans need to embrace these changes as our neighbors to the north already do. We have to understand that we need immigrants. Tantonites have to let this one go. All parts of SANE must be implemented together.

POLITICAL WILL

The sad truth about passing a comprehensive immigration reform act—a national initiative that allows for undocumented aliens to come forward and become legal participants with a possible path toward citizenship—is that neither party wants to let their rivals take credit for such life-changing legislation. Immigration in America isn't so much an economic issue or a human rights issue or a quality of life issue as it is *a political issue*. It is pregnant with politics. There are an estimated eleven million undocumented immigrants in the U.S. If a Democratic administration makes eleven million people citizens, well, they have likely earned themselves eleven million new voters. The same thing would happen if a Republican administration were able to push through naturalization for this same group living in the shadows. Then they, too, would earn eternal gratitude at the ballot box. But the Republicans, as we've seen, have thrown their weight against those eleven million and against a Democratic platform. And so, nothing gets done. It is amazing to think that in 1986 the Democratic-controlled House cooperated with Reagan's bill that gave citizenship to three million immigrants. Although conservatives and liberals both opposed the bill—many opposed the bill ban on hiring undocumented workers—it garnered significant bipartisan support.[9] Coming as it did, in the wake of Reagan's 1984 landslide, forty-nine-state victory against Mondale, some Democrats were evidently invested in staking out a centrist position.

The only way to achieve this in our messy, often combative democratic form of government is for a groundswell of political will. This occurs when a critical mass of voters get in the face of politicians. Then, decision makers will work toward a common vision and feel empowered to act for the public in a certain way. Recent examples of political will include bipartisan reactions to national disasters. After the September 11 attacks, President Bush was able to harness a tremendous amount of political will. He could do whatever he wanted, from passing the Patriot Act to justifying the invasion of Iraq using dubious intelligence about weapons of mass destruction. More recently, COVID-19 has generated tremendous political will to push through numerous financial aid packages, such as the two trillion-dollar stimulus bailout that dwarfed all previous emergency bills.

Disaster can come in many forms. Sometimes it comes as a chilling terrorist attack; sometimes it arises from financial policy; sometimes it comes with war; sometimes it comes from misguided social policy.

Sometimes, as with the COVID-19 pandemic, disaster snowballs as lax health screening policies at our airports and a lack of testing capacity stoked the spread of a disease that led to a medical crisis, which set in motion a financial meltdown.

In Arizona, SB 1070 and the Horseshoe Virus acted similarly. Legal policy, stirred by the misguided social policies of outside influencers like FAIR and other divisive organizations, married with a bully like Russell Pearce, created a disaster. Because it was localized in Arizona and we didn't see any falling buildings or reports of a body count that would generate political will at the national level, the Gang of Eight Senate bill died in the Republican-majority House. Even in Arizona, many people were slow to understand the implications of the law. Although SB 1070 only targeted "illegals," residents can be excused from not realizing the law would impact the entire state. But that is exactly what happened. When millions of media stories portray a state as racist, it affects the economy and the general morale.

The people who convinced me to run against Russell Pearce inspired Christi and me to act because we heard and felt their pain. They had been affected. They did not want to be party to the suffering and loss they witnessed and experienced as they watched loved ones and close friends flee or be arrested. They wanted it stopped. There was also a community level of outright embarrassment for the wrong-headed passions of Russell Pearce.

Russell Pearce and SB 1070 subjected the state to boycotts that hurt our economy. But that was just part of damage. Business formation rates *declined*, forcing 200,000 people out of the state and annihilating the real estate market. Housing prices in the Phoenix-area dipped 20 percent lower than the national average.[10]

Now, thanks to President Trump, Steven Miller, and his team of advisors who consciously tap into nativist and racist sentiments, the same Horseshoe Virus that drove SB 1070 has spread into a pandemic at a national level.

Multiple economic studies tell us we are shooting ourselves in the foot by limiting immigration, and that Tanton talking points about job loss and salary reductions and increased crime rates are utter fiction.

And yet here we are.

Separating children from their mothers and locking them in cages.

If that image, which recalls Nazi acts of inhumanity, doesn't embarrass our nation, I don't know what will.

President Trump's immigration policy has embarrassed America. Our nation is exhausted. But he has ridden the Horseshoe Virus to power, and it is incumbent upon the voters of America to create the political will to stop the misinformed policy that spreads like a sickness.

We do that by getting involved.

When I began my campaign to unseat Pearce, I started attending monthly Republican Party precinct political meetings in Mesa. Anywhere from seventy to 200 people would show up, ninety-five percent of whom were Tea Party extremists. They were full of anger and vitriol, spewing conspiracy theories—even chemtrail theories about government control of the weather that makes people gay.

In Mesa, embarrassed by Russell Pearce and SB 1070, the middle became far more powerful and more active than the fringe. First, people were activated by Randy Parraz's mission to force a recall election. Then, Jerry Lewis inspired people to come to the polls and vote in that recall. Four months later, I continued their work with a message that was the opposite of embarrassment: Let's Elevate.

I believe America's voters are tired of being embarrassed. They are horrified by children in cages, by constant lying and the denial of scientific and empirical research, and by the weaponization of us versus them tribalism—as opposed to respect, compassion, and unity. We understand the need to stop the shameful immigration policy of our nation. We need to mass at the polls and create political will to bring necessary change. We will collapse without a robust immigration policy. We can't focus on maintaining a WASP majority in America—and we shouldn't.

We *need to vote*. That means me, you, your spouse or partner, your friends, the young adults you know who may have never cast a ballot before, the elderly who may struggle to get out of the house.

And we need to vote not just to change leadership, but to support down-ballot candidates who will challenge and defeat the ignorance that has engulfed us. Unless the one hundred senators and 435 members of the House of Representatives become more willing to compromise and look at reality, like they did after 9/11, they will not feel compelled by political will to create a safer, securer, wealthier, unified nation that draws strength from our differences instead of weakness from division and fears of "race suicide."

Chapter Twelve
THE OVERVIEW EFFECT

SOMETIMES THE SOLUTION TO A problem can come from its very source. Fighting viruses can work that way. Vaccines that protect us from killer diseases like smallpox, cholera, the flu, and, hopefully, COVID-19, are made from weakened or dead forms of virus, or a protein removed from a viral strand.

One of the inspirations for extremist environmentalism and the push for zero population growth that led John Tanton to create the anti-immigrant movement actually came from—and this may sound strange at first—space travel. It turns out space exploration helped focus humans on earth.

Astrophysicist Neil DeGrasse Tyson speaks very movingly about the impact space programs have had on the human race. "We go to the moon to explore the moon, and then we turn around and discover the earth for the first time... And there it was, alone, in the vacuum dark of space.

And if you see it not as the social studies classroom globe—there were no color-coded countries on it. All you saw was blue oceans and dry land and clouds. And at that moment, everyone changed. Everybody said, 'Oh my gosh, pollution is not just this river behind my house or this lake. It is global. We have to think of earth as a planet.'"[1]

Less than a year after Neil Armstrong took those first steps on the moon, on April 22, 1970, Earth Day was founded. Many conservationist initiatives were launched soon after as well. The Environmental Protection Agency and the National Oceanic and Atmospheric Administration were founded. Leaded gas was banned. Clean air and water acts were passed.

"You know why we go to space?" Tyson asked "Because a cosmic perspective can descend upon you in such a way that you are realigned with your survival and the survival of others in such a way that maybe you're going to do something about it."[2]

And around this same time, John Tanton, focusing on the environment, decided that immigrants would be bad for America.

John Tanton and his eco-fascist pal, Garrett Hardin, refused to align their survival with the survival of others. We are all passengers on the "blue dot." The planet is vitally important but so are *all* its passengers, not just those who will sustain "northern European" culture—whatever that is.

The epiphany that Tyson described is an almost universal experience for space explorers, according to philosopher Frank White, who dubbed it "The Overview Effect" in his book of the same title. The first man in space, Russian Cosmonaut Yuri Gagarin, returned to earth on April 12, 1961, and immediately expressed a kind of global awareness: "Circling the Earth in my orbital spaceship, I marveled at the beauty of our planet. People of the world, let us safeguard and enhance this beauty—not destroy it."[3]

I believe the ugliness of SB 1070, the cruelty and racism driving this administration and Stephen Miller's war on foreigners, and the white supremacy dreams fueled by John Tanton's organizations can give us a new perspective. Pointing out symptoms of the virus are the first steps to killing it. First seeing the Horseshoe Virus as the ugly disaster that it represents is critical. Creating the political will to remove people with these ideologies is critical at the ballot box. With that newfound political will, we must then act in bipartisan ways to adopt "SANE" immigration policies and find a pathway for those who are here.

Dr. Brené Brown, a popular researcher and author, gave a Sunday sermon at Washington National Cathedral on January 21, 2018, that was a chilling and deeply moving distillation of the fragmenting and divided state of our union. Dr. Brown noted that we have recently been "sorting" ourselves and hunkering down in factions. "I think that behind the barricades of belief is not real connection. I think we just hate the same people," she said. "I call it the Common Enemy Intimacy. 'I don't know you, don't particularly like you, I'm not interested in knowing you but I'm glad you hate those people too.'"[4] This form of polarization comes as a spiritual crisis.

> The definition of spirituality in my work, and it crosses every religion, is the deeply held belief that we are inextricably connected to each other by something greater than us. It is something that is rooted in love and compassion. I call that God.
>
> Here's the thing about the connection between me and you and the Syrian refugee and the mother in the Congo. It cannot be severed, but it can be forgotten and we have forgotten that we are inextricably connected to each other....
>
> We are in a time of rampant dehumanization... We're not wired to kill and maim and torture and rape and hurt and belittle and shame people. It actually goes against our wiring. So when we feel extreme hatred, or more likely fear, we engage in a process of dehumanization. We take groups of humanity and start moving them outside of what we see as human. If you move a group out of being human, you have permission to do whatever you want to them. What is the very first stage of every act of global dehumanization? Language and words. Every genocide in history started with a dehumanization campaign of a group of people and that began with words.

Dr. Brown concluded her sermon urging us to reject our tribal divisions. "It's not a question of which side of politics you are on, it's a question of what side of humanity we are on. If we continue down this path, we will get to the place where we don't see humanity in each other much less connection," she said. "If you are a person of faith, you are called to find the face of God in every single person you meet. There is really nothing more unholy than stripping humanity away from a person through language or any other endeavor."

Her final words were stirring:

> What God has brought together, let no bigot pull apart.
> This is about love.

Is it okay for politicians to talk about love? As COVID-19 upended our nation, I was surprised and pleased to hear one politician turn repeatedly to this word that we often hear on Sundays and forget about for the rest of the week. On a regular basis, New York Governor Andrew Cuomo would hold daily press conferences about the battle to stop the spread of the disease that threatened to decimate the state of New York. This included the city that has been the gateway to America for the majority of our history and remains our nation's financial capital. In appropriately somber and serious tones, he shared the disturbing daily death tolls for his state and urged citizens to protect themselves and each other. He avoided self-aggrandizing statements and political grandstanding; he stuck to facts, and he described seemingly insurmountable challenges. On March 24, as the entire state struggled to prepare for the oncoming peak of the crisis, Cuomo ended his address declaring the state would endure "because we are united, and when you are united, there is nothing you can't do. And because we are New York tough... New York loves all of you. Black and white and brown and Asian and short and tall and gay and straight. New York loves everyone. That's why I love New York. It always has, it always will. And at the end of the day, my friends, even if it is a long day, and this is a long day, love wins. Always. And it will win again through this virus."[5]

On April 10, as the infection rate seemed to be flattening, Cuomo used the word again to explain why the infection, hospitalization, and mortality numbers were lower than the terrifying worst-case projections made by so many experts. Noting there was no way to gauge the compliance of New Yorkers to enact social distancing and isolation protocols, the experts "didn't know how unified New Yorkers can be and how responsible they can be and how caring they are... and that's what they couldn't count in those models. They couldn't count the spirit of New Yorkers and the love of New Yorkers—to step up and do the right thing."[6]

Love—an intense commitment to unity and respect—is critical to the overview effect and to stopping that other plague: the Horseshoe Virus.

On a personal level, Christi and I have been married forty-three years and we have a large family of six married children, twenty-nine grandchildren and two great-grandchildren. We are not models of the perfect small family sizes espoused by John and Mary Lou Tanton. In 1996, we bought a thirty-five-acre, forested, 7,000-foot elevation, secluded homestead in northeast Arizona just 125 miles from our home in the desert in Mesa. We are eight miles from any town and close to Black Canyon Lake. We wanted a place to get away from the world, spend sacred time around the fire, to listen and connect, and to raise our kids, where they could host their friends on weekends and holidays.

The time at our "Ranch" enriched our relationship with each other. Raising our kids was pretty easy; they seldom had discipline issues and we are remarkably close. We built and called our place Legacy Lodge, to honor and celebrate our own family history. Each room is decorated in an authentic style to honor a country of one of our ancestors. Christi's mother's maiden name is Wilde. It seemed only fitting to name the space where our grandchildren play after their great great-grandfather. It is known as the "Wilde" loft. We finished and moved in just in time to celebrate Thanksgiving Day 2000. On the inside of the lodge over the front door we had the words of English historian Lord Thomas Macaulay carved into a log: "The people who do not revere the deeds of their ancestors will never do anything to be remembered by their descendants." The intention was to have our posterity remember the sacrifices of those before them and in so doing they would likely have greater character and live a life worth remembering.

We always listen to country and Broadway music on family trips. One particular song would cause Christi to reach and squeeze my hand—"Love Remains," sung by Collin Raye and written by Tom Douglas and Jim Daddario. The words always hit a chord for us at our ranch where we have blood in the ground. (Our grandson Peter Hunt passed away at childbirth and we created a family graveyard for him at Legacy Ranch.) We love the lines about how kingdoms will perish and the future quickly becomes the past. That's why we inscribed the final words from this song above the entrance to our house:

> In spite of what's been lost or what's been gained
> We are living proof that love remains

For us, "Love Remains" recalls stories of struggle and joy and everything in between in our family legacy. And it likely resonates with many other families as well. The Overview Effect teaches us that we are, like it or not, a global family.

The COVID-19 virus hammers this point home. It does not look to the science of eugenics for its victims. Its target is us—all of us—regardless of borders and country of origin. The good news is that we are not powerless against unseen enemies. If we lead with both our heads and our hearts, we can create the vaccine, the antidote to these viruses, whether they are an attack on our health or our humanity. It is clear that we will not find all the solutions in the halls of government. We will find it in our inextricable hardwiring to connection, to caring, to feeling and showing compassion. Because, in the end, love remains.

My audit of the Horseshoe Virus will continue. My hope is that, as Americans become aware of this man-made infection, they will experience an awakening, as I did, and that a kind of Overview Effect like the one Neil DeGrasse Tyson describes—realigning your survival with the survival of others—will take hold of our hearts and minds and our votes. We must remember and aspire to the beautiful, elevating message that begins in our Constitution and makes it such a comforting, inspirational document. Why did "We the people" want "to establish Justice, ensure domestic Tranquility, provide for the common defense, promote the general Welfare, and secure the Blessings of Liberty to ourselves and our Posterity?"

To form a more perfect union.

That formation, that perfect union, is the opposite of the nativism and bigotry that has for so much of our history been used to wound and divide, to stop us from being a nation that is truly united, that is out of many, one.

OTHER POLITICAL OBSERVATIONS BEYOND IMMIGRATION

I DID NOT RUN FOR state Senate looking for other alarming practices and policies. But my short political life exposed me to other issues besides immigration reform that also urgently need to be addressed.

- Fake news, driven by "clickbait" to drive corporate profits of media empires, is destroying our democracy. We need to support new ideas to validate news before it is circulated. Did this come from a Russian bot? Are these facts or hyperbole or just lies? Maybe some kind of blockchain public ledger, like those that track Bitcoin and other cyber currency transactions, can be used to source, prove or audit the veracity of news. If we can keep numbers accurate for banks and Bitcoin, then we can check and triple check news sources.

- The two-party system has a death grip on our democracy. Our major parties are simply tired old arcane unions that need to go or be reinvented. President George Washington complained about this in his Farewell Address: "However [political parties] may now and then answer popular ends, they are likely in the course of time and things, to become potent engines, by which cunning, ambitious, and unprincipled men will be enabled to subvert the power of the people and to usurp for themselves the reins of government, destroying afterwards the very engines which have lifted them to unjust dominion." Think about the planks of the Republican Party just forty months ago compared to what the party now embraces, and you will have a powerful example of what Washington feared could happen. The destruction of the old GOP is nearly complete. I mourn our loss. The Electoral College system is arcane and needs to go, since it is overruling the will of the majority of Americans. There is an arrogance of lawmakers that only they have the facts necessary to make good decisions. They believe that masses of voters are uninformed. Using the argument that we are a "republic" not a democracy shows the level of disdain many feel toward voters. Truthfully, many lawmakers do not read bills themselves and won't meet with both sides of issues before voting. Instead, they say, "I know my policy and I don't need to hear from that side of things." They then vote with the party or their caucus blindly—not for "We the People."

- Party caucuses should be banned and replaced with legitimate primaries by the voters. We should not allow extreme groups of party insiders to decide our candidates for any office.

- Gerrymandering is evil and should be managed by each state, like Arizona, with an independent redistricting commission doing all the mapping to make it fair.

- On-line or mail-in voting must be implemented in each state, with a paper ballot backup to audit each vote. The reason why this is not allowed everywhere is an attempt to discourage voters who may not have the time to wait in long lines, as opposed to political extremists who will drive long distances and stand in line for hours to vote.

- The Citizens United case must be overturned to get anonymous big money out of our elections.

- Judicial packing of courts, legislative harassment of the executive, and autocratic executive refusal to be investigated by Congress are all recently-exposed fault lines. After Trump leaves office, a commission to strengthen the Constitution's separation of powers should be formed to make recommendations to the American people. Congress should take up new laws that will strengthen the constitutional separation of powers, even if it means states need to ratify needed change.

- We need to eliminate the election of county sheriffs, judges, assessors, and attorneys in local elections. These offices should be appointed and hired by heads of counties after careful search and screening processes, like most city- and state-level best hiring practices. This should end Arpaio-type characters and insane elections of judges all over our country! Conflicts of interest and corruption exist at the county level all over America.

ACKNOWLEDGMENTS

MANY PEOPLE HELPED SHAPE THIS book. I would like to extend my gratitude to the following:

Seth Kaufman for all his work researching and shaping the vast amount of material in this book.

Heidi Beirich and Caleb Kiefer for sharing the collection of John Tanton documents amassed by the Southern Poverty Law Center.

Historian Andreas Killen for his insight into the rise of eugenics in Europe.

Criminal justice scholar Judith A. Greene for her take on Arizona, SB 1070, and American immigration policy.

Early reader Maureen Williams, who also designed the Horseshoe Virus Cast of Characters that maps the key figures in this book.

Roger Conner, Tyler Montague, and Randy Parraz for sharing their stories.

Chad Heywood, Jerry Lewis, Tyler and Dea Montague, Ken Smith,

Brent Ellsworth, the Wheelers, and Alan Soelberg for getting me into politics.

My brother Dan and his wife Lori for helping with sign logistics and donating hundreds of hours of their time.

Nina Spahn, John Parsons, and the entire team at Amplify.

The small army of Mesa supporters who joined the campaign and hosted meet-and-greets in their homes for me.

A stateful of terrific reporters at Arizona's newspapers for documenting the lows and highs of our complicated state. Thank you for all you do, even when you disagree with me.

The entire community of Mesa, which inspired me to elevate my own expectations and honored me by electing me to serve them. I am so grateful. You set me off on this journey.

That journey was made that much smoother by my beloved children and grandchildren, and of course, my muse, advisor, and soulmate for over four decades, Christi.

HORSESHOE VIRUS

Population control and eugenics movements arose from the writings of these men:

Gregor Mendel
1822–1884, Austria; friar whose study of botanical hereditary traits launched genetics and unwittingly inspired eugenics

Thomas Malthus
1766–1834, UK; his *Essays on the Principles of Population* questioned human sustainability

Francis Galton
1822–1911, UK; prolific author (and Charles Darwin's cousin), coined "Eugenics" from the Latin for "good in stock"

Garrett Hardin
1915–2003, TX population extremist, & ecologist author of *Tragedy of the Commons*

Wickliffe Draper
1891–1972, MA millionaire, funded racist studies and organizations

1921 Emergency Quota Act
Grant backed and lobbied Albert Johnson, WA, Chair of House Immigration and Naturalization Committee

Eugenics Committee of USA (ECUSA)
1922–1926 board member

IRL Immigration Restriction League,
1922–1937 Grant and Tanton each served as vice-presidents

AES - Eugenics Eugenics Society,
1926–1972 transformed from ECUSA with Laughlin

ERA - Eugenics Research Association,
1913–1936 founded by Davenport, with Grant as president & board member

Madison Grant
1865–1937, NY zoologist, lawyer, eugenicist: *The Passing of the Great Race* (Hitler's "bible")

Earnest Sevier Cox
1880–1966, TN white supremacist; *White America*, and *Let My People Go* published by Draper

Committee on Eugenics American Breeders' Association
created at the request of Davenport in 1906

Greater Liberia Act,
1939 – repatriation of blacks to Africa, backed by MS Senator T. Bilbo (never adopted)

lobbied for Virginia's **Preserve Racial Integrity Act of 1924**

Charles Davenport
1866–1944, CT *Heredity in Relation to Eugenics*

Immigration Act of 1924
imposed quotas on immigrants pushed by Grant and Laughlin

Harry Laughlin
1910–1938 proponent: Eugenics & Compulsory Sterilization

Race Betterment Foundation
1906–1932 (approx) Battle Creek, MI – cereal millionaire John Harvey Kellogg and Davenport founded this eugenics propaganda organization

ERO Eugenics Record Office
1910–1938 founder: Davenport; director Laughlin

THE CAST OF PLAYERS

Colcom Foundation
1996–present
John Rohe, VP
(biographer of Tantons)

Cordelia Scaife May
1928–2005, PA
Tanton's Bankroller heiress
to Mellon-Scaife fortune,
gave millions to Tanton's
organizations

Margaret Sanger
1879–1966, NY
women's healthcare
activist, founder Planned
Parenthood, was a hero to
May, and was backed by
Madison Grant's AES

Social Contract Press
1990–present
publisher of the inflammatory
magazine *Social Contract Journal* and
racist novel *The Camp of the Saints*

AICF American Immigration Control Foundation
1983–present

NumbersUSA
1997–present
co-founded with Roy Beck

U.S. English
1983–present
founded by Tanton and
Senator S.I. Hayakawa

Pioneer Fund
1937–present
Draper, with guidance from Laughlin,
created a "charity" to finance
racist/eugenicist studies to prove white
supremacy; funded FAIR and dozens of
race-obsessed "academics"

John Tanton
1934–2019, MI
mastermind of modern
anti-immigration movement,
environmentalist,
extremist-turned-white
nationalist; founder and
fundraiser of 13+
anti-immigrant
organizations

CIS Center for Immigration Studies
1985–present
with Otis Graham

U.S. Inc.
1981–present
Tanton's tax-exempt "educational
foundation," which funds many of his
anti-immigrant organizations,
including The Social Contract

ProEnglish
1983–present
founded by Tanton to push
for English-only laws

F.A.I.R Federation for American Immigration Reform
1979–present
launched D.C.-based anti-immigrant
lobbying group with Roger Conner

Zero Population Growth
National President
1975–1977
(ZPG renamed: Population
Connection in 2002)

Key figures in modern
anti-immigration movements

Kris Kobach
1966–present, WI
studied under Huntington, shaped
Arizona's SB 1070 and other states'
laws on behalf of Tanton and FAIR;
as Kansas Secretary of State, he
pushed restrictive voting laws

Samuel Huntington
1927–2008, NY
Harvard political scientist, his
book *Who Are We?* demonized
Latino and Islamic
immigrants, resurrected
"race suicide" fears, and
hurt his once-lauded
reputation

Stephen Miller
1985–present, CA
pal of white supremacist Richard
Spencer and nationalist Steve
Bannon; fed anti-immigrant stories
to Breitbart and Fox; worked for
Jeff Sessions; architect of Trump
anti-immigration policy

Russell Pearce
1947–present, AZ
divisive Arizona state senator, sponsored SB 1070
and other bills targeting immigrant population;
worked with Kobach, FAIR, and The Social
Contract

ENDNOTES

PREFACE

1   John Higham, *Strangers in the Land: Patterns of American Nativism, 1860-1925* (New Brunswick, NJ: Rutgers University Press, 1955).

CHAPTER ONE: MY IMMIGRANT STORY

1   "United States Congress, 'An Act to Establish a Uniform Rule of Naturalization,' March 26, 1790," *George Washington's Mount Vernon*, Mount Vernon Ladies' Association, https://www.mountvernon.org/education/primary-sources-2/article/naturalization-acts-of-1790-and-1795/.
2   Ann Hafen and LeRoy Hafen, *Handcarts to Zion* (Lincoln, NE: University of Nebraska Press, 1993).

3   Joseph Smith, "The Articles of Faith of The Church of Jesus Christ of Latter-day Saints," *Pearl of Great Price*, https://www.churchofjesuschrist.org/study/scriptures/pgp/a-of-f/1?lang=eng.

4   Andrew Jenson, *Encyclopedic History of The Church of Jesus Christ of Latter-day Saints* (Salt Lake City: Deseret News Publishing Company, 1941), 426, https://contentdm.lib.byu.edu/digital/collection/BYUIBooks/id/2249.

5   Ethan Epstein, "Are Conservative Cities Better?" *Politico*, September 17, 2014, https://www.politico.com/magazine/story/2014/09/mesa-arizona-are-conservative-cities-better-111069.

6   "Immigration Reform and Control Act of 1986," S. 1200, 99th U.S. Congress, Senate, November 6, 1986, https://www.congress.gov/bill/99th-congress/senate-bill/1200.

7   "The Facts about the Individual Tax Identification Number (ITIN)," American Immigration Council, January 2, 2018, https://www.americanimmigrationcouncil.org/research/facts-about-individual-tax-identification-number-itin#:~:text=The%20Facts%20About%20the%20Individual%20Tax%20Identification%20Number,government%20otherwise%20would%20have%20no%20way%20of%20collecting.

8   Jason De León, *The Land of Open Graves: Living and Dying on the Migrant Trail* (Oakland: University of California Press, 2015).

9   Ibid.

10 Marc Lacey and Katharine Q. Seelye, "Recall Election Claims Arizona Anti-Immigration Champion," *New York Times*, November 10, 2011, https://www.nytimes.com/2011/11/10/us/politics/russell-pearce-arizonas-anti-immgration-champion-is-recalled.html.

11 Tim Gaynor, "Hispanic Firms Hurt by Arizona Migrant Crackdown," Reuters, November 18, 2007, https://www.reuters.com/article/us-immigration-businesses-idUSN1639175520071118.

12 Stephen Lemons, "Russell Pearce Seems Incapable of Telling the Truth, Evenabout His Own Religion," *Phoenix New Times*, March 29, 2012, https://www.phoenixnewtimes.com/news/russell-pearce-seems-incapable-of-telling-the-truth-even-about-his-own-religion-6452820.

13 Ibid.

14 "Church Supports Principles of *Utah Compact* on Immigration," Press Office, Church of Jesus Christ of the Latter Day Saints, November 11, 2010, https://newsroom.churchofjesuschrist.org/article/church-supports-principles-of-utah-compact-on-immigration.

15 "Official Text of Utah Compact Declaration on Immigration Reform," *Deseret News*, November 12, 2010, https://www.deseret.com/2010/11/12/20152257/ official-text-of-utah-compact-declaration-on-immigration-reform.

CHAPTER TWO: RAZING ARIZONA

1 Tonya Moreno, "Your Guide to State Income Tax Rates," *The Balance*, January 27, 2020, https://www.thebalance.com/state-income-tax-rates-3193320.

2 Marc Lacey, "Hispanics Are Surging in Arizona," *New York Times*, March 10, 2011, https://www.nytimes.com/2011/03/11/us/11arizona.html.

3 Anna Brown and Mark Hugo Lopez, "Appendix Tables from Mapping the Latino Population by State, County and City," Pew Research Center, https://www. pewresearch.org/

4 Timothy J. Dunn, *Blockading the Border and Human Rights: The El Paso Operation that Remade Immigration Enforcement* (Austin: University of Texas Press, 2009), 60.

5 Joel Brinkley, "A Rare Success at the Border Brought Scant Official Praise," *New York Times*, September 14, 1994, https://www.nytimes.com/1994/09/14/us/a-rare-success-at-the-border-brought-scant-official-praise.html.

6 De León, *Land of Open Graves*, 30-31.

7 "Border Patrol Strategic Plan 1994 and Beyond: National Strategy," *Homeland Security Digital Library*, July 1994, https://www.hsdl.org/?abstract&did=721845.

8 Manny Fernandex, "'You Have to Pay with Your Body': The Hidden Nightmare of Sexual Violence on the Border," *New York Times*, March 3, 2019, https://www. nytimes.com/2019/03/03/us/border-rapes-migrant-women.html.

9 De León, *Land of Open Graves*, 6.

10 "Total Illegal Alien Apprehensions by Month," 2000-2018, United States Border Patrol, https://www.cbp.gov/sites/default/files/assets/documents/2019-Mar/ bp-total-monthly-apps-sector-area-fy2018.pdf.

11 De León, *Land of Open Graves*, 7.

12 "Arizona: Analysis of U.S. Decennial Census Data through 2010," CensusScope, http://censusscope.org/2010Census/states.php?state=AZ&name=Arizona.

13 Alexis Bergelt, "Arizonans Recall Fight for State MLK Holiday," *Tucson Sentinel*, October 16, 2011, http://www.tucsonsentinel.com/local/report/101611_az_ mlk_dedication/arizonans-recall-fight-state-mlk-holiday/.

14 Linda Greenhouse, "Supreme Court Roundup; Appeal to Save English-Only Law Fails," *New York Times*, January 12, 1999, https://www.nytimes.com/1999/01/12/us/supreme-court-roundup-appeal-to-save-english-only-law-fails.html?auth=login-email&login=email&pagewanted=all.

15 Ron Unz is now the publisher of the Unz Review website. When John Tanton died, Unz republished a tribute to the controversial English language crusader written by Peter Brimelow, a friend of Tanton's who runs VDARE.com, which has been called an "anti-immigration hate website" and frequently publishes articles by white supremacists. The article was titled "Brimelow Remembers Tanton: A Citizen Who Took up Arms for His Country," https://www.unz.com/article/brimelow-remembers-tanton-a-citizen-who-took-up-arms-for-his-country/.

16 Judith Ann Warner, ed., *Battleground Immigration*, *Vol 2* (Santa Barbara, CA: Greenwood Press, 2008), 32.

17 "Proposition 203 Ballot," Arizona Secretary of State, https://web.archive.org/web/20101119091831/http://www.azsos.gov/election/2000/info/PubPamphlet/english/prop203.htm.

18 Kathy Hoffman, "Arizona Is the Only State with an English-Only Education Law. It's Time to Repeal It," *Arizona Republic*, November 17, 2019, https://www.azcentral.com/story/opinion/op-ed/2019/11/17/arizona-only-state-english-only-law-werepeal-it/2564675001/.

19 Nicolas Riccardi, "Arizona's Relentless Conservative Voice," *Los Angeles Times*, January 17, 2011.

20 Russell Pearce, "Resume," Russell Pearce, https://russellpearce.com/frontpage/full-bio/.

21 Jacques Billeaud, "Arizona Sheriff to Shut down Famed Tent City Jails Complex," *Arizona Capitol Times*, April 4, 2017, https://azcapitoltimes.com/news/2017/04/04/arizona-sheriff-to-shut-down-famed-tent-city-jails-complex/.

22 Judy Greene, interview with author, January 2020.

23 Dennis Welch, "Arpaio, Pearce Setting Their Dispute Aside," *East Valley Tribune*, November 1, 2007, https://tucson.com/news/state-and-regional/arpaio-pearcesetting-their-dispute-aside/article_a81591f9-d453-5e5c-bf0e-36b735c404f6.html.

24 Lemons, "Russell Pearce Seems Incapable of Telling the Truth."

25 Gary Grado, "MVD Employees Charged with Selling Fake IDs," *East Valley Tribune*, September 23, 2004, https://www.eastvalleytribune.com/news/mvd-employees-charged-with-selling-fake-ids/article_151d73a6-6b49-5ff3-a37b-4ecd6de612c3.html.

26 Kyrsten Sinema, "No Surprises: The Evolution of Anti-Immigration Legislation in Arizona," in *Punishing Immigrants: Policy, Politics, and Injustice*, eds. Charis E. Kurbrin, Marjorie S. Zatz, and Ramiro Martínez, Jr. (New York University Press, 2012).

27 Ibid., 66.

28 Bryon Wells, "Migrant Foe Tied to Racism," *East Valley Tribune*, August 16, 2004, https://www.eastvalleytribune.com/news/article_bb6cb865-a006-5636-915d-89e501942701.html.

29 Riccardi, "Arizona's Relentless Conservative Voice."

30 Judith A. Greene, "Local Democracy on ICE: The Arizona Laboratory," in *Outside Justice: Immigration and the Criminalizing Impact of Changing Policy and Practice*, ed. David C. Brotherton (New York: Springer Books, 2013).

31 Gary Nelson, "Arizona Immigration Law Sponsor Russell Pearce Thrusts State into Political Storm," *Arizona Republic*, June 6, 2010, http://archive.azcentral.com/arizonarepublic/news/articles/2010/06/06/20100606arizona-immigration-law-russell-pearce.html.

32 Russell Pearce, "Arizona Takes the Lead on Illegal Immigration Enforcement," *The Social Contract*, 20:4 (Summer 2010), http://www.thesocialcontract.com/artman2/publish/tsc_20_4/tsc_20_4_pearce.shtml.

33 Sinema, "No Surprises."

34 E. Ann Carson and Daniela Golinelli, "Prisoners in 2012 - Advanced Counts," U.S. Department of Justice, Bureau of Justice Statistics, July 2013, https://www.bjs.gov/content/pub/pdf/p12ac.pdf.

35 "J.T. Ready," *Extremist Files*, Southern Poverty Law Center, https://www.splcenter.org/fighting-hate/extremist-files/individual/jt-ready.

36 Jimmy Zuma, "The Ignoble Death of Arizona Racist J.T. Ready," *Tucson Sentinel*, May 3, 2012, http://www.tucsonsentinel.com/opinion/report/050312_jjt_ready/the-ignoble-death-arizona-racist-jt-ready.

37 "J. T. Ready: Neo-Nazi and Anti-Immigrant Extremist," Anti-Defamation League, May 3, 2012, https://www.adl.org/news/article/j-t-ready-neo-nazi-and-anti-immigrant-extremist.

38 Stephen Lemons, "Triumph of the Swill: White-Pride Poster Boy J.T. Ready Rocks the Rabble at Saturday's Anti-Immigrant Fest," *Phoenix New Times*, June 18, 2007, https://www.phoenixnewtimes.com/news/triumph-of-the-swill-white-pride-poster-boy-jt-ready-rocks-the-rabble-at-saturdays-anti-immigrant-fest-6499544.

39 David Neiwert, "A Little Local Fascism," *Orcinus*, November 21, 2007, https://dneiwert.blogspot.com/2007/11/little-local-fascism.html.

40 Stephen Lemons, "When Valley Neo-Nazi J.T. Ready Converted to Mormonism, Guess Which Prominent Politico Ordained Him an 'Elder,'" *Phoenix New Times*, December 16, 2010, https://www.phoenixnewtimes.com/news/when-valley-neo-nazi-jt-ready-converted-to-mormonism-guess-which-prominent-politico-ordained-him-an-elder-6446907.

41 Lemons, "Triumph of the Swill."

42 Kris Kobach, "Retainer Agreement between Kobach and Ogletree Deakins," October 13, 2009, https://www.documentcloud.org/documents/4623369-Kobach-Maricopa-Contract.html.

CHAPTER THREE: ARIZONA RISING

1 Molly O'Toole, "Arizona State Senator Russell Pearce Discusses Illegal Immigration, SB 1070, and Elections," *Latin America News Dispatch*, September 9, 2010, https://latindispatch.com/2010/09/09/russell-pearce-discusses-illegal-immigration-sb-1070-and-elections-interview/.

2 The state legislature had deemed its budget inadequate to spend on capital improvements like new prison beds, so leasing or contracting new beds from for-profit prisons was the exclusive result for new prisoners. Since 2000, Arizona has ranked number one in increases to private prisons with a 479 percent increase, while the national average increase was only 39.3 percent. Federal use of private prisons increased 77 percent over the same time period.

3 Howard Fischer, "Pearce, Brewer Stand Firm behind Immigration Law," *East Valley Tribune*, April 17, 2011, https://www.eastvalleytribune.com/arizona/immigration/pearce-brewer-stand-firm-behind-immigration-law/article_6f7b7284-67bb-11e0-8d6c-001cc4c03286.html.

4 David Neiwert, "Was SB1070 a Success for Arizona? Pearce Claims U-Haul Rentals Prove It Was. Problem Is, He's Lying," *Crooks and Liars*, April 25, 2011, https://crooksandliars.com/david-neiwert/was-sb1070-success-arizona-pearce-cl.

5 Randy Parraz, interview with author, January 2020.

6 Alia Beard Rau, "Russell Pearce Recall: Enough Signatures to Force Election," *The Arizona Republic*, July 9, 2011, http://archive.azcentral.com/arizonarepublic/news/articles/2011/07/08/20110708russell-pearce-recall-signatures-certified.html.

7   Tyler Montague, interview with author, January 2020.

8   Craig Harris and Ginger Rough, "Two Officials Stand Out in Fiesta Bowl Gifts Scandal," *Arizona Republic*, May 13, 2020, http://archive.azcentral.com/ arizonarepublic/news/articles/2011/05/13/20110513fiesta-bowl-gifts-scandal-pearce- arredondo.html#ixzz1MGDhpRCn.

9   "Statement by Senate President Russell Pearce Responding to Questions Posed by Craig Harris of the *Arizona Republic*," *Arizona Republic*, May 11, 2011, http:// archive.azcentral.com/ic/pdf/0512pearceresponse.pdf.

10 Stephen Lemons, "Russell Pearce's Mystery 'Challenger' Olivia Cortes Speaks, Kinda-Sorta," *Phoenix New Times*, August 4, 2011, https://www. phoenixnewtimes.com/news/russell-pearces-mystery-challenger-olivia-cortes-speaks-kinda-sorta-6502635.

11 Sean McMinn and Renee Klahr, "Where Does Illegal Immigration Mostly Occur? Here's What the Data Tell Us," *National Public Radio*, January 10, 2019, https:// www.npr.org/2019/01/10/683662691/where-does-illegal-immigration-mostly-occur-heres-what-the-data-tell-us.

12 Anna Flagg, "The Myth of the Criminal Immigrant," *New York Times*, March 30, 2018, https://www.nytimes.com/interactive/2018/03/30/upshot/crime-immigration- myth.html.

13 Alex Nowrasteh, "Myths and Facts of Immigration Policy," *Cato Institute Policy Report* (January/February 2019), https://www.cato.org/policy-report/ januaryfebruary-2019/myths-facts-immigration-policy.

14 Mary Jo Dudley, "These U.S. Industries Can't Work without Illegal Immigrants," *CBS News*, January 10, 2019, https://www.cbsnews.com/news/illegal-immigrants- us-jobs-economy-farm-workers-taxes/.

15 Associated Press, "Chilling 911 Calls Detail Last Moments in Gilbert Shooting," *KJZZ News*, May 7, 2012, https://kjzz.org/content/1574/chilling-911-calls-detail- last-moments-gilbert-shooting.

16 "J.T. Ready," Southern Poverty Law Center.

17 Elise Foley, "Russell Pearce Distances Himself from J.T. Ready, Shootings in Gilbert, Arizona," *HuffPost*, May 3, 2012, https://www.huffpost.com/entry/ russell-pearce-jt-ready-gilbert-arizona-shootings-immigration_n_1474251.

CHAPTER FOUR: THE EDUCATION OF BOB WORSLEY

1   "ALEC & Immigration," *ALEC Exposed*, The Center for Media and Democracy, February 23, 2017, https://www.alecexposed.org/wiki/ALEC_%26_Immigration.

2   "ALEC Public Safety and Elections Task Force," *Sourcewatch*, The Center for Media and Democracy, December 25, 2019, https://www.sourcewatch.org/index.php/ALEC_Public_Safety_and_Elections_Task_Force.

3   Stephanie Condon, "ALEC Backs down in Wake of Backlash over Voter ID, 'Stand Your Ground' Laws," *CBS News*, April 17, 2012, https://www.cbsnews.com/news/alec-backs-down-in-wake-of-backlash-over-voter-id-stand-your-groundlaws/.

4   "Welcome to Arizona Lobbyists," *Arizona Capitol Times*, https://azcapitoltimes.com/azlobbyists/.

5   Amy Howe, "SB1070: In Plain English," *SCOTUSBLOG*, June 25, 2012, https://www.scotusblog.com/2012/06/s-b-1070-in-plain-english/.

6   Fernanda Santos, "Arizona Limits Police Actions in Enforcing Immigration Law," *New York Times*, September 15, 2016, https://www.nytimes.com/2016/09/16/us/arizona-limits-police-enforce-immigration.html.

7   "Search: Russell Pearce," Arizona Campaign Finance Database, March 15, 2020, https://apps.azsos.gov/apps/election/cfs/search/CandidateSearch.aspx.

8   Tal Axelrod, "Bloomberg Spent over $900M on Presidential Campaign," *The Hill*, March 20, 2020, https://thehill.com/homenews/campaign/488767-bloomberg-spent-over-900-million-on-presidential-campaign.

9   Laurie Roberts, "Roberts: Russell Pearce's Triple Dip Just Got Sweeter," *Arizona Republic*, January 13, 2017, https://www.azcentral.com/story/opinion/op-ed/laurieroberts/2017/01/13/roberts-russell-pearces-triple-dip-just-got-sweeter/96548646/.

10 Ibid.

11 Yvonne Wingett Sanchez, "Russell Pearce Resigns Post with Republican Party," *Arizona Republic*, September 14, 2014, https://www.azcentral.com/story/news/politics/2014/09/14/pearce-contraception-remarks-denounced/15645837/.

12 Ibid.

13 Bob Worsley, "Sen. Bob Worsley Is Done with Arizona Politics. Here's What He Hopes We Learn from That," *Arizona Republic*, June 18, 2018, https://www.azcentral.com/story/opinion/op-ed/2018/06/18/bob-worsley-arizona-senate-reelection-done-partisanship/707126002/.

CHAPTER FIVE: THE ROOTS OF ANTI-IMMIGRATION

1   "Overview of Race and Hispanic Origin: 2010," U.S. Census, March 2011, https://www.census.gov/prod/cen2010/briefs/c2010br-02.pdf.

2   "Naturalization Act of 1802," *A Century of Lawmaking for a New Nation: U.S. Congressional Documents and Debates, 1774 – 1875*, U.S. Statutes at Large, 7th Congress, 1st Session (1802), https://memory.loc.gov/cgi-bin/ampage?collId=llsl&fileName=002/llsl002.db&recNum=190.

3   "An Act to Prevent the Importation of Certain Persons into Certain States, Where, by the Laws Thereof, Their Admission Is Prohibited," *A Century of Lawmaking for a New Nation: U.S. Congressional Documents and Debates, 1774 – 1875*, U.S. Statutes at Large (February 28, 1803), http://www.loc.gov/law/help/statutes-at-large/7th-congress/session-2/c7s2ch10.pdf.

4   "An Act to Prohibit the Importation of Slaves into Any Port or Place within the Jurisdiction of the United States, from and after the First Day of January, in the Year of Our Lord One Thousand Eight Hundred and Eight," *A Century of Lawmaking for a New Nation: U.S. Congressional Documents and Debates, 1774 – 1875*, U.S. Statutes at Large, 9th Congress (March 2, 1807), https://avalon.law.yale.edu/19th_century/sl004.asp.

5   Hidetaka Hirota, *Expelling the Poor: Atlantic Seaboard States and the 19th-Century Origins of Anti-Immigration Policy* (Oxford University Press, 2017).

6   Lorraine Boissoneault, "How the 19th-Century Know Nothing Party Reshaped American Politics," *Smithsonian*, January 26, 2017, https://www.smithsonianmag.com/history/immigrants-conspiracies-and-secret-society-launched-american-nativism- 180961915/.

7   Amy Briggs, "The Know-Nothings: The United States' First Anti-Immigration Party," *National Geographic History*, July/August 2017, https://www.nationalgeographic. com/history/magazine/2017/07-08/know-nothings-and-nativism/.

8   Thomas R. Whitney, *A Defense of the American Policy, as Opposed to the Encroachments of Foreign Influence, and Especially to the Interference of the Papacy in the Political Interests and Affairs of the United States* (Dewitt & Davenport Publishers, 1856).

9   "The Pugilists' Encounter," *New York Times*, March 9, 1855.

10 Abraham Lincoln, "Lincoln on the Know Nothing Party," Letter to Joshua F. Speed, August 24, 1855, Lincoln Home, National Park Service, https://www. nps.gov/liho/learn/historyculture/knownothingparty.htm.

11 "Cooper's Clarksburg Register (Clarksburg, Va. [W. Va.]), Image 2," April 26, 1854, *Chronicling America: Historic American Newspapers*, Library of Congress, https:// chroniclingamerica.loc.gov/lccn/sn85059716/1854-04-26/ed-1/seq-2/.

12 "The Daily Dispatch. (Richmond [Va.]), Image 2," April 3 1854, *Chronicling America: Historic American Newspapers*, Library of Congress, https:// chroniclingamerica.loc.gov/lccn/sn84024738/1854-04-03/ed-1/seq-2/.

13 Statutes of California (1850), 230, https://clerk.assembly.ca.gov/sites/clerk. assembly.ca.gov/files/archive/Statutes/1850/1850.pdf.

14 Ling Sing vs. Washburn, 20 Cal. 534 (1862).

15 "The Page Act of 1875 (Immigration Act)," Public Law 43-141, U.S. Statutes at Large, 18 (1875), 477, https://loveman.sdsu.edu/docs/1875Immigration%20 Act.pdf.

16 "An Act to Execute Certain Treaty Stipulations Relating to Chinese," Public Law 47-126, U.S. Statutes at Large, 22 (1882), 58, https://www.loc.gov/law/help/ statutes-at-large/47th-congress/session-1/c47s1ch126.pdf.

17 "An Act to Regulate Immigration," Public Law 47-376, U.S. Statutes at Large, 22 (1889), 214-15, https://www.loc.gov/law/help/statutes-at-large/47th-congress/ session-1/c47s1ch376.pdf.

18 Joyce E. Chaplin, "Is Greatness Finite?" *Aeon*, January 26, 2017, https://aeon.co/ essays/how-more-and-malthus-light-the-way-towards-humanitys-future.

19 "Paul Broca (1824-80)," The Science Museum, http://broughttolife. sciencemuseum.org.uk/broughttolife/people/paulbroca.

20 Francis Galton, *Hereditary Genius: An Inquiry into Its Laws and Consequences* (London: Macmillan, 1869), 1, http://galton.org/books/hereditary-genius/text/ pdf/galton-1869-genius-v3.pdf.

21 Francis Galton, *Inquiries into Human Faculty and Its Development* (London: Macmillan, 1883), 17, http://galton.org/books/human-faculty/text/human-faculty.pdf.

CHAPTER SIX: THE MAINSTREAMING AND POLITICIZATION OF EUGENICS

1 S.J. Holmes, "Some Misconceptions of Eugenics," *The Atlantic*, February, 1915, https://www.theatlantic.com/magazine/archive/1915/02/somemisconceptions-of-eugenics/376211/.

2 Charles Benedict Davenport, *Heredity in Relation to Eugenics* (Henry Holt & Company, 1911), p. iii.

3 Ibid., 219.

4 Stephen Jay Gould, *Hen's Teeth and Horse's Toes: Further Reflections in Natural History* (New York: W.W. Norton & Company, 1983), 23.

5 Jonathan Spiro, *Defending the Master Race: Conservation, Eugenics, and the Legacy of Madison Grant* (Lebanon, NH: University Press of New England, 2009), 391.

6 Stefan Kuhl, *The Nazi Connection: Eugenics, American Racism and German National Socialism* (Oxford University Press, 1994), 85.

7 Madison Grant, *The Passing of the Great Race* (New York: Charles Scribner & Sons, Fourth Revised Edition, 1934), 238.

8 Ibid., xxiii-xxix.

9 Edward A. Ross, "The Value Rank of the American People," *The Independent*, November, 1904, 57.

10 Theodore Roosevelt to Marie Van Horst, October 18, 1902.

11 Thomas Leonard, *Illiberal Reformers; Race, Eugenics & American Economics in the Progressive Era* (Princeton University Press, 2016), 7.

12 Ibid.

13 Margaret Sanger, "Suppression," *The Women Rebel*, 1914, https://www.nyu.edu/projects/sanger/webedition/app/documents/show.php?sangerDoc=420004.xml.

14 Margaret Sanger, "The Eugenic Value of Birth Control Propaganda," *Birth Control Review* (October 1921), 5, https://www.nyu.edu/projects/sanger/webedition/app/documents/show.php?sangerDoc=238946.xml.

15 Mark Crutcher, "Racial Targeting and Population Control," Life Dynamics Incorporated, https://www.klannedparenthood.com/wp-content/themes/trellis/ PDFs/Racial-Targeting-Population-Control.pdf.

16 Karen Pazol, Andreea A. Creanga, Kim D. Burley, and Denise J. Jamieson, "Abortion Surveillance — United States, 2011," *CDC Morbidity and Mortality Weekly Report*, November 28, 2014, https://www.cdc.gov/mmwr/preview/mmwrhtml/ ss6311a1.htm.

17 "Birth and Population Control," Eugenics Archive, http://www.eugenicsarchive.org/eugenics/topicsfs. pl?theme=42&search=sanger&matches=1614,1607,1616,1615,1606.

18 Leonard, *Illiberal Reformers*, 111.

19 "PPFA Margaret Sanger Award Winners," Planned Parenthood, https://www.plannedparenthood.org/about-us/newsroom/campaigns/ppfa-margaret-sangeraward-winners.

20 "An Act to Regulate the Immigration of Aliens to, and the Residence of Aliens in the United States," Public Law 301, U.S. Statutes at Large, 874-98 (1917), https://www.loc.gov/law/help/statutes-at-large/64th-congress/session-2/c64s2ch29.pdf.

21 Andrew Glass, "Senate Approves Harsh Immigration Bill, Dec. 14, 1916," *Politico*, December 14, 2018, https://www.politico.com/story/2018/12/14/senate-approves-immigration-bill-1916-1055011.

22 Spiro, *Master Race*, 203-210.

23 "How Many Refugees Came to the United States from 1933-1945?" *Americans and the Holocaust*, United States Holocaust Memorial Museum, https:// exhibitions.ushmm.org/americans-and-the-holocaust/how-many-refugees-came- to-the-united-states-from-1933-1945.

24 Spiro, *Master Race*, 204.

25 Harry Hamilton Laughlin, *Eugenical Sterilization in the United States*, Psychopathic Laboratory of the Municipal Court of Chicago, 1922, 446-447, https://repository.library.georgetown.edu/bitstream/handle/10822/556984/EugenicalSterilizationInTheUS.pdf.

26 Buck vs. Bell, 274 U.S. 200 (1927).

27 Adam Cohen, *Imbeciles: The Supreme Court, American Eugenics, and the Sterilization of Carrie Buck* (New York: Penguin Books, 2016).

28 William H. Tucker, *The Funding of Scientific Racism* (University of Illinois Press, 2002), 30.

29 Ibid., 33.

30 "Charles Davenport's *Race Crossing in Jamaica*," *Eugenics in America*, https://library.missouri.edu/exhibits/eugenics/jamaica.htm.

31 Paul A. Lombardo, *Three Generations, No Imbeciles: Eugenics, the Supreme Court, and Buck v. Bell* (Baltimore, MD: JHU Press, 2008), 202.

32 "U.S. Eugenist Hails Nazi Racial Policy," *New York Times*, August 29, 1935.

33 A.E. Samaan, *H.H. Laughlin: American Scientist. American Progressive. Nazi Collaborator* (A.E. Samaan: 2015), 242.

34 Paul Lombardo, "The American Breed," *Albany Law Review*, Vol. 65, No. 3 (June 2, 2002).

35 Douglas Smith, "Earnest Sevier Cox (1880–1966)," *Encyclopedia Virginia*, October 12, 2009. https://www.encyclopediavirginia.org/cox_earnest_sevier_1880-1966.

36 Lombardo, "The American Breed."

37 Tucker, *Scientific Racism*, 122-129.

38 Kuhl, *Nazi Connection*, 82.

39 F. Scott Fitzgerald, *The Great Gatsby* (Toronto, Ontario: Broadview Editions, 2007), 58.

40 Lombardo, "The American Breed."

41 Tucker, *Scientific Racism*, 63-64.

42 "Pioneer Fund," *Extremist Files*, Southern Poverty Law Center, https://www. splcenter.org/fighting-hate/extremist-files/group/pioneer-fund.

43 Tucker, *Scientific Racism*, 167.

44 Charles Lane, "The Tainted Sources of 'The Bell Curve,'" *New York Review of Books*, December 1, 1994.

CHAPTER SEVEN: JOHN TANTON, THE PUPPET MASTER

1 John Tanton homepage, https://www.johntanton.org/.

2 John Rohe, *Mary Lou & John Tanton: A Journey into American Conservation* (FAIR Horizon Press, 2000).

3 Betsy Hartmann, *Reproductive Rights and Wrongs: The Global Politics of Population Control* (Chicago: Haymarket Books, 2016), 94-95.

4 Paul R. Ehrlich, *The Population Bomb* (New York: A Sierra Club Ballantine Book, 1968), xi.

5 John Bevilaqua, "Maj. Gen. William H. Draper, Jr. - Dillon, Read and Eugenics," *Education Forum*, November 21, 2007, http://educationforum.ipbhost.com/ topic/11642-maj-gen-william-h-draper-jr-dillon-read-and-eugenics/.

6 Paul R. Ehrlich and Anne H. Ehrlich, "The Population Bomb Revisited," *The Electronic Journal of Sustainable Development* (2009).

7 Rohe, *American Conservation*, 37.

8 Gretchen Livingston, "Is U.S. Fertility at an All-Time Low? Two of Three Measures Point to Yes," Pew Research Center, May 22, 2019, https://www. pewresearch. org/fact-tank/2019/05/22/u-s-fertility-rate-explained/.

9 John Tanton to James Greene, December 2, 1974.

10 John Tanton to (and from) Alan Blaustein, May 1, 1975.

11 John Tanton, "The Case for Passive Eugenics," April, 24, 1975.

12 Matthew Day, "'Shocking' Holocaust Study Claims Nazis Killed up to 20 Million People," *The Telegraph*, March 3, 2013, https://www.businessinsider. com/ shocking-new-holocaust-study-claims-nazis-killed-up-to-20-millionpeople-2013-3.

13 John Tanton, "RE: Establishment of The Society for Genetic Education (SAGE)," March 22, 1996.

14 John Tanton, "International Migration as an Obstacle to Achieving World Stability," *Ecologist*, No. 6 (July 1976), https://www.johntanton.org/ articles/ mitchell_essay_immigration.html#overview.

15 Doug Saunders, "The World Has a Surplus of Food. So Why Can't We Eliminate Hunger?" *The Globe and Mail*, April 15, 2017, https://www.theglobeandmail.com/ opinion/the-world-has-a-surplus-of-food-so-why-cant-we-eliminate-hunger/ article34709360/.

16 Roger Conner, interview with author, March 4, 2020.

17 Ibid.

18 Rohe, *American Conservation*, 46.

19 "Federation for American Immigration Reform," *Extremist Files*, Southern Poverty Law Center, https://www.splcenter.org/fighting-hate/extremist-files/ group/ federation-american-immigration-reform.

20 Nicholas Kulish and Mike McIntire, "Why an Heiress Spent Her Fortune to Keep Immigrants Out," *New York Times*, August 14, 2019, https://www.nytimes. com/2019/08/14/us/anti-immigration-cordelia-scaife-may.html.

21 Ibid.

22 Roger Conner and John Tanton, "A Proposal for The Federation for American Immigration Reform," January 9, 1979.

23 Rohe, *American Conservation*, 47.

24 Jason DeParle, "The Anti-Immigration Crusader," *New York Times*, April 17, 2011, https://www.nytimes.com/2011/04/17/us/17immig.html.

25 Wayne Lutton and John Tanton, *Immigration Invasion* (Petosky, MI: The Social Contract Press, 1994), 61.

26 Matt O'Brien, Spencer Raley, and Casey Ryan, "SCAAP Data Suggest Illegal Aliens Commit Crime at a Much Higher Rate Than Citizens and Lawful Immigrants," Federation for American Immigration Reform, February 3, 2019, https://www.fairus.org/issue/illegal-immigration/scaap-data-suggest-illegal-aliens-commit-crime-much-higher-rate-citizens.

27 Hans A. von Spakovsky, "What the Media Won't Tell You About Illegal Immigration and Criminal Activity," Heritage Foundation, March 13, 2017, https://www.heritage.org/immigration/commentary/what-the-media-wont-tell-you- about-illegal-immigration-and-criminal-activity.

28 Lutton and Tanton, *Immigration Invasion*, 62.

29 "The Nativist Lobby: Three Faces of Intolerance," *Intelligence Project*, Southern Poverty Law Center, February, 2009, https://www. splcenter.org/sites/default/files/d6_legacy_files/downloads/splc_nativistlobby. pdf.

30 Sarah Jones, "The Notorious Book That Ties the Right to the Far Right," *New Republic*, February 2, 2018, https://newrepublic.com/article/146925/notoriousbook- ties-right-far-right.

31 Kulish and McIntire, "Heiress."

32 Jean Raspail, *The Camp of the Saints*, trans. Norman Shapiro (Petoskey, MI: The Social Contract Press, 1995), https://www.thesocialcontract.com/artman2/publish/tsc0402/article_321.shtml.

33 Russell Pearce, "Arizona Takes the Lead on Illegal Immigration Enforcement," *The Hill*, June 28, 2010, https://thehill.com/blogs/congress-blog/politics/105931-arizona- takes-the-lead-on-illegal-immigration-enforcement-ariz-gop-state-sen-russell-pearce.

34 Robert Farley, "Will Trump's Wall Pay for Itself?" Factcheck Posts, March 16, 2018, https://www.factcheck.org/2018/03/will-trumps-wall-pay-for-itself/.

35 Heidi Beirich, "The Nativist Lobby," Southern Poverty Law Center, February 1, 2009, https://www.splcenter.org/20090131/nativist-lobby-three-faces-intolerance.

36 Jessica Huseman, Blake Paterson, Bryan Lowry, and Hunter Woodall, "Kris Kobach's Lucrative Trail of Courtroom Defeats," *ProPublica*, August 8, 2018, https://www.salon.com/2018/08/08/kris-kobachs-lucrative-trail-of-courtroom-defeats_partner/.

37 "John Tanton's Network," *Intelligence Report*, Southern Poverty Law Center, https://www.splcenter.org/fighting-hate/intelligence-report/2015/john-tantons-network.

38 In the spirit of full disclosure, The Southern Poverty Law Center has been termed a hate group by The Social Contract. There are, of course, vast differences between the two groups. Most notably, the SPLC, which has worked closely with the Anti-Defamation League and other well-respected civil rights organizations, is not a politically focused, single-issue lobbying organization, as so many of Tanton's organizations are.

39 "John Tanton Is the Mastermind behind the Organized Anti-Immigration Movement," *Intelligence Report*, Southern Poverty Law Center, June 18, 2002, https://www.splcenter.org/fighting-hate/intelligence-report/2002/john-tanton-mastermind-behindorganized-anti-immigration-movement.

40 Ibid.

41 Kulish and McIntire, "Heiress." *Oxford English Dictionary*, 2nd ed., s.v. "witenagemot."

42 *Oxford English Dictionary*, 2nd ed., s.v. "witenagemot."

43 Conner interview.

44 John Tanton, "'WITAN Memo' I," *Intelligence Report*, Southern Poverty Law Center, https://www.splcenter.org/fighting-hate/intelligence-report/2015/witan-memo-i.

45 Roger Conner, "'WITAN Memo' II," *Intelligence Report*, Southern Poverty Law Center, https://www.splcenter.org/fighting-hate/intelligence-report/2015/witan-memo-ii.

46 John Tanton, "'WITAN Memo' III," *Intelligence Report*, Southern Poverty Law Center, https://www.splcenter.org/fighting-hate/intelligence-report/2015/witan-memo-iii.

47 Tom Gjelten, *A Nation of Nations: A Great American Immigration Story* (New York: Simon & Schuster, 2015), 253.

48 "Chavez Quits U.S. English Over 'Repugnant' Memo," *Education Week*, October 26, 1988, https://www.edweek.org/ew/articles/1988/10/26/08440014.h08.html.

49 John Tanton, "RE: Update on English Language Advocates (ELA)," January 23, 1998.

50 Conner interview.

51 Sonia Khaleel, "Appeal Court Rules against U-M in Case to Keep Anti-Immigration Leader's Documents Sealed," *Detroit Metro Times*, June 22, 2019, https://www.metrotimes.com/news-hits/archives/2019/06/22/appeal-court-rules-against-u-m-in-case-to-keep-anti-immigration-leaders-documents-sealed.

52 John Tanton to Samuel Huntington, August 8, 1997.

53 John Tanton, "Memo for Buffett File," April 18, 1984.

54 John Tanton to Charles Munger, September 22, 1993.

55 John Tanton to Robert Graham, March 22, 1996.

56 Marian Van Court, "Reflections on My Life as a Eugenicist, Part 3," Counter-Currents Publishing, January 8, 2016, https://www.counter-currents.com/2016/01/reflections-on-my-life-as-a-eugenicist-part-3/.

57 John Tanton to Donna Panazzi, January 9, 2001.

58 John Tanton to Donna Panazzi, June 29, September 29, 1998.

59 Kulish and McIntire, "Heiress."

60 Ibid.

61 Ibid.

62 Richard Brookhiser, "III Cheers for the WASP," *Time*, December 2, 1993, http://content.time.com/time/magazine/article/0,9171,979728,00.html.

63 John Tanton to Garrett Hardin, December 10, 1993.

CHAPTER EIGHT: DECODING THE HORSESHOE VIRUS

1   Kulish and McIntire, "Heiress."

2   Issie Lapowsky, "Trump's Campaign CEO's Little Known World of Warcraft Career," *Wired*, September 2, 2016, https://www.wired.com/2016/09/trumps-campaign- ceos-little-known-world-warcraft-career/.

3   Joshua Green, *Devil's Bargain: Steve Bannon, Donald Trump, and the Nationalist Uprising* (New York: Penguin Press, 2017), 81.

4   Ibid.

5   Elinor Ostrom, *Governing the Commons: The Evolution of Institutions for Collective Action* (Cambridge University Press, 2015).

6   Scott Steepleton, "Pioneering Professor, Wife Die in Apparent Double Suicide," The Garrett Hardin Society, September 18, 2003, https://www.garretthardinsociety.org/tributes/obit_sbnews_2003sep18.html.

7   Kulish and McIntire, "Heiress."

8   Ibid.

9   "Garrett Hardin," *Extremist Files*, Southern Poverty Law Center, https://www.splcenter.org/fighting-hate/extremist-files/individual/garrett-hardin.

10 "Emmet County, MI," Data USA, https://datausa.io/profile/geo/emmet-county-mi.

11 "1970 Census of Population and Housing," U.S. Census Bureau, https://www2.census.gov/library/publications/decennial/1970/phc- 1/39204513p20ch03.pdf.

12 Matthew Kyle Yates, "The Conscience of a Movement: American Conservatism, the Vietnam War, and the Politics of Natural Law," Dissertation (Ohio State University, 2011), https://etd.ohiolink.edu/!etd.send_file?accession=osu1313108426.

13 Jean Pierre Fay, *Le Siecle des Ideologies* (Paris: Armand Colin,1996), 36.

14 Jean-Luc Steinmetz, *Pétrus Borel, Un Auteur Provisoire* (Presses Universitaires du Septentrion, 1986), 181, https://www.google.com/books/edition/P%C3%A9trus_Borel/zDxEcDlG5m4C?hl=en&gbpv=0.

15 Chip Berlet and Matthew N. Lyons, "Repression and Ideology: The Legacy of Discredited Centrist/Extremist Theory," *Political Research*, November 17, 1998, https://www.politicalresearch.org/1998/11/17/repression-and-ideology-the-legacy-of-discredited-centristextremist-theory.

16 Tucker Carlson, "The Intellectual Roots of Nativism," *Wall Street Journal*, October 2, 1997.

17 Mario H. Lopez, "Hijacking Immigration?" *The Human Life Review*, October 28, 2012, https://humanlifereview.com/hijacking-immigration/.

18 Elizabeth F. Cohen, *Illegal: How America's Lawless Immigration Regime Threatens Us All* (New York: Basic Books, 2020), 148-149.

CHAPTER NINE: DIVIDED WE STAND

1 Robert E. Scott, "Growth in U.S.–China trade Deficit between 2001 and 2015 Cost 3.4 Million Jobs," Economic Policy Institute, January 31, 2017, https://www.epi. org/publication/growth-in-u-s-china-trade-deficit-between-2001-and-2015- cost-3-4-million-jobs-heres-how-to-rebalance-trade-and-rebuild-american-manufacturing/.

2 Juliana Menasce Horowitz, Ruth Igielnik, and Rakesh Kochhar, "Most Americans Say There Is Too Much Economic Inequality in the U.S., but Fewer Than Half Call It a Top Priority," Pew Research Center, January 9, 2020, https://www. pewsocialtrends.org/2020/01/09/most-americans-say-there-is-too-mucheconomic- inequality-in-the-u-s-but-fewer-than-half-call-it-a-top-priority/.

3 Miriam Jordan, "8 Million People Are Working Illegally in the U.S. Here's Why That's Unlikely to Change," *New York Times*, December 11, 2018, https://www.nytimes.com/2018/12/11/us/undocumented-immigrant-workers.html?.

4 Bob Price, "John Tanton Networks like FAIR, NumbersUSA and CIS - Leftist Groups Manipulating Republicans," Texas GOP Vote, December 19, 2012, https://www.texasgopvote.com/family/john-tanton-networks-fair-numbersusa-and- cis-leftist-groups-manipulating-004942.

5   Steven A. Camarota, "The Wages of Immigration," Center for Immigration Studies, January 1, 1998, https://cis.org/Report/Wages-Immigration.

6   Steven A. Camarota, "Immigration Is Hurting the U.S. Worker," Center for Immigration Studies, April 1, 2007, https://cis.org/Immigration-Hurting-USWorker.

7   "Table 1. Persons Obtaining Lawful Permanent Resident Status: Fiscal Years 1820 to 2014," *2014 Yearbook of Immigration Statistics*, Department of Homeland Security, https://www.dhs.gov/immigration-statistics/yearbook/2014/table1.

8   Steven A. Camarota and Karen Zeigler, "Immigration Continues to Surge," Center for Immigration Studies, October 31, 2018, https://cis.org/Report/Immigration-Continues-Surge.

9   "Illegal Aliens Taking U.S. Jobs," Federation for American Immigration Reform, March 2020, https://www.fairus.org/issue/workforce-economy/illegal-aliens-taking-us-jobs.

10 Jeffrey Sparshott, "Immigration Does More Good Than Harm to Economy, Study Finds," *Wall Street Journal*, September 22, 2016, https://www.wsj.com/articles/immigration-does-more-good-than-harm-to-economy-study-finds-1474568991.

11 Vernon M. Briggs, Jr., "American Unionism and U.S. Immigration Policy," Center for Immigration Studies, August 1, 2001, https://cis.org/Report/American-Unionism-and-US-Immigration-Policy.

12 Jennifer Ludden, "1965 Immigration Law Changed Face of America," *National Public Radio*, May 9, 2006, https://www.npr.org/templates/story/story.php?storyId=5391395.

13 Daniel Denvir, *All-American Nativism: How the Bipartisan War on Immigrants Explains Politics as We Know It* (New York: Verso, 2020), 46.

14 Conner interview.

15 Ximena Clark, Timothy J. Hatton, and Jeffrey G. Williamson, "Explaining U.S. Immigration, 1971-1998," *The Review of Economics and Statistics*, 89, No. 2 (May 2007), 359-373.

16 John Tanton, "Memo to FAIR Board of Directors and Dan Stein," February 17, 1994.

17 Barbara Jordan, "U.S. Commission on Immigration Reform," *In Defense of the Alien*, 18 (1995), 3–7.

18 Eric Schmidt, "Milestones and Missteps on Immigration," *New York Times*, October 26, 1996, https://www.nytimes.com/1996/10/26/us/milestones-and-missteps-on-immigration.html?.

19 "Barbara Jordan's Vision of Immigration Reform," NumbersUSA, October 7, 2015.

20 Jerry Kammer, "Remembering Barbara Jordan and Her Immigration Legacy," Center for Immigration Studies, January 17, 2016, https://cis.org/Report/ Remembering-Barbara-Jordan-and-Her-Immigration-Legacy.

21 Bruce Morrison, "The Jordan Commission Wasn't Anti-Immigration," Letters to the Editor, *Washington Post*, December 23, 2016, https://www. washingtonpost.com/opinions/the-jordan-commission-wasnt-antiimmigration/ 2016/12/23/543e0968-c864-11e6-acda-59924caa2450_story.html.

22 Dara Lind, "The Disastrous, Forgotten 1996 Law That Created Today's Immigration Problem," *Vox*, April 28, 2016, https://www.vox. com/2016/4/28/11515132/ iirira-clinton-immigration.

23 "Table 39. Aliens Removed or Returned: Fiscal Years 1892 To 2014," *2014 Yearbook of Immigration Statistics*, Department of Homeland Security, https://www. dhs.gov/immigration-statistics/yearbook/2014/table39.

24 "Politico 50: Jeff Sessions; Stephen Miller," *Politico*, 2016, https://www. politico. com/magazine/politico50/2016/jeff-sessions-stephen-miller.

CHAPTER TEN: "OUR COUNTRY IS FULL"

1   Brett Samuels, "Cohen: Trump Described His Campaign as 'The Greatest Infomercial in Political History,'" *The Hill*, February 27, 2019, https://thehill. com/homenews/house/431802-cohen-trump-described-his-campaign-as-the- greatest-infomercial-in-political.

2   Marc Fisher and Will Hobson, "Donald Trump Masqueraded as Publicist to Brag about Himself," *Washington Post*, May 13, 2016, https://www.washingtonpost. com/politics/donald-trump-alter-ego-barron/2016/05/12/02ac99ec-16fe-11e6- aa55-670cabef46e0_story.html.

3   "Full Text: Donald Trump Announces a Presidential Bid," *Washington Post*, June 16, 2015, https://www.washingtonpost.com/news/post-politics/ wp/2015/06/16/full-text-donald-trump-announces-a-presidential-bid/.

4   Associated Press, "Jeff Sessions among Republicans Criticizing 14th Amendment's Birthright Provisions," AL.com, August 3, 2010, https://www. al.com/ wire/2010/08/jeff_sessions_among_republican.html.

5   Julie Hirschfeld Davis and Michael D. Shear, *Border Wars: Inside Trump's Assault on Immigration* (New York: Simon & Schuster, 2019), 17.

6   Robert Draper, "Trump vs. Congress: Now What?" *New York Times*, March 26, 2017, https://www.nytimes.com/2017/03/26/magazine/trump-vs-congress-now-what.html.

7   Jonathan Bitzer, "How Stephen Miller Manipulates Donald Trump to Further His Immigration Obsession," *The New Yorker*, February 21, 2020, https://www.newyorker.com/magazine/2020/03/02/how-stephen-miller-manipulates-donald- trump-to-further-his-immigration-obsession.

8   Lisa Mascaro, "How a Liberal Santa Monica High School Produced a Top Trump Advisor and Speechwriter," *Los Angeles Times*, January 17, 2017, https://www.latimes.com/politics/la-na-pol-trump-speechwriter-santamonica-20170117-story.html.

9   William D. Cohan, "How Stephen Miller Rode White Rage from Duke's Campus to Trump's West Wing," *Vanity Fair*, May 30, 2017, https://www.vanityfair.com/news/2017/05/stephen-miller-duke-donald-trump.

10 Ibid.

11 Pat Doyle, "Thursday: Bachmann, Tinklenberg Air It Out," *Star Tribune*, October 18, 2008, http://www.startribune.com/thursday-bachmann-tinklenberg-air-it-out/31145584.

12 Nick Miroff and Josh Dawsey, "The Adviser Who Scripts Trump's Immigration Policy," *Washington Post*, August 17, 2019, https://www.washingtonpost.com/graphics/2019/politics/stephen-miller-trump-immigration.

13 Julia Hahn, "Camp of the Saints' Seen Mirrored in Pope's Message," *Breitbart*, September 24, 2015, https://www.breitbart.com/politics/2015/09/24/camp-saints-seen-mirrored-popes-message/.

14 Michael Edison Hayden, "Emails Confirm Miller's Twin Obsessions: Immigrants and Crime," *Hatewatch*, Southern Poverty Law Center, November 25, 2019, https://www.splcenter.org/hatewatch/2019/11/25/emails-confirm-millers-twin- obsessions-immigrants-and-crime.

15 Jason L. Riley, "The Mythical Connection Between Immigrants and Crime," *Wall Street Journal*, July 14, 2015, https://www.wsj.com/articles/the-mythical-connection-between-immigrants-and-crime-1436916798.

16 "Mass shootings in the U.S.: Shooters by Race, as of February 2020," *Statistica*, March 2, 2020, https://www.statista.com/ statistics/476456/mass-shootings-in-the-us-by-shooter-s-race.

17 David Fitzgerald, "This Proves Donald Trump Is Lying: Here Are the Actual Facts on Immigrants and Crime," *Salon*, July 7, 2015, https://www.salon.com/2015/07/07/this_proves_donald_trump_is_lying_here_are_the_actual_facts_on_immigrants_and_crime/.

18 "Victims of Immigration Crime Engagement (VOICE) Office," U.S. Immigration Customs and Enforcement, https://www.ice.gov/voice.

19 "Victims of Immigration Crime Engagement (VOICE) 2018 Quarterly Report," U.S. Immigration Customs and Enforcement, https://www.ice.gov/doclib/voice/voiceQrtlyRptQ4FY18.pdf.

20 "Executive Order 13768 of January 25, 2017, Enhancing Public Safety in the Interior of the United States," *Code of Federal Regulations*, Title 3 (2017): 8799-8803, http://www.gpo.gov/fdsys/pkg/FR-2017-01-30/pdf/2017-02102.pdf.

21 "Executive Order 13767 of January 25, 2017, Border Security and Immigration Enforcement Improvement," *Federal Register* vol. 82, no. 18 (2017), 8793-97, http://www.gpo.gov/fdsys/pkg/FR-2017-01-30/pdf/2017-02095.pdf.

22 "Executive Order 13780 of January 27, 2017 (revised March 26, 2017), Protecting the Nation from Foreign Terrorist Entry into the United States," *Code of Federal Regulations*, Title 3 (2017): 13209-19, http://www.gpo.gov/fdsys/pkg/FR-2017-03-09/pdf/2017-04837.pdf.

23 Jonathan Blitzer, "How Stephen Miller Single-Handedly Got the U.S. to Accept Fewer Refugees," *The New Yorker*, October 13, 2017, https://www.newyorker.com/news/news-desk/how-stephen-miller-single-handedly-got-the-us-to-accept-fewer- refugees.

24 Julie Hirschfeld Davis and Somini Sengupta, "Trump Administration Rejects Study Showing Positive Impact of Refugees," *New York Times*, September 18, 2017, https://www.nytimes.com/2017/09/18/us/politics/refugees-revenue-cost-report- trump.html.

25 Bitzer, "Obsession."

26 Rosie Gray, "Emails Link Former Homeland Security Official to White Nationalists," *The Atlantic*, August 28, 2018, https://www.theatlantic.com/politics/archive/2018/08/emails-link-former-dhs-policy-analyst-to-white-nationalists/ 568843/.

27 Stephen Miller, "2015 Katz Award Ceremony Transcript," Center for Immigration Studies, May 31, 2015.

28 Fish v. Kobach, 16-2105-JAR-JPO, Findings of Fact and Conclusions of Law (D. Kans., June 18, 2018).

29 Donald Trump, "Remarks by President Trump at the 2019 Conservative Political Action Conference," White House, March 3, 2019, https://www.whitehouse.gov/briefings-statements/remarks-president-trump-2019-conservative-political-action- conference/.

30 Alex Nowrasteh, "Criminal Immigrants in Texas: Illegal Immigrant Conviction and Arrest Rates for Homicide, Sex Crimes, Larceny, and Other Crimes," *Cato Institute Immigration Research and Policy Brief*, Number 4, February 26, 2018, https://www.cato.org/sites/cato.org/files/pubs/pdf/irpb-4-updated.pdf.

31 David S. Glosser, "Stephen Miller Is an Immigration Hypocrite. I Know Because I'm His Uncle," *Politico*, August 13, 2018, https://www.politico.com/magazine/story/2018/08/13/stephen-miller-is-an-immigration-hypocrite-i-know-because-im-his-uncle-219351.

32 Lisa Riordan Seville and Hannah Rappleye, "Trump Admin Ran 'Pilot Program' for Separating Migrant Families in 2017," *NBC News*, June 29, 2018, https://www.nbcnews.com/storyline/immigration-border-crisis/trump-admin-ran-pilot-program-separating-migrant-families-2017-n887616.

33 Miles Parks, "Trump Signs Order to End Family Separations," *National Public Radio*, June 20, 2018, https://www.npr.org/2018/06/20/621798823/speaker-ryan-plans-immigration-votes-amid-doubts-that-bills-can-pass.

34 Donica Phifer, "Donald Trump Tweets 'Our Country Is Full,' Calls on Mexico to Stop Illegal Immigration Hours after Kirstjen Nielsen Resigns as DHS Secretary," *Newsweek*, May 8, 2019, https://www.newsweek.com/donald-trump-tweets-our-country-full-calls-mexico-stop-illegal-immigration-1388503.

35 "H-2A Temporary Agricultural Labor Certification Program - Selected Statistics, FY 2018," https://www.foreignlaborcert.doleta.gov/pdf/PerformanceData/2018/H-2A_Selected_Statistics_FY2018_Q4.pdf.

36 Heather Long, "Trump Administration Nearly Doubles H-2B Guest Visa Program, Which Brings Many Mexican Workers," *Washington Post*, April 6, 2019, https://www.washingtonpost.com/business/2019/04/06/trump-administration-nearly-doubles-h-b-guest-visa-program-which-brings-many-mexican-workers/.

37 Ibid.

38 Ian Kullgren, "CBP: Border Arrests Doubled in 2019," *Politico*, October 29, 2019, https://www.politico.com/news/2019/10/29/us-mexico-border-2019-arrests-061168.

39 "Southwest Border Migration FY 2020," U.S. Customs and Border Protection, https://www.cbp.gov/newsroom/stats/sw-border-migration.

40 Nick Miroff and Josh Dawsey, "Mulvaney Says U.S. Is 'Desperate' for More Legal Immigrants," *Washington Post*, February 20, 2020, https://www.washingtonpost.com/politics/mulvaney-says-us-is-desperate-for-more-legal-immigrants/2020/02/20/946292b2-5401-11ea-87b2-101dc5477dd7_story.html.

41 Maggie Haberman, "Mick Mulvaney Says He Often Disagrees with Trump (Just Never Publicly)," *New York Times*, February 20, 2020, https://www.nytimes.com/2020/02/20/us/politics/mulvaney-trump.html.

42 Janet Adamy and Paul Overberg, "Growth in Retiring Baby Boomers Strains U.S. Entitlement Programs," *Wall Street Journal*, June 21, 2018, https://www.wsj.com/articles/retiring-baby-boomers-leave-the-u-s-with-fewer-workers -to-support-the-elderly-1529553660.

43 "Births: Provisional Data for 2018," National Center for Health Statistics Division of Vital Statistics, May 2019.

CHAPTER ELEVEN: A SANE SOLUTION

1 Marshall Fitz and Angela Maria Kelley, "Stop the Conference: The Economic and Fiscal Consequences of Conference Cancellations Due to Arizona's S.B. 1070," Center for American Progress, November 18, 2010, https://www.americanprogress.org/issues/immigration/reports/2010/11/18/8657/stopthe-conference/.

2 Denise D. Resnik and Lisa Urias, "The Story behind the Real Arizona Coalition," *KTAR News*, April 23, 2013, https://ktar.com/story/290799/the-story-behind-the- real-arizona-coalition/.

3 Marisa Peñaloza, "For a Stark Contrast to U.S. Immigration Policy, Try Canada," *National Public Radio*, January 26, 2017, https://www.npr.org/sections/parallels/2017/01/26/511625609/for-a-stark-contrast-to-u-s-immigration-policy- try-canada.

4 "How We Rank Your Express Entry Profile," Government of Canada, https://www. canada.ca/en/immigration-refugees-citizenship/services/immigrate-canada/ express-entry/eligibility/criteria-comprehensive-ranking-system.html.

5 "Directory of Visa Categories," U.S. Department of State, Bureau of Consular Affairs, https://travel.state.gov/content/travel/en/us-visas/visa-information-resources/all-visa-categories.html.

6 "Green Card Eligibility Categories," U.S. Citizenship and Immigration Services, https://www.uscis.gov/greencard/eligibility-categories.

7 Ana Castro, "Immigration: The US vs. Canada," *USA Latino*, March 22, 2017, https://www.latinousa.org/2017/03/22/immigration-us-vs-canada/.

8 The Real Arizona Coalition, "SANE Immigration Platform."

9   Robert Pear, "Congress, Winding up Work, Votes Sweeping Aliens Bill; Reagan Expected to Sign It," *New York Times*, October 18, 1986, https://www.nytimes.com/1986/10/18/us/congress-winding-up-work-votes-sweeping-aliens-bill-reagan-expected-to-sign-it.html.

10 Alex Nowrasteh, "Arizona-Style Immigration Laws Hurt the Economy," *Forbes*, October 12, 2012, https://www.forbes.com/sites/alexnowrasteh/2012/10/12/arizona-style-immigration-laws-hurt-the-economy/#4d8e436e15b9.

CHAPTER TWELVE: THE OVERVIEW EFFECT

1   "Neil deGrasse Tyson on Coronavirus: Will People Listen to Science?" *The Late Show with Stephen Colbert*, March 7, 2020, https://www.youtube.com/watch?v=jB4FUHHMI24.

2   Ibid.

3   Denise Lineberry, "Celebrate with the World for One Night: Yuri's Night," *Researcher News*, NASA Langley Research Center, January 6, 2009, https://www.nasa.gov/centers/langley/news/researchernews/rn_yurisnight.html.

4   Dr. Brené Brown, "Sunday Sermon by Dr. Brené Brown at Washington National Cathedral," YouTube, January 21, 2018, https://www.youtube.com/watch?v=ndP1XDskXHY.

5   Andrew Cuomo, "In New York, 'Love Wins and it Will Win Again through This Virus,'" Office of the Governor Pressroom, March 24, 2020, https://www.governor.ny.gov/news/video-audio-photosrush-transcript-governor-cuomo-new-york-love-wins-and-it-will-win-again.

6   "Gov. Cuomo's Office Presents a Video Showing What "New York Tough" Looks Like," *ABC News*, April 10, 2020, https://www.youtube.com/watch?v=ilMDAc-yqr4.

INDEX

Repository for Germinal Choice, 165-6

Republican Party, 64, 67-8, 72, 80, 84, 104-5, 169-71, 176, 181-2, 186, 191, 193-4, 231-3, 244

Resnik, Denise D., 224

Reyes, Silvestre, 32

Riley, Jason L., 203-4

Rockefeller, John D. III, 119, 166

Rohe, John, 146, 148, 155, 167

Ronnebeck, Grant, 205-6

Roosevelt, Theodore, 120, 122

Ross, Edward A., 121-2

Rubio, Marco, 197. *See also* Gang of Eight

Rushton, J. Philippe, 141

Ruth, Babe, 137

Ryan, Charles, 53

S

sanctuary cities, 85, 207, 230

Sanders, Bernie, 6, 178

SANE Immigration Platform, 9, 225-30

Sanger, Margaret, 123-6, 166, 172

SB 1070. *See* legislation

Schumer, Chuck, 197. *See also* Gang of Eight

Schweikert, David, 227

Scott, Ralph, 141

Second Amendment, 86. *See also* Constitution

Sessions, Jeff, 197, 200-3, 206

Sherwood, Andrew, 63

Shockley, Will, 141

Sierra Club, 147, 182

SkyMall, 3, 20. *See also* Worsley, Bob

slavery, 100-2, 104-6, 108

Smith, Al, 137

Smith, Ian M., 211

Smith, Joseph, 16, 107

Smith, Ken, 3

Smith, Steve, 205-6

Social Contract Press (SCP), 156-8, 165, 203

social media, 75-6, 159, 174, 214-5, 243-4

Social Security, 22, 196, 217, 219-20, 227-8

Society for the Advancement of Genetics Education (SAGE), 151, 166

Sonoran Desert, 24-5, 30, 33. *See also* borders

Southern Poverty Law Center, 148, 158-9

Sovereignty Commission, 135-6

Spencer, Richard, 202, 211

Stanback, Fred Jr., 186

stand your ground. *See* American Legislative Exchange Council (ALEC); legislation

State Innovation Exchange, 86. *See also* legislation; lobbyists

Station for Experimental Evolution, 119

Stein, Dan, 179-81

sterilization, 91-2, 130, 133-4. *See also* eugenics

Stewart, Warren H. Sr., 37

Support Our Law Enforcement and Safe Neighborhoods Act. *See* SB 1070

Supreme Court, 87, 90, 106, 131, 139, 207-8. *See also* legislation

Swensrud, Sydney, 154

Symington, John Fife, 44

T

Taft, William Howard, 120

Tanton, John, 7-8, 37, 46, 94, 141, 143-68, 171-6, 182, 185-92, 212, 215, 219-21, 235-6

Tanton, Mary Lou (Brow), 146, 148

Taylor, Jared, 211

Tea Party, 40, 68, 70, 79, 84, 87-8, 170, 202, 227, 229, 233

Templeton, John M., 165

think tanks, 8, 73, 145, 157, 170, 189, 215, 217, 224

trespassing, 52-3, 60-1

Trump, Donald, 73, 92-3, 173-4, 187, 199-203, 206-20, 232-3, 245

Tuchman, Gloria, 39

Tunney, Gene, 137

U

United for a Sovereign America, 55

Unz, Ron, 38-9, 256